Dr. and Master Sha: Miracle Soul Healer

Dr. and Master Sha: Miracle Soul Healer

Documenting a Legend

William Gladstone

Waterside Productions

WATERSIDE PRODUCTIONS
CARDIFF, CALIFORNIA

Waterside Productions

Waterside Productions
2055 Oxford Ave.
Cardiff, CA 92007
www.waterside.com

ISBN: 978-1-958848-07-4 print-on-demand
ISBN: 978-1-958848-09-8 e-book
ISBN: 978-1-958848-08-1 hardcover

Design: Lynda Chaplin
Cover: Henderson Ong

Contents

PART TWO: Exploring Master Sha's Service

PART THREE: Stories from Master Teachers and Tao Soul Healers

PART FOUR: Master Sha's Growing Influence as a World-renowned Healer

Foreword by Queen Diambi

I T IS MY great honor to provide the foreword to this new edition of *Miracle Soul Healer*. I met Dr. and Master Sha for the first time at the Tao Healing Concert held in Toronto, Canada on July 22, 2022. I served as host and my sister, Princess Isabelle Kabuta, an acclaimed opera singer, also performed. This was an amazing concert in which Master Sha created a healing calligraphy and performed three of his Tao healing songs. The audience, both live and online, responded with heartfelt emotion and enthusiasm. Many reported spontaneous healings and everyone was lifted by the high energy of the concert.

My first interaction with Master Sha came when I attended one of his online quantum healing sessions. I was visiting my good friends, William and Gayle Gladstone and was experiencing muscle spasms and cramps, especially in my back, caused by a car accident a few months earlier. William and Gayle had just published Master Sha's most recent book, *Tao Calligraphy to Heal and Rejuvenate Your Back*. William handed me this small book and said, "Put this book on your back. It will likely help you be more comfortable." I was skeptical but saw no reason not to try this so I did. Within twenty minutes my back felt significantly better. Now I was intrigued. How could this be and who is this Master Sha who can put healing energy into a book?

Next thing I knew, William and Gayle were connecting us with the quantum healing hour. I saw Master Sha and relaxed during the session. It truly felt like receiving a deep cleansing massage for all the cells in my body. When I had an opportunity to interact online with Master Sha after the session, he explained that through his Tao Calligraphy and Tao Song he is able to open a vortex that allows each of us to connect with the Tao. When connecting with the Tao, we can remove the negative information that in most instances is responsible for illness and other life challenges.

As Queen of the Order of the Leopard of the Bakwa Luntu People of Central Kasaï in the Democratic Republic of the Congo, I am thoughtful of the indigenous traditions and wisdom of my own people. Much of our belief in the sacredness of all living beings parallels the principles utilized by Master Sha in his Tao teachings and healings. I resonate with the teachings of Lao Zi, one of Master Sha's sources for his own teachings about the nature of the Source and advice on how to access the Source in daily life. There is much more to investigate to truly understand the nature and principles of Master Sha's unique healing abilities.

The book you are about to read will provide answers to many of the questions raised by the thousands of miracle healings acknowledged and attributed to Master Sha and his master teachers and healers. Who is Master Sha? How did he develop his abilities? What do scientists think of his achievements? Can his results be replicated? These and many other questions will be answered in the following pages.

Enjoy this elegantly written book and pursue your own connection to Master Sha and the Divine. Master Sha is a true Tao Grandmaster and gift to humanity. *Miracle Soul Healer: Documenting a Legend* is the best introduction to Master Sha and his unique service.

Queen Diambi Kabatusuila Tshiyoyo Muata

Prelude

Jules:	I just been sittin' here thinkin'.
Vincent:	About what?
Jules:	The miracle we witnessed.
Vincent:	The miracle you witnessed. I witnessed a freak occurrence.
Jules:	Do you know what a miracle is?
Vincent:	An act of God.
Jules:	What's an act of God?
Vincent:	I guess it's when God makes the impossible possible.

—*Pulp Fiction*. Dir. Quentin Tarantino. Perf. John Travolta,
Samuel L. Jackson. Miramax, 1994.

PART ONE

Beginning My Journey
with Dr. and Master Sha

Introduction

IN 1973, AS a young man and recent graduate from Yale College, I was chosen by Rod Serling, the creator of the fabulously provocative and successful television series *The Twilight Zone*, as his researcher and production coordinator for the NBC television documentary *In Search of Ancient Mysteries*. In my capacity as researcher, I traveled from the Nazca Lines in the deserts of Peru to the primitive art caves of Lascaux in France, to the ancient astrological observatory outside of Delhi, India, and to locations in the Middle East and all parts of the globe. In all those travels I never encountered a mystery more puzzling than that of Dr. and Master Sha. How could reports of instant healings of deafness, cancer, lupus, back injuries, and knee injuries be true? How could the reports of his ability to empower others to also perform such healings be true?

I was determined to discover the truth or falsehood of this mystery. I left no stone unturned. I have a degree in anthropology from Harvard University. I studied medical anthropology with the foremost authorities in this subject area. I knew what to look for. I was not going to be fooled or easily convinced. I interviewed dozens of Dr. Sha's students, scores of those whom he had claimed to heal. The following is my report on this incredible mystery and my own journey of discovery. But let's start our story at the beginning.

I was driving to the Polo Lounge at the Beverly Hills Hotel to meet with my new client Dr. and Master Sha. Dr. and Master are both terms of respect. Dr. Sha did not achieve them without effort. Dr. Sha had studied and earned a medical degree in Western medicine, a doctorate of traditional Chinese medicine, including Chinese herbs, acupuncture, and Chinese massage (Tui Na), in his native country of China, as well as a certified doctorate of traditional Chinese medicine and acupuncture in British Columbia, Canada. Dr. Sha was also a grandmaster of tai chi, qi gong, kung fu, *I Ching*, and feng shui. In China such experts are given the honorific of Master. Dr. Sha was therefore both Dr. and Master Sha. He was not born with either title but merited both. As I was approaching Beverly Hills, I received a phone call from a colleague, Amish Shah, who would be attending the meeting. His name ironically was also Shah, but spelled with an extra "h." Amish Shah is an internet marketing executive. I had asked him to join the meeting to advise Dr. Sha on developing a more accessible website and internet strategy to reach the wide general audience for whom he was writing his books.

Amish apologized as he asked me, "Bill, I know this is short notice, but I have a friend, Naada Guerra, who was in a terrible bus accident a month ago. She has heard about Dr. Sha and would like to know if she could join us for lunch."

"We are scheduled to meet Dr. Sha in twenty minutes, and I am not sure I can get a bigger table since we are already ten people for lunch, but bring your friend. Knowing Dr. Sha, I'm sure he will meet with her even if only in the lobby of the hotel," I replied.

I turned out to be correct. Dr. Sha told the others to go ahead and sit down, and he would meet with Amish's friend and give her a healing right there in the lobby of the plush Beverly Hills Hotel. He had never met this woman before. Since I was the one setting up the meeting, I knew that neither she nor Dr. Sha could have had any idea that they would be meeting that day.

When I met Naada, I saw a lovely young woman with a hideous Frankenstein-like left eye. She had been riding in a two-deck open-air bus a month previously. A tree branch had struck her left eye and shattered her eye socket. The left side of her face was somewhat deformed and she had no movement whatsoever in her left eye. Her doctors had explained that they had done all they could to save the eye but that it would take at least six months before the eye would heal sufficiently for movement and the possibility of a second operation to restore her vision. I am somewhat squeamish and could hardly bear to look at Naada's deformed eye and stood to the side while Dr. Sha began his healing.

He placed his hands over her head and began a chant. He put his hands over her damaged eye and continued to chant. The entire healing took less than twenty minutes. When the procedure was complete, I looked at this young woman and her eye was able to move. Her face was no longer stiff and deformed. Dr. Sha explained that she was not yet healed but that he had been able to release the paralysis of the eye and neighboring area in one short session. He suggested that she return to her doctors and see what the prognosis would be for recovering her vision and for accelerating the operation that they had suggested could not be considered for at least six months.

Before leaving, Naada confirmed that she felt better than she ever had since her accident and that she could feel her face and eye for the first time since then. While I was prepared to accept that Master Sha might be a genuine healer, it was still somewhat shocking. Did I witness a freak occurrence or a genuine miracle? (In Part Three I will provide a more detailed analysis of Naada's experience, as well as a progress report.)

There are many so-called healers making extraordinary claims. Some generate millions of dollars from such claims only to fail to perform the cures for which well-intentioned but gullible patients and their families spend tens of thousands of dollars. I am no more skeptical than the average person, but on first encountering Dr. Sha's claims, my scientific mind immediately wanted proof. Having studied medical anthropology at Harvard University, the concept of spiritual healing and self-healing was not unknown to me. I was aware of the experiments that have been done authenticating the positive impact of prayer on successful medical surgeries performed by mainstream medical doctors. I was also aware that the placebo effect and the belief of a patient in a doctor, healer, or shaman can have a strong positive impact on the effectiveness of any therapeutic intervention. Still, if I have an illness I am going to rely on traditional Western medicine and seek out the most prestigious medical doctors and hospitals I can find.

But as Dr. Sha's literary agent and now friend, I have witnessed with my own eyes miracle healings that defy Western scientific principles and all that I know of traditional medicine. I have since witnessed dozens of healings. Over a thousand healings are available for viewing on YouTube. I am beginning to falter in my conviction that Western medical science is superior to the "soul healing" techniques Dr. Sha has mastered. Perhaps it is time for Western medicine and spiritual healing to enter a dialogue so that the best of both traditions can be utilized. Given the health-care crisis in America and throughout the world, this is more than just a passing interest. If soul healing can be taught to others as Dr. Sha claims it can, if patients themselves can learn to perform their own "soul healing miracles," then this is a pursuit that demands our immediate attention and scientific exploration.

As I've said, I am increasingly convinced that Dr. Sha is providing genuine healing. But how? What does Dr. Sha do to help these people? How does he do it? What are the limits on his ability to heal?

This book is my journey and exploration to answer these questions. Dr. and Master Sha looks and acts like an ordinary human, but the results he achieves are far from ordinary. My goal in this book is to explore how and why Dr. and Master Sha generates the results and adoration from those whom he has trained. The most extraordinary finding may be that Dr. and Master Sha believes he can train others to perform even greater soul healing miracles than he can perform.

In this book I am going to explore the basic principles upon which Dr. Sha has created his program, and I am also going to introduce you to the man himself, as well as to many of his students and advocates. I will also explore the science behind Dr. Sha's claims and methods. I do not understand everything that Dr. Sha has attempted to teach me about his healing technique, but I am impressed by his results and his obvious sincerity and commitment to helping heal individuals and our planet. I encourage you to be skeptical as you read this book but to also be open. As Dr. Sha says, "If you want to know if a pear is *sweet, taste* it." Keep an open mind, and if you like what you hear, try the exercise in chapter fifteen. Decide for yourself whether you agree with my findings.

1

My First Encounter
with Dr. and Master Sha

I N NOVEMBER 2012 I received a phone call from my good friend Rick Frishman, who was formerly the head of Planned Television Arts, a major New York City-based publicity firm. "Bill, I have a wonderful new client for you. His name is Dr. and Master Sha. Have you ever heard of him?"

"No, I am not aware of Dr. Sha or his books," I replied. "Have his previous books sold well?"

"Yes. I think they have all been *New York Times* best sellers. Simon & Schuster has published his last nine or ten books, but I just spoke with him and he is thinking of working with a literary agent if he can find the right one. I think you are probably the right one," Rick continued.

"Well, I will be happy to speak with him. We can use the Waterside conference line. Just let me know when it will be convenient," I offered.

A few days later I was on the phone with Dr. and Master Sha, his attorney, Rick, and the CEO of Dr. Sha's company. Dr. Sha asked a few questions, his attorney asked additional questions, and I explained how my literary agency operates. The call seemed to go well and the first action step was for me to send my standard author/agent agreement to Dr. Sha's attorney for review. The attorney reviewed the agreement and said he would present the agreement to Dr. Sha to sign.

I heard nothing for seven months, and then in late June 2013 Rick called again and said that Dr. Sha was ready to sign and engage my services as his literary agent. I had almost forgotten about Dr. Sha and had assumed that he had decided that he did not really need an agent. I told Rick that I needed to look at Dr. Sha's present book-publishing contract with Simon & Schuster since I wanted to know the terms of that agreement and to also check to see if there was the standard option clause that requires authors to submit their next book project to their present book publisher.

After going through the Simon & Schuster contract I was uncertain whether or not Dr. Sha actually needed my services. His contract was one of the best I had ever seen, with terms far superior to standard author/publisher contracts from major New York houses. By now Dr. Sha had signed my literary representation agreement and we had set up a time for a phone call. I was not sure why, but that call was scheduled for 9 p.m. Apparently Dr. Sha was in the middle of a major conference, and that was the only time he was free to speak.

Although I found the call somewhat tedious since I had to explain many basic book publishing definitions, I found myself laughing almost every five minutes at the enthusiasm and attitude Dr. Sha was expressing through both his questions and his asides. Dr. Sha had consulted with his divine sources before choosing me as his literary agent. I was pleased that I had received good marks even though I was still unsure whether I subscribed to the idea of consulting angels and heavenly guardians on business matters.

The longer the dialogue continued, the merrier it became. I was not sure exactly why, but the energy of the call was very light even when I explained that despite the wonderful terms Simon & Schuster was offering, I knew I could obtain much better terms if he was willing to explore non-New York City-based book publishers whose overheads were less than those of the large New York houses. I explained that we would honor the option clause and attempt to improve terms with Simon & Schuster, but that I could only be effective if he might be ready to switch publishers. We agreed that this was a viable option and then I asked, "So how much of the new book have you written?"

"Oh, I have not started on the new book yet. I have a big conference that will start in November and we need at least five hundred printed books to give to my students in early November," he replied.

"Except in rare instances, big publishers require a minimum of nine months' advance notice to publish a book. It is already early July, and without a manuscript it is going to be impossible to have your book published for November, at least if we publish in the usual way," I explained.

"There is nothing to worry about. I do this all the time with Simon & Schuster. They know how I work. They will make sure we have books in November if we ask," Dr. Sha assured me.

Since printing and shipping books takes a minimum of six weeks, I had to explain that that left Dr. Sha at most eight weeks to write and edit the book. The short timeline concerned me, but it didn't concern him.

"Oh, eight weeks is plenty of time. I work with the Divine and will have the book finished within three weeks from starting. We have lots of time," Dr. Sha assured me.

Still amazed, I inquired if the book was to be full-sized or if he was thinking of just a short book.

"It will be a full-sized book. My students can help us with the editing. They can also help with the layout and design," Dr. Sha responded.

"Well, then you are not just authoring the book, you're also packaging," I observed. "The timeframe is still going to be a challenge, but I will see what I can do. Get me the book proposal as soon as you finish your conference and we will see what can be achieved," I concluded.

"Very good, and thank you, Bill. I know we are going to be successful together. When I checked with the Divine, I was told that you have wonderful connections. You represented the For Dummies books and other big successful book series. That is my goal. I intend to write lots of books and sell millions of copies. I am a servant for the Divine and I have promised the Divine that I will heal as many people as I can. That is why my books are so important. They are not just books but soul healing miracles themselves. You will see. We will put soul healing calligraphy in each book, and the calligraphy itself will help heal people. You will help me find a television producer and we will also create health shows and events to heal people. You are going to have an important role in all of this, Bill," Dr. Sha confirmed enthusiastically.

I thanked Dr. Sha for his time and put down the phone.

The call had gone on for more than three hours. It was after midnight in California. I only learned later that week that Dr. Sha had been in Toronto, Canada, during the call and had not gotten off the phone until 3 a.m. his time. This was while he was at a healing conference providing healings from 8 a.m. to 11 p.m. for days at a time. Two months later when I had my first physical meeting with Dr. Sha, I learned that this kind of drive and energy that enabled him to work at times for thirty-six hours or more without rest was not unusual for him.

I did not yet know that I would be observing soul healing miracles myself, but I was already aware that I was about to embark on a journey with a most unusual and highly gifted client.

In early September 2013 I had the pleasure of meeting Dr. and Master Sha in person. We had, after much discussion, decided to publish *Soul Healing Miracles* not with Simon & Schuster but with BenBella instead. The book had already been written, just as Dr. Sha had promised, and the final editing was taking place with almost a week to spare to ensure that the book would arrive on time.

That first week in September Dr. Sha had arranged for a healing retreat for his students and student teachers at Asilomar on the beautiful Monterey Peninsula. Asilomar is a rustic meeting place with individual units spread over many acres, a quaint non-luxury convention center. Its location, however, is one of beauty and high energy near the ocean, with large open tracts of land just off the famous Carmel 17-Mile Drive. I had decided to drive up and meet Dr. Sha after spending the weekend in

Santa Barbara with other clients. The drive from Santa Barbara was relatively short, just a few hours, and we had agreed to meet for dinner. My fiancée, Gayle Newhouse, accompanied me both on the trip and for the dinner meeting that had previously been arranged.

Although I found the Asilomar site easily, it was not so easy finding the specific building and room. I quickly became lost, and while lost looked up and saw a man in a business suit sitting in front of a small cottage basking in the sun. I am not sure why, but I instantly knew, even though I was not close enough to make out any facial features, that this suited man was Dr. Sha. He had a simple air about him, and if not for the business suit I would have thought he was just an ordinary person on vacation taking a moment to relax in the sun.

I soon found my room and called Dr. Sha's assistant to reconfirm our dinner plans. Dr. Sha had made reservations at a simple Chinese restaurant in town, just a mile from the Asilomar center. During dinner I was impressed with how simple and gentle a man I was representing. On the phone Dr. Sha had done some of his "divine transmissions," which are loud and full of strong energy, so I was expecting someone a bit more excitable and extroverted. But in reality, Dr. Sha was soft-spoken and more of a listener than speaker. He had many questions for me and asked if I would be willing to get up onstage to address his students for five or ten minutes after dinner. He asked Gayle to join me onstage since he rightfully felt that energetically we were partners, if not business partners. There was going to be an evening session that would start at 10 p.m. and go until 5 a.m. Gayle and I would not be expected to stay past 11 p.m. so we could get a good night's sleep, but he felt it important with so many of his students in attendance that I explain the genesis and purpose of his forthcoming book, *Soul Healing Miracles*.

Of course, I agreed.

Before going onstage, there was a session for a man in his eighties who had been diagnosed with cancer. He had a visible tumor the size of a baseball that was protruding from his chest. Dr. Sha performed a healing and had six of his top students participate as well. The healing took about twenty minutes, and after the healing it was visible that the tumor had shrunk by at least 20 percent. I was not sure what this meant medically, but I was impressed.

When the healing session was over, Gayle and I were invited onstage. I was given a wonderful greeting and then explained why I thought *Soul Healing Miracles* would be the most important book Dr. and Master Sha had ever written. When I completed my short remarks, I was treated to the most incredible experience I have ever had with a group of five hundred people. All five hundred started chanting, "We love you, Bill. We thank you, Bill." The chanting must have lasted a full minute or more. That is a long time to have people you don't know telling you they love you. I felt an enormous glow and sense of ebullience; really, I guess, a sense of being truly loved. Then Gayle was asked to make a few remarks and they gave her the same ovation with chants of "We love you, Gayle. We thank you, Gayle."

We were able to exit the stage and return to our room for a good night's sleep, but it was clear to me that Dr. Sha had not only amazing abilities himself but had trained his students well.

I share these details of my first encounter with Dr. Sha because in exploring the life and work of Dr. and Master Sha, it is important that I reveal the circumstances surrounding my personal experiences. I believe that I remain objective in all that I will be reporting on in this book, but those who are skeptical should know that I am not pretending to be completely unbiased. In reality no ethnographer ever is completely unbiased; there is always some existing bias. But anthropologists rarely share the unique circumstances under which their data is gathered. I do not believe that this first or any subsequent encounter has distorted my view of Dr. Sha and his students; but if it has, at least the degree and nature of such bias has been revealed.

The only slightly jarring observation I made in this first meeting with Dr. Sha was that his students had a level of devotion resembling that which I have only witnessed at the ashram of Sri Sri Ravi Shankar and other spiritual teachers. I am not saying this is a bad thing, but as we explore the medical efficacy of Dr. Sha, it is important to realize that for many of his students, Dr. Sha is held at a level of devotion and admiration that only saints and gurus are accorded. I did not observe any behavior by Dr. Sha that encouraged this level of adoration, but we should acknowledge that this level of adoration and esteem is present whenever Dr. Sha is with his students. Perhaps it is the inevitable response of people who in most cases have had their lives saved or altered because of specific miracle soul healings that Dr. Sha has performed for them and their loved ones.

The next morning Gayle and I ducked in just before breakfast ended. We had made our goodbyes to Dr. Sha the night before and we were on a tight schedule to get to our next meeting. We joined a table of students and were relieved to encounter normal people. They were devoted to Dr. Sha. But otherwise, they were just everyday people who had personal experiences with Dr. Sha that had been transformational and who, because of these experiences, were motivated to learn the essence of soul healing miracles. We will get to these miracles shortly, but first let's explore the background and personality of this miracle soul healer, Dr. and Master Sha.

Who Is Dr. and Master Sha?

PSYCHOLOGISTS TELL US that the first seven years of life shape our personalities. In working with Dr. Sha, I was fortunate to have many opportunities to learn about him not just as a healer but also as a person. And I came to recognize how his early years shaped not only his personality but his interest in healing.

Dr. Sha was born in China in 1956 in what he refers to as The New China. This of course was the China of Mao Zedong, communism, and a rural economy. It was not yet a major economic power.

Born in a small town in Northwest China, when he was six years old his parents and family moved to Xi'an City, Shaanxi Province, a world-renowned ancient city of about two million people. His father was the top executive of a coal mine with ten thousand employees. His mother was a technician who worked at the mine. We can imagine that it was through their work at the mine that they met, fell in love, and married. Their relationship was traditional in every sense, and Dr. Sha was their firstborn at a time when there were no limits on the number of children a family could have. Later Dr. Sha would have three sisters and a brother.

Dr. Sha is very proud of his parents. His father was the type of hands-on executive who stood with his workers. Whenever there was a cave-in or other crisis at the mine, his father would be the first to risk his own life to organize a rescue crew to save the other miners. In every instance his employees would literally bar his way and try to prevent him from risking his own life. But he would say, "If I do not go down, who will go down to save the miners?" This sense of responsibility and care for others, so easily felt in the presence of Dr. Sha, comes from his earliest role model, his father.

When Dr. Sha was born, he was in very poor health. He suffered from allergies, fatigue, and insufficient appetite. When he was just five years old, he caught a cold and had a severe fever. His parents took him to the town's best Western medical doctor, where he was given an injection. Soon after he returned home, had a severe allergic reaction and he fell into a coma. His parents were not at home. His grandmother feared he would die. She ran to a neighbor who was an acupuncturist and the acupuncture brought the young boy out of his coma. His parents and grandparents were convinced that it was the acupuncture that had saved his life, and Dr. Sha developed an early appreciation for acupuncture that in his later life would direct him to learn the art himself.

Dr. Sha was still a sickly child, and shortly after moving to Xi'an his primary physical activity was taking walks in the park with his parents on Sundays. One Sunday in the park when he was just six years old, he observed an old tai chi grandmaster teaching three students. The tai chi master was instructing them on what is known as "the pushing hands practice." The master would do a movement and even without making physical contact, the student would be pushed several feet away. The six-year-old observed this exercise with each of the three students and could hardly believe his eyes. This was magic, and he wanted to learn how to use this tai chi power himself. He went running up to the grandmaster and, bowing as is customary with masters in China at that time, shouted, "Ye ye, I want to do this. Will you be my teacher?"

The grandmaster looked at the young boy for a while, thinking, and with a pleasant, yet stern smile told him, "You are too young to learn tai chi."

"No, no, I am not too young. I will be a good student. I so much want to learn. Please accept me as your student," the boy pleaded.

Surprised with the intensity of the entreaty, the grandmaster reconsidered. "Let me speak with your parents and perhaps I will make an exception."

The young Dr. Sha did not need a second opportunity. He ran back to his parents, brought them to meet the tai chi master, and after a brief conversation in which the tai chi master realized that Dr. Sha was from an important family, he relented and took the boy on as his youngest student ever.

Starting the very next Saturday, the young Dr. Sha would practice tai chi for four hours each and every Saturday and Sunday for the next ten years. As a six-year-old it was very difficult to meet the demands of his Tai Chi master. The training included holding positions for up to thirty minutes at a time. After five minutes, Dr. Sha's feet would ache. After ten minutes, his entire body would feel as if it were on fire. As Dr. Sha reflected back on his early tai chi training, he commented, "Tai chi taught me persistence and internal power. I learned at a very young age that I could push myself beyond pain and accomplish great control of my body."

With his health improving from tai chi and good nutrition as well as other exercises, the young boy quickly became a model for his siblings and a strong student at school. He was a dutiful son and would always show respect to his parents and their neighbors. He would help serve tea and would show respect by calling his neighbors Auntie and Uncle and following their guidance whenever it was offered. In school the young boy's favorite subject was literature, but he excelled in all subjects and was chosen to be the class monitor. This was a position of honor even for a six or seven-year-old, and Dr. Sha took the responsibility with serious intent to be the best class monitor he could be. In the class of fifty students there would always be one or two who were having difficulties with a particular lesson. As class monitor, Dr. Sha would stay after school to tutor these weaker students. It was, he felt, part of his responsibility to ensure that the entire class would progress and perform well on the school exams, not just he alone. Thus, we see from a very young age Dr. Sha's dedication to others, his intelligence, and his willingness to work hard. Dr. Sha's own reflection on these early years and experiences was, "I learned patience from working with the students who needed my help. None of us were even ten years old at the time, but I had compassion for the slower students and enjoyed helping them. They said I had a good heart; I never felt superior to them or that I was doing anything special in helping them."

In high school Dr. Sha's favorite subject was mathematics. He was the top student in every subject and was poised to go to any university he chose. As a teenager he had witnessed a neighbor who had terrible asthma. He asked the neighbor, "Have you seen a doctor? Has the doctor given you medicine? Is it helping you?" She said, "I have seen the doctor and am taking the medicine, but I am still suffering like this." Another day the teenager saw a man with swollen legs who complained that he had problems with his heart and kidneys. He asked, "What is wrong with you? You have such swollen legs. Have you gotten help from the doctor?" He said, "I have heart and kidney problems. I have gone to the doctor but the medicine does not help this." Intuitively the young boy felt that the doctors could help this man and woman, but he was disappointed that they were not getting enough help from the medical doctors. It was at that moment that the teenager thought that he wanted to be a good doctor to help people like this man and woman to remove their suffering. In the 1950s and 1960s most Chinese focused on Western medical treatments for all ailments. Although there were still acupuncture, massage, and herbal medical specialists, the government pushed Western medicine as the primary viable and rational approach to curing and healing major and even minor illnesses. If this teenager was really going to learn to help heal and cure his neighbors, then only a top medical school would do.

But Mao Zedong had other plans. This was during the time of the Cultural Revolution, and it was mandatory for all Chinese youths to go to the countryside to learn and work on farms immediately after high school. Dr. Sha found himself working first on a farm for two years and then in a factory for another year. Fortunately, the Chinese government reinstated the university system in 1977 and millions of students sat for the board exam. Based on his outstanding performance on the exam, Dr. Sha gained entry to the medical college of his choice.

Again Dr. Sha was a very good student and excelled. He learned all he could about Western medicine while also taking courses in traditional Chinese herbal medicine and developing his acupuncture skills. His interest in acupuncture increased due to a severe case of food poisoning that he experienced his first year at medical college.

As Dr. Sha explained the incident to me, "I ate some pork for lunch and it must have been spoiled or diseased. Within hours of eating, I had severe diarrhea and was vomiting. I went to the medical doctor on campus, and he gave me an injection. I went back to my dorm, but I could not even keep water down. I was still vomiting. One of my great friends who was in the same grade studying with me was ten years older than I and had studied traditional Chinese medicine from his family lineage. When I was in such pain and vomiting, I asked my roommate to call him and come to me at 3 a.m. He immediately came."

"He asked me to lie on my stomach. He then moved the big tendon on my back and my inner thigh. When he pinched the tendon, I shouted 'Wow!' It was extremely painful. He then asked me to get up and drink some water. I protested that I would just vomit the water again but he insisted. I drank the water and did not vomit. Shortly thereafter the excruciating pain I had been suffering disappeared. I was so shocked."

From that day forth, even while he pursued the latest techniques and findings emphasized in Western medicine, Dr. Sha made a commitment to master traditional Chinese medicine including Chinese herbs, acupuncture, and Chinese massage. He was fascinated by special techniques such as adjusting the tendon and acupuncture points that he had experienced himself. He had learned a profound lesson. Western medicine is not always the best approach. Western medicine and traditional Chinese medicine and other styles of traditional spiritual and energy healing can complement each other in specific situations. Just as he had always been a very good student in every class he took in medical school, soon Dr. Sha was an exceptional acupuncturist.

Master Sha learned special techniques from a professor of acupuncture. He studied traditional Chinese medicine with his full love and effort. He learned and mastered a few special healing techniques including acupuncture for strokes, deafness, slipped discs, and serious back pain.

1984–1989

AFTER GRADUATING FROM medical college, Dr. and Master Sha had an opportunity to go to the University of the Philippines to study and receive a master's degree in hospital administration. Before he went to the Philippines, he received one year of English training at the Beijing Foreign Language Institute. One day in 1984 his classmates were playing basketball. A senior physician of the hospital with expertise in traditional Chinese medicine in Shanghai jumped up and fell down. Instantly he could not move. Master Sha went to him and said, "Can I help you?" This traditional Chinese medicine doctor said, "Do not touch me." Ten students took him from the basketball court to his home. At dinner Master Sha went to this doctor's room to deliver a newspaper. The doctor asked, "Can you help me?" Master Sha said, "I offered my service to you when you were injured six to seven hours ago. You told me not to touch you." The man said, "I apologize." He continued and said, "I received acupuncture and Chinese massage from some experts. No one helped me. I still cannot move at all." The doctor then continued, "Dr. Sha, I fell down a few years ago and I lay in bed for a few months. This time I feel the same injury and pain." Dr. Sha went to his bed and put his hands on his inner thigh, asking him to inhale deeply; and then he pulled the tendon of his inner thigh. The doctor shouted in intense pain. Dr. Sha then asked him to try to sit up. The doctor said that he could not move at all. Dr. Sha continued and told him to try to sit up. The doctor then turned his body and sat up. Instantly he not only sat up but stood up and walked like a normal person. He said, "Wow!" Because this was a special training class for high-level senior doctors of traditional Chinese medicine to study English, this miracle case was instantly reported to the Ministry of Traditional Chinese Medicine. The leader of the Ministry of Traditional Chinese Medicine heard the story and kept Master Sha for one year more at the Academy of Traditional Chinese medicine in Beijing, China. A three-month international acupuncture training course for foreign physicians was held there, with hundreds of foreign physicians from all over the world studying in this institute. Master Sha offered his tai chi and qi gong training. He also offered special healing for those who were deaf and for stroke victims. There was a man who suffered a stroke. After one year he was still unable to move his arm. This patient was a relative of the institute office manager. Master Sha placed a few needles into his body. The man instantly was able to move his arm. This happened in the top institute of traditional Chinese medicine in China. The top professor of acupuncture could not help this man move his arm. They would treat a deaf patient with acupuncture for one year to restore his hearing. Dr. and Master Sha's unique acupuncture, which is called Sha's Acupuncture, combines energy and spiritual healing with acupuncture technique. Traditional Chinese acupuncturists usually insert the needles and leave them there for fifteen to thirty minutes. Dr. Sha's acupuncture technique was to quickly insert a needle, make a healing sound of "Ha!," and then instantly remove the needle. Within a few sessions, many deaf patients received remarkable healing, and many felt instant improvement. People were moved to tears and shocked. Therefore, Dr. Sha's reputation as a "miracle healer" was widespread in one of China's top institutes of acupuncture, as well as in the Ministry of Traditional Chinese Medicine.

Ten years later when Dr. and Master Sha visited the International Acupuncture Training Center for Foreign Physicians under the World Health Organization, the president of the institute told Dr. Sha, "Dr. Sha, come back. I will create a hospital for the deaf for you. The way you treat the deaf is amazing." Master Sha smiled and said, "Thank you so much for the offer. I have my unique mission for the world. I cannot accept your kind offer now."

By 1985, Dr. and Master Sha's miracle healing stories had reached the top Chinese government officials. A vice prime minister and a top military general had invited Dr. Sha to the Chinese leader's residence to give him acupuncture. In one session, this senior with back and leg issues could walk much better. He said, "Dr. Sha, you are so young and have excellent healing abilities. Why don't you come to 301 Hospital?" 301 Hospital was the top hospital in China for Chinese leaders, but Dr. Sha wanted to go abroad to gain more knowledge. Dr. Sha asked the deputy of this leader to please let him go abroad. This deputy helped. Otherwise, this leader in one sentence could have ordered Dr. Sha to be permanently stationed at 301 Hospital.

In 1986 Dr. Sha went to the Philippines to matriculate at the University of the Philippines for a master's degree in hospital administration. Because of Master Sha's miracle healing reputation in the Ministry of Health, this opportunity for studying at the University of the Philippines was granted. One leader introduced Master Sha to a Philippine traditional Chinese medical doctor who was the physician for the president of the Philippines. One day the Chinese embassy called this doctor and said, "The driver for the Chinese ambassador fell and has been lying on his stomach in bed for ten hours and cannot move." The Chinese embassy thought about sending a private airplane to take the driver back to China. When this doctor received the call from the Chinese embassy, he asked Dr. Sha to go with him. Master Sha said *yes* and went to the embassy with the doctor. When they went to the room, the ambassador's driver was lying flat on the bed. This traditional Chinese medicine doctor held both ankles and he wanted to push. Master Sha stopped him and said, "If you do not mind, let me do it." The doctor said, "Please." Master Sha used his unique technique on the man's inner thigh to help his back. Master Sha asked him to breathe and adjusted a tendon on his inner thigh. Master Sha did not tell him that it could be painful. He yelled out in pain. Master Sha then asked him to get up. The driver insisted, "I cannot get up." Master Sha said, "Please give it a try." The man turned his body slowly and had no pain. He sat up and had no pain. He was then assured enough to stand and walk. He had no pain! This shocked the Chinese ambassador. Right away, twenty to thirty Chinese embassy officials got in line to receive healing from Master Sha. Many officials and their wives received amazing healings. This miracle healing of the ambassador's driver astonished everyone at the embassy.

About one month later, the renowned overseas touring Chinese ballet troupe was performing, and the Chinese embassy invited the most prominent and important families to attend. One prominent Chinese woman called the embassy saying, "I am truly sorry, I cannot go tonight. My daughter has a slipped disc. She has cannot stand, sit, or lie down without excruciating pain. She may need an operation." The Chinese embassy instantly shared the story of the ambassador's driver. The woman's family called Dr. Sha and asked if he could come to them. As an unconditional servant, Dr. and Master Sha went without hesitation. Master Sha used his unique technique to adjust her back and inner thigh. After the adjustment he asked the daughter to get up. She said, "I cannot move." The same thing happened again. She then sat up, stood up, and walked normally. She was the sister of the wealthiest person in the Philippines. Dr. and Master Sha quickly became the doctor and healer for their whole family and for all of their renowned friends. The Chinese in the Philippines controlled the country's economy at the time. This news soon came to the attention of the Philippine government. The mother-in-law of the president, the speaker of the house, the Senate president, several top military generals, and many millionaires and billionaires invited Dr. and Master Sha to heal them. Master Sha created so many healing miracles. He became widely known as a miracle healer in the Philippines. Many newspapers and magazines wrote about these healings.

Dr. Sha not only treated government officials, millionaires, and billionaires; he also treated the poor. On weekends, he would give hundreds of the poor free healing. With his unique techniques, Dr. Sha could treat more than one hundred patients a day. He was a miracle healer in the Philippines from 1986 to 1990. He was so popular that even today many people, rich and poor, hold Dr. Sha in the highest regard and greatest gratitude for the healings they received.

Canada

IN 1989 A Chinese friend and client whom Dr. Sha had met in the Philippines invited Dr. Sha to visit his family in Canada. Dr. Sha went to the Canadian embassy in the Philippines. His tourist visa was refused. The reason was simple. Dr. Sha held a Chinese passport. In 1989 Chinese passports were not popular. Some people told Dr. Sha that he would never have a chance to go to Canada because the word "refused" would be in the computer system within Immigration. They said that he would have a difficult time getting to Canada and it would in turn affect his going to the United States and other countries. Dr. Sha was concerned.

A few months later, another family friend went to an immigration expert attorney in Canada. One member of this friend's family met the lawyer to be interviewed. This family friend asked Dr. Sha to go with him. When Dr. Sha was interviewed by the lawyer he asked, "What do you do?" Dr. Sha replied, "I am an acupuncturist." The family friend then shared that Dr. Sha was a doctor for the wealthiest family in the Philippines. The lawyer's office building was on the property of this wealthy family. The lawyer asked again, "What more can you do?" Dr. Sha answered, "I can do tai chi." The lawyer asked him to demonstrate, and Dr. Sha did. The lawyer said, "Give me your passport. I will make sure you can enter Canada." The next day Dr. Sha gave his passport to the lawyer, who took it to the Canadian embassy in the same building. The lawyer was the godfather of one of the consuls and told the consulate that he was personally inviting Dr. Sha to Canada as his guest with his guarantee. The consulate stamped Dr. Sha's visa and gave Dr. Sha permission to visit Canada.

After Dr. Sha arrived in Canada, the lawyer arranged for him to offer acupuncture for the Stroke Foundation. The left hand and fingers of the president of the Stroke Foundation's were stiff and could not open. Dr. Sha placed one needle in the president's palm and his hand instantly opened. This was such a miracle that no one could believe the result if they had not seen it with their own eyes. Dr. Sha received a letter of support from the Stroke Foundation. Various other organizations also gave supportive references. With this support, Dr. Sha received a work permit as an acupuncturist.

After Master Sha received his work permit, he started to practice. Because of his unique technique, in a short time he had many patients and great success. CBC News, the Canadian Broadcasting Corporation, interviewed Dr. Sha in his office and broadcast to the public. This program announced that Dr. Sha was a new immigrant with acupuncture skills. This broadcast brought great attention to his practice.

In 1992 a multimillionaire business entrepreneur, Sylvia, was visiting Toronto. She had sprained her ankle and asked one of the Chinese leaders to connect her with the best doctor in Toronto. The Chinese leader said, "See Dr. Sha." It was 9 p.m. Sylvia felt it was too late to visit Dr. Sha. The Chinese leader said, "Dr. Sha will serve patients at any time," and then he called Dr. Sha, who accepted the appointment. Dr. Sha gave Sylvia acupuncture and special Chinese massage for the ankle injury. She received instant release and continued to receive healing for a few more days.

During the weekend, Dr. and Master Sha gave a speech at one of the largest Buddhist temples in Toronto. Sylvia attended. At the end of the workshop, she stayed until almost everyone had left and then went to Dr. Sha to say, "Congratulations, great lecture." They had a brief conversation. A few days later, Sylvia returned to her home in British Columbia. One of Sylvia's relatives developed complications from a medical operation. Sylvia explained that she had met Dr. and Master Sha, an expert acupuncturist and qi gong master, who could offer remote energy healing. The relative did not believe it, but Sylvia immediately called Dr. Sha, who offered remote qi gong energy healing. The relative instantly felt better. Another one of Sylvia's employees also received great results through remote energy healing. Master Sha then requested that Sylvia arrange for him to go to British Columbia. He said that he could come within a few days. Sylvia had great connections in Vancouver and the province. She organized three or four events for Dr. Sha at the Buddhist society and other spiritual organizations. Every session was attended by more than one hundred participants.

During his visit, Dr. Sha offered many healings. One older gentleman was deaf and needed two hearing aids. Master Sha gave him an acupuncture treatment and he could hear. The man picked up a phone, called his daughter, and started to cry. He had not ever heard his daughter's voice without his hearing aids. After the acupuncture treatment he could hear his daughter clearly.

Another man suffered from serious back pain and had had quite a few acupuncture treatments from other doctors, yet received no relief from his pain. He heard of Dr. Sha through a major radio interview. This radio interview generated more than one hundred patients a day for Dr. Sha to offer acupuncture, so Dr. Sha decided to stay in Vancouver for a few more weeks. Because of the great results from Dr. and Master Sha's acupuncture treatments, one of the major local radio stations interviewed Dr. Sha regularly. Dr. Sha became one of the most visible and renowned acupuncturists in Vancouver. His practice was extremely successful and he achieved all of the material success he needed.

Dr. and Master Sha visited Vancouver regularly, three times a year. Each visit was for one month. Every time he had numerous patients. They would tell Dr. Sha that he was the "typhoon master," drawing attention to the storm of energy and success that Dr. Sha brought to his acupuncture treatments.

Dr. and Master Zhi Chen Guo

I N 1988 WHEN Master Sha was in the Philippines, his father sent him a book titled *Dong Yi Gong*. Dong (pronounced *dōng*) means *using*. Yi (pronounced *yee*) means *thinking*. Gong (pronounced *gōng*) means *practice*. Dong Yi Gong is one kind of Chinese qi gong. Qi gong is the ancient energy practice to boost energy, stamina, vitality, and immunity; to rejuvenate the body; to prolong life; and to heal sickness. As I shared earlier, Master Sha began studying qi gong at the age of ten. He taught qi gong to foreign physicians at the Beijing International Acupuncture Training Center under the World Health Organization. Dr. Sha's father was very proud of his son's teachings and knew that this book by Dr. and Master Guo would be of interest to him.

Master Sha read *Dong Yi Gong*. In this book Dr. and Master Guo shared many miracle healings created through thinking. Dr. Sha was intrigued. Dr. Sha was fascinated that qi gong had such unbelievable power to create such miracle healings. Dr. Sha wanted to learn from Dr. Guo. Shortly after reading the book, Dr. Sha sent a group of people who were sick to Dr. Guo's clinic because Dr. Sha was not able to go himself at that time. One of the patients had been shot in the shoulder and suffered constant shoulder and neck pain. Miraculously, after just one session with Dr. Guo, the pain disappeared. When Master Sha heard of this result, he could not wait to learn from Master Guo. He phoned Master Guo's center in China and was able to speak to Master Guo, saying, "Guo Lao Shi [Lao Shi means *teacher*], I was so moved by your book and so many miracle healing stories within the book. I truly want to learn from you. I have such a desire to become your disciple. Can you accept me as your disciple?"

Master Guo replied, "Just be a student."

Dr. Sha was not satisfied with that answer and in an interview he explained why. "Being Chinese, I understood in my heart that if you are a disciple, you learn the true secrets. If you are a regular student, you could study for thirty to fifty years and may not be taught the true secrets. How many thirty to fifty years does one have in their life? Having studied tai chi from age six, I had personally experienced that disciples learn the true secrets. My tai chi master's daughter was slight and young, but because my master taught his daughter self-defense, she could throw a tall, powerful man very far because she had learned the true secrets from her father. A regular student could take ten to twenty years of obedience and devotion to win the teacher's trust. Unfortunately, this kind of condition has lasted for thousands of years in China. Some great healers and great spiritual masters wait until just before they transition to pass on their secrets and power. They usually pass the secrets and knowledge to only one or at most two lineage holders. That is why I desired to be a disciple, not just a student, because I wanted to learn the secrets. I wanted the power to help and heal others the way Dr. Guo was helping and healing others. I did not give up when he told me to just be a student. I called one week later. Master Guo was in Xinjiang province holding an event with over fifteen thousand people. I was lucky to have a conversation with him again. I said, 'Guo Lao Shi, since childhood I have studied tai chi, qi gong, and Shaolin gong fu. I love ancient Chinese arts. The profound secrets and power of ancient Chinese arts have touched my heart so deeply, but when I read your book and sent the group of people to you, I was so fascinated. I wanted to be your disciple.' I spoke passionately with tears in my eyes and said, 'Could you accept me?' Master Guo paused a moment on the phone and said, 'I wrote a letter to you. I seldom write a letter to anyone. Prepare to receive the letter.' I was so moved I instantly bowed down to the floor." Master Sha explained to me that Chinese custom requires students to bow down and put their head on the floor to show respect to the teacher. Master Sha bowed down to his teacher, showing his love and respect to Master Guo even though Master Guo was thousands of miles away in China and they had never physically met.

One week passed. Master Sha did not receive the letter. He called Master Guo again and said, "Guo Lao Shi, I have not received your letter yet." Dr. Guo said, "Patience, the letter is on the way." Three days later Dr. Sha received the letter. He was excited and instantly opened the letter. The letter was only one page with a few sentences. It said, "Zhi Gang, disciple." Dr. Sha picks up the story: "I instantly bowed to the floor without reading any further. I was sobbing with joy. I felt such honor. I read his letter again after crying. The letter said, 'Do not forget your mother.' I felt, 'Wow!' The next sentence was 'Do not forget your country.' The letter continued, 'Use 3396815 to communicate between you and me.' I thought, 'What is 3396815? Is this a telephone number?' The letter did not explain how this number could be used for communication. The letter concluded, 'Serve humanity and serve wan ling.'" Master Sha explained that wan means *ten thousand*. In Chinese, ten thousand means *countless*. Ling means *soul*. Wan ling (pronounced *wahn ling*) means *countless souls, including countless planets, stars, galaxies, and universes.*

Master Sha told me, "I was so moved and touched that I could not express fully the deep gratitude and honor I felt when Master Guo accepted me as his disciple."

In 1993, before Dr. Sha met Master Guo in China, he started offering his service in other countries. Sylvia arranged workshops for Master Sha in Los Angeles. One of the largest Buddhist temples there is named Buddha Mountain. Master Sha gave the monks and Buddhist followers amazing healing and received their admiration. Right away, Sylvia helped Master Sha to give a teaching in Taiwan. This was before Master Sha went to mainland China. In Taiwan, Master Sha gave teaching and healing to two of the biggest Buddhist organizations. At that time his workshops reached more than one thousand people. Three major television stations in Taiwan and more than thirty newspapers broadcast Master Sha's healing. There was a man in Taoyuan City who suffered from serious psoriasis. The doctors said that his next step was to develop liver disease. He was very pale, very tired, and very sick. Master Sha gave him acupuncture and taught him how to do a special qi gong practice. He recovered very quickly, surprising everyone. According to Dr. Sha, to this day he has remained free of psoriasis and liver problems.

During Master Sha's one-month visit to Taiwan, he was completely booked with appointments every day from 9 a.m. to midnight. He gave healings to many of the country's leaders and business leaders. Word of mouth about Master Sha's healings reached many all across Taiwan. In October 1993, Master Sha and Sylvia went to Master Guo's healing center in China. They brought fifty people to join them at Master Guo's center. In Dr. Sha's words, "Master Guo offered daily teaching for ten days. Twenty thousand people packed in the courtyard of his center. There were so many people at the center that at night people would sleep in the hallways of the four-story center. Master Guo lacked the funds to complete the construction of his center. Sylvia gifted Master Guo the monies to complete the construction. Master Guo asked Sylvia if she wanted a share of the center or some land around the property. Sylvia said, 'No, I want nothing.' When I went back to Taiwan later, one of Sylvia's relatives told me, 'Sylvia is crazy. She gave all of her savings unconditionally to Master Guo, with no interest, and did not know when it would be returned.' I asked Sylvia why she did this. She said, 'There were so many people suffering and sleeping in the hallways. I felt such compassion that I wanted to support Master Guo. There were also so many miracle healings that were seen with so many people that had chronic pain and cancer.'"

Master Sha continued his own story:

"The next year, in October 1994, I returned to Master Guo's clinic for ten days. Master Guo had two annual gatherings, one in April and the other in October. Sylvia and I brought another seventy people to the center. Master Guo gave a healing for twenty thousand people. His center could only hold twenty thousand people and it was completely packed. Master Guo raised his hands, moving them from left to right and then right to left. He did this three times. He kept silent. I stood in the audience to face Master Guo. Every time his hands faced my direction, my body shook uncontrollably. I had seen many people's bodies shake uncontrollably during qi gong practice, but my body had never moved. I did not know why, but my body started to shake uncontrollably when Master Guo's hands were facing me. I felt heat and was sweating from every pore of my skin. I had a 'wow!' feeling in my heart and my heart opened. I thought, 'Wow, such power.' I could not express it enough. During that year Master Guo taught Soul Language. He asked twenty thousand people to chant 3396815 (*sahn sahn jeo leo bah yow woo*). He asked them to chant fast. Then, he asked all twenty thousand people to chant 3396815 (*sahn sahn jeo leo bah yow woo*) as fast as they could. This was his technique for bringing out one's own Soul Language. Soul Language is so dynamic and so fast. Everyone was wild and shouting. It was dynamic and powerful. Everyone carried a different voice. I chanted so fast and yet, my soul voice did not come out. No matter how hard I tried, it could not come out. Now I would like to share about 3396815.

"In 1978 at around 3 a.m. one morning, Master Guo received the number sequence 3396815 from the Divine. He woke his third daughter and asked her what number she might receive from the Divine. She received the same number, 3396815. The Divine taught Master Guo that this is the sacred divine code to bring out Soul Language. This sacred code carries divine sacred healing power and the power to transform all life, including relationships and finances. Thousands of soul healing miracles have occurred in Master Guo's Center. People have thrown their canes away. People have recovered from chronic pain, cancer, and blindness. The miraculous results had totally shocked me. I was in such an exciting situation and was so fascinated all of the time. I had the most amazing feeling in my heart when Master Guo waved his hands in the air a few times and miracles happened. How did he do this? I truly wanted to learn. Master Guo only performed his power and did not share his secrets with anyone.

"In 1998, I went back to Master Guo's clinic for the third time. I brought another group of people with me. I witnessed more soul healing miracles. I still did not know how to offer healing like Master Guo.

"In 2005, I went back to China for the fourth time to visit Master Guo. I brought with me about one hundred students from all over the world. We were filming a documentary called *Soul Masters: Dr. Guo and Dr. Sha.* One day I had a private consultation with Master Guo in his office. He said, 'Zhi Gang, for twelve years I have tested you on your love, compassion, commitment, and loyalty. Now I am passing the secrets to you on how to offer and do soul healing to the masses and do remote healings.' I was moved to tears and bowed down, touching my head to the floor. I did not want to get up. I felt the wisdom and sacred power was priceless. Millions of dollars could not buy this power and sacred wisdom, this sacred soul healing power. They were truly priceless in my heart. Therefore, my head was on the floor and I could not get up. I was deeply moved that I could use this sacred power to save people's lives. People's lives are priceless.

"After I returned to Canada from China, I communicated with Master Guo and he said, 'I am going to give you regular teachings for two hours per day.' It was summertime in China when I arrived, with temperatures over 40°C. Air conditioners were rare in China. They only used fans at Master Guo's clinic. It was so hot, but Master Guo gave me teachings daily. He taught me what the soul is. In Master Guo's teaching, the soul was called the subconscious. It was not proper to use the word *soul* in China. Master Guo explained to me the characteristics of the subconscious and the power of consciousness and how to communicate with the subconscious. He also taught me how to interpret dreams. It was such profound secret teaching. The dreams are the message. We know some people have such powerful dreams. For some people dreams are prophetic. There were profound secrets on how to interpret dreams. It was twelve years after meeting Master Guo that I started to learn the secrets of the soul and the power of the soul. I have shared a lot of essence from his teaching in my Soul Power Series of ten books. I would like to share with humanity that to meet a true Master is a great honor. To receive the true teaching, delivery, and sacred power from a true Master is beyond a blessing. The testing was very serious. I followed Master Guo for twelve years after our first face-to-face meeting. During a break after one of my early meetings, I came out from one building and Dr. Guo came out from another building. We walked toward one another. I am his adopted son and first disciple. I smiled to my teacher as I was walking toward him. As we almost met one another, his face became cold and he turned his head away from me and walked away. I felt such pain in my heart. How could my adopted father and spiritual father give me such an angry face, treating me like this? I had given my heart and soul to him. I was afraid to say anything. Before I left his center, he was playing ping pong. I went to him and bowed down. He did not even look at me. I said, 'Baba, I am leaving.' He did not say anything. It hurt me so deeply. I did not know that he was testing me. He told me twelve years later, 'Zhi Gang, I gave you a cold face and tested you in every way for your loyalty to me; your love and compassion to humanity; your kindness; and your persistence with no fear in moving forward. Your compassion has moved me. You have passed my test and therefore, I now pass my secrets to you.'

"Master Guo, Mama Guo, their five daughters, and all the teachers at Master Guo's clinic have given me such love, blessing, and teachings. When Master Guo purposely tested me, he did so with great compassion and love for me. The entire Guo family gave me so much love all of the time. For Master Guo, Mama Guo, the five daughters, and all of their teachers, I cannot give enough love and blessings. And for Master Guo's three months of daily teaching to me in such hot weather, I am forever grateful. I am speechless when I contemplate the great gifts I received from my teacher. I want to share with the whole world the ancient Chinese teaching, 'One day teacher, whole life father.' Master Guo is my most honored, respected spiritual father, and his wife is my most beloved spiritual mother. His five daughters are my most loved sisters. Their teachers are also my teachers and friends. I honor them forever.

"The more successful I am now and in the future, the more I remember their teachings and the teachings from other masters. I want to share with your readers a most powerful ancient Chinese phrase:

yin shui si yuan

Yin means *drink*. Shui means *water*. Si means *think*. Yuan means *source of the water*. Yin shui si yuan (pronounced *yeen shway sz ywen*) means *when you drink water, think of the source*. Now I am serving so many people worldwide. The source is Master Guo and all of my great teachers, the Divine, and the Source, are all the source of the wisdom and the power of my service. How can I thank them enough? I am a humble servant for them and for all humanity."

"Thank you. Thank you. Thank you from the bottom of my heart and soul."

Dr. Sha's Divine Encounter

ONE OF THE most interesting aspects of Dr. Sha's story and his emergence as a miracle soul healer is that even as he was completely dedicated as a disciple of Dr. Guo, he continued to have his own direct experience of the Divine. Dr. Sha was teaching a workshop in Soquel, California, at Land of Medicine Buddha in April 2003 when he had a direct encounter with the Divine.

Dr. Sha remembers the time and place vividly. In the words of Dr. Sha, "During my teaching of the workshop, the Divine appeared. I told all of the students that I grew up in China and bowed down to my tai chi and gong fu masters. Divine is here. Please allow me to bow down to Divine and let me show my respect. Please sit and allow me these few minutes. I bowed down and saw the Divine above my head."

I interrupted and asked Dr. Sha, "What did the Divine look like?"

Master Sha said, "The Divine looked like a human being."

> *Bill:* Was it a man or a woman?
>
> *Master Sha:* It looked male. The Divine was short and handsome. He wore a golden robe. The Medicine Buddha, Guan Yin, and a few other Buddhas were with him.
>
> *Bill:* What color eyes and hair did he have?
>
> *Master Sha:* He had black hair and his eyes were brown. He was Asian-looking. He had such dignity.

Bill:	In other spiritual traditions, they have said they could not look into the eyes of the Divine. But you could?
Master Sha:	Yes.
Bill:	What did you feel?
Master Sha:	I felt a vibration. I also felt such love and compassion from his eyes.
Bill:	Was he floating in the air?
Master Sha:	Yes, he was a light being in the air. It was a human being form that was standing in the air.
Bill:	Even though he was short, he was above you?
Master Sha:	Yes.
Bill:	So you bowed down?
Master Sha:	Yes.
Bill:	What happened next?
Master Sha:	Divine started to speak with me.
Bill:	What did he say?
Master Sha:	"Zhi Gang, today I came to share with you a spiritual law. This law is named the Universal Law of Universal Service. It is one of the highest spiritual laws in the universe. It applies to the spiritual world and the physical world." Then the Divine pointed to himself with his right hand and said, "I am a universal servant." Then he pointed to me. I was bowing down. He said, "You are a universal servant." He swept his hands over everyone. With additional slight movements for emphasis, the Divine continued, "Everyone and everything is a universal servant to share universal love, forgiveness, peace, healing, blessing, harmony, and enlightenment."

I looked at the Divine in awe of this revelation and the Divine continued, "If one offers a little service, one receives a little reward from the universe and me. If one offers more service, one receives more rewards. If one offers unconditional service, one receives unlimited rewards."

Then the Divine added, "In history there are unpleasant services including killing, harming, taking advantage of others, cheating, stealing, and more. If one offers a little unpleasant service, one learns a little lesson." I interrupted the Divine and said, "What kind of lessons does one learn?" He asked, "Are you a doctor?" I said, "Yes." He said, "Sicknesses are the lessons. People have relationship challenges, financial challenges, challenges with children, and many challenges in their lives. These are the lessons also. If one offers more unpleasant service, one learns more lessons. If one offers huge unpleasant services, one learns huge lessons." I instantly asked the Divine, "Dear Divine, are you teaching me the karma law?"

Divine replied, "The Universal Law of Universal Service I am sharing with you now is the karma law. This is how Heaven operates with Mother Earth and humanity." I said, "Thank you so much for the teaching." I instantly bowed down and made a vow. "Dear Divine, I want to be an unconditional universal servant. I am giving my life for service. If I cannot accomplish the task that you and Heaven give to me, I am willing to learn the heaviest lessons, including sending my soul to the deepest place. I am okay." Divine smiled and instantly disappeared.

What had Dr. Sha agreed to do, and how can we possibly ascertain that what Dr. Sha believes was an actual encounter with the Divine was not a hallucination or some form of self-delusion? The reality is we cannot scientifically prove that this event happened. The moment was not recorded. I know that Dr. Sha believes the encounter actually occurred. More important, Dr. Sha began to act on the vow that he undertook and miracles started to happen in his healings.

Just three months later, in July 2003, the Divine appeared again to Dr. Sha at a conference in Toronto.

According to Dr. Sha, the Divine spoke to him with these words: "Dear my son Zhi Gang, today I come to choose you as my direct servant." Master Sha replied, "I am honored to be your servant." The Divine said, "This service is unique. From today, when you offer healing. I will do the job." "I (Master Sha) was moved to tears about how blessed I was that the Divine was going to do this. I asked, 'How?' The Divine said, 'Choose a person with a challenging condition.' I chose a person named Walter, who had a new medical diagnosis of liver cancer with a three-centimeter malignant tumor that had been diagnosed from a biopsy. Walter stood on the stage and the Divine was above our heads. I said, 'Divine, please do it.' Divine told me, 'You share with the public and say *Divine Order, Divine Liver. Transmission.*' I said, 'Divine Order, Divine Liver. Transmission.' With my spiritual eye, I saw the Divine's heart radiate a beam of light to Walter's liver. I saw the dark shadow leave his liver and a golden light ball rotating in his liver. I asked the Divine, 'What is this golden light ball?' The Divine said, 'This is a golden new soul of the liver. Tell Walter to chant *Divine Liver* for two hours per day.' I told Walter that the Divine wanted him to chant *Divine Liver* repeatedly for two hours a day. He could divide the time into ten-minute, twenty-minute, or longer chanting sessions to total two hours a day. I asked Walter if he could do this and he replied that he could do more than two hours a day. The Divine said, 'If Walter can chant two hours a day, his liver cancer could disappear.' Walter did more than two hours a day of practice. Two-and-a-half months later, he went for a medical checkup. A CT scan and an MRI showed his cancer had disappeared. Walter has been cancer-free to this day."

The practice of soul healing miracles had begun.

It is curious to me that the information received by Dr. Sha from the Divine was focused on healing and learning lessons. Dr. Sha would later formulate his concept of "karma cleansing" to describe the mechanism that he believes empowers soul healing miracles. In the brief encounters with the Divine, the message was that the more you give, the more you get, whether it be giving love or healing energy. Those who give unconditionally receive unconditionally. The ultimate gift is to be able to be of unconditional service to others. When in this state, miracles can and do happen. This is Dr. Sha's belief and practice. In fact, the generation of unlimited abundance and joy through giving is not a belief for Dr. Sha, but a law of the universe, a law that governs his every waking moment and action. Dr. Sha believes that we live in a world of unlimited joy and abundance. Dr. Sha believes that the universe itself abounds with joy. It is only human beings misbehaving that creates illness and sorrow.

In this context I am reminded of the author of *The Master Key System*, Charles Haanel, who was the first Western writer to describe the law of attraction. The popular film *The Secret* oversimplified the presentation of the concepts of the law of attraction. For Charles Haanel, the law of attraction was the law of love. Haanel wrote of his belief that the universal law of the universe was that like attracted like. Love attracted love. Goodness attracted goodness. For Charles Haanel, this was the basic principle upon which he developed his Master Key System, which was later modified by Napoleon Hill and others to create programs for creating material wealth and health.

From a very different source, Dr. Sha discovered and emphasizes the law of karma. Given his background as both a medical doctor and acupuncturist, he has been able to apply this law in a practical way to enhance his own life and those of all he teaches and heals.

But is this concept of being a universal servant as the key to creating soul healing miracles verifiable on any scientific or measurable level? Is there any scientific data that might provide greater evidence that Dr. Sha has in fact communicated with the Divine and that his soul healing miracles are based on universal laws and not just the power of suggestion? We will explore these questions in future chapters, but in the next chapter we need to provide some of the basic principles upon which Chinese medicine in particular and energy medicine in general are based.

What Is Energy Medicine?

D R. SHA'S SOUL healing techniques have been developed from ancient Chinese practices of qi gong, tai chi, acupuncture, and other
traditional healing practices that are often considered "energy medicine." When I first heard the term *energy medicine*, I had visions of nu-
clear-powered contraptions sending energy to our bodies and healing
us with the latest and greatest technology. Energy medicine is, however,
completely low-tech. No machines are used and, in some cases, there is
barely even any touching. Reiki is perhaps the best-known modality of
energy medicine, but many practitioners have developed their own
techniques under a variety of names ranging from vibrational medicine
to white magic. From a traditional Western medical perspective, none of
these practices are medicine at all, and many would prefer that the name
energy medicine not be used. I am fine with that and will just use the term
energy healing.

While still a young boy in China, Dr. Sha was exposed to energy healing.
There are many such traditions within ancient Chinese practices including, of course, the acupuncture techniques that Dr. Sha later learned. The
principle behind acupuncture and other energy healing techniques is
that we all possess qi, or energy, and that when our qi is blocked, we
become ill. The essence of all energy healing is to remove the blockages
and get our qi moving again. Many herbal remedies throughout Asia
are based on this concept of qi and removing blockages. The difference
between herbal remedies and pure energy healing is that much can be
accomplished with mental and emotional intentionality even if the
herbal concoctions are not available. For many healers, having a positive

intention is essential for any form of herbal or energy healing to be effective. This positive intention is ideally shared by both healer and patient. There is no conflict between herbal remedies and movement work or acupuncture work when the healers are in agreement. In many healings, including those performed by Dr. Sha's own teacher Dr. Guo, both herbal and energy movement therapies are performed by the same therapist.

Modern scientists have studied the impact of intentionality. Removing stress enhances health. Focusing your mind can have a direct impact on improving the health of your body. Experiments by modern Western physicians have demonstrated a positive correlation between emotional therapies and the reduction of cancer cells in patients playing specially created video games. There is clearly a connection between emotional health and physical health. Traditional Western physicians are not sure how strong that connection is and have not been able to scientifically prove that for every patient the emotional component is significant. Few medical physicians have studied the emotional component of healing. The majority of practitioners and medical research dollars are devoted to finding and testing new drugs and exploring the ability to create new remedies based on cellular and even molecular research.

Holistic medicine is practiced by doctors who are traditionally trained MDs who feel that a patient's entire situation needs to be treated, not just the symptoms being presented in any specific moment. For these doctors it is important to treat the whole person, even if they are suffering from cancer or heart disease. The perspective is one that includes body, mind, and soul when treating a patient, not just the body. Dr. Sha's techniques are in this tradition of holistic medicine, and within this approach to healing it is clear that meditation, stress reduction, and other "soft therapies" have had and continue to have profound healing impact.

Paraphrasing Dr. Sha, the world is made of matter, energy, soul, and mind. Western medicine has not yet recognized the soul and focuses on matter in the physical body. Master Sha teaches there are three bodies in the human being: matter body, energy body, and soul body. Western medicine only focuses on the matter body. Dr. Sha told me, "When there is focus on the physical there can be healing on the physical, but that healing is often limited to the physical symptoms only and not the spiritual cause. In many cases the physical problem will return. When I focus on the spiritual cause of illness, that is the root cause of sickness."

"But how do you know when you are correct with your treatment?" I asked Dr. Sha.

"I offer divine soul readings to find out the soul mind body blockages of the person and offer divine soul healing" was his answer.

"But how do you know it is the Divine giving you this information?" I pushed.

"I am with the Divine. The Divine chose me as a servant. He is with me all of the time" was his matter-of-fact reply.

"But for a scientist that is a subjective feeling that cannot be measured and codified," I insisted.

"I use Einstein as the example. In the later stage of Einstein's life, he could not explain the phenomenon of the law of relativity and his findings. Then he started to believe in the Divine. There are many renowned scientists who cannot explain the phenomenon in a scientific way and then they turn to the Divine. What I want to share with humanity is the Divine is the creator for us. The Divine is the spiritual father and mother for us. Science is developing. Science will continue to develop. Science is always behind the spiritual development. You may agree with me. You may not agree with me. That is my internal understanding," was Dr. Sha's explanation.

"I believe you, but in this book I want to be able to explain your technique in a way that will pass scientific scrutiny," I explained.

"Well, scientists can study my patients. I have healed leukemia, cancer, heart disease, deafness, and stroke. I have healed thousands of chronic and life-threatening conditions," Dr. Sha went on enthusiastically.

"Can anyone learn how to do soul healing miracles?" I asked.

"Yes. Everyone can create soul healing miracles. They need to learn the secrets, wisdom, knowledge, and practical techniques to create their own soul healing miracles," Dr. Sha explained.

"Okay. Let's explore in more detail what you call karma cleansing and how you heal people."

Karma Cleansing

"SO DR. SHA, tell me about karma cleansing. What is it and how does it work?" I asked.

"Karma is the record of services in all lifetimes, including previous lifetimes and this lifetime. Karma is divided into two kinds: good karma and negative karma. Having good karma means a person has offered service to make others happier and healthier. The person has offered love, care, compassion, sincerity, honesty, kindness, generosity, integrity, grace, and much more to others. Negative karma means that a person offers unpleasant services to others including killing, harming, taking advantage of others, cheating, stealing, and more. How does karma work? If one accumulates good karma, one receives good health, good relationships, flourishing finances, good children, good intelligence, and they flourish in every aspect of life. If a person has accumulated negative karma, the person could learn lessons from challenges to their health, relationships, children, finances, intelligence, and every aspect of life."

I asked Dr. Sha, "Some people like me believe in karma from this lifetime, but I am not sure I believe in karma from past lifetimes. Does a karma cleansing still work for me?"

Dr. Sha explained. "When you speak about karma, it includes past lifetimes and the current lifetime. How karma works? The past lifetimes of negative karma affect this lifetime. The negative karma from this lifetime affects this lifetime. They all also affect the future lifetimes. If some people have very heavy karma, the person could learn lessons in hundreds or thousands of lifetimes. If you only believe negative karma for this lifetime, karma cleansing will work for you. If you do not believe in past lifetimes of negative karma and you do not clear the negative karma, you will learn lessons. This is the karma law regardless of whether you believe or not."

I then interjected and said, "As long as I am of service in this lifetime, I receive the benefits of karma cleansing even if I don't believe in reincarnation?"

Dr. Sha answered, "Yes, if you offer unconditional service, you will clear negative karma naturally regardless of whether you believe in negative karma or not; regardless of whether you believe in reincarnation or not. If you do not believe, it does not mean it does not exist. Karma is one of the most important spiritual laws. It operates by itself."

"This is very reassuring and makes me feel somewhat more protected because I and the majority of people I know do not believe in reincarnation, so it is very reassuring that if we do not believe in reincarnation, we can still receive the benefits of karma cleansing," was my answer to Dr. Sha.

When I expressed my desire to learn more about the science behind karma cleansing, Dr. Sha suggested that I meet with his student Rulin Xiu.

Dr. Rulin Xiu

I N MY PURSUIT to learn of the science behind soul healing miracles I asked Dr. Sha to introduce me to Rulin Xiu. Rulin had been mentioned to me as a former academic with a Ph.D. in theoretical physics from the University of California at Berkeley. Rulin was one of the world's leading authorities on string theory and grand unification theory. The search for a grand unification theory is the domain of the great physicist Albert Einstein and other luminary physicists. This is not the type of endeavor for people with little brainpower. Rulin had written many scientific papers on string theory while at Berkeley. Dr. Sha was attracting some of the best and brightest minds in the world to learn and study his soul healing practices. Rulin at the time I met her was a fit, attractive, petite woman with black hair in her early fifties. She looked much younger and at five feet two inches could not have weighed more than 105 pounds. She dressed simply with the cheerful colors typical of the clothing worn in Hawaii, where she now lives.

Rulin was able to fly to the mainland for our meeting. I thought it important to learn as much as I could about Rulin's personal history before delving into the science, so I did my normal ethnographic background study of who she was, what type of family she came from, and what her key values were. I learned that Rulin had been born in Yulin, a city in northwest China next to Inner Mongolia. Her father had been a geologist and her mother taught at a university. She was born in the 1960s, so Mao's Cultural Revolution had ended prior to her entering high school. As a young girl her favorite hobbies were picking herbs, reading, singing, and dancing. In elementary and high school her favorite subject was mathematics, and in college and graduate school she pursued theoretical physics. She learned English in middle school in China, and by the time I met her thirty years later her English was impeccable, no doubt because of the time she had spent at Berkeley and living near Hilo on the island of Hawaii.

Although Rulin had been a top-notch string theorist expert at Berkeley in 1996, she was offered an opportunity to start a business, which she would run from Washington, D.C. with family members in China, that would produce and process nutritional herbs. This business became quite successful, and Rulin put on hold her academic dreams of working out the details of a grand unification theory. In 2003 Rulin relocated to Hawaii, where she continues to oversee a factory she set up to process Hawaiian-grown herbal supplements. It was at a retreat held by Dr. Sha in Hawaii a few years later on September 9, 2009, that Rulin first met Dr. Sha. This meeting changed her life forever.

Rulin describes the meeting in this way: "My life was going very smoothly. My business was extremely successful and I had achieved every material desire I had ever had. I was living in one of the most beautiful places in the world and able to pursue my hobbies and intellectual interests. I went to Dr. Sha's workshop not because of any specific desire I had for a personal healing but because of my general interest in healing itself. My herbal business was directly related to the healing properties of our products, and it was intellectual curiosity that piqued my interest in attending the workshop. Besides, the workshop was quite close to where I was living, so it was not a great effort on my part to attend and was a nice change of pace from my daily routine. Of course, there was a spiritual element to my decision to attend as well. I had befriended two Hawaiian kahunas, and each of them told me it was important for me to attend the workshop.

"I was impressed by Dr. Sha's healing power and inspired by his dedication to serving humanity. At the end of the workshop, when he was signing books for me, I told him I wanted to become his student. I did not realize this in that moment, but his acceptance of me as his student altered my life in ways that I could never have imagined. I continue to prosper in my business, but his teachings have taken my life to a much higher level. From Dr. Sha I have learned how to truly live and how to serve humanity. In that process I have connected with my higher purpose and am now able to unleash my true potential. For me, since meeting and working with Dr. Sha, I now live a life full of love on multiple levels, a life of joy of unlimited possibilities."

Intrigued by this high praise I asked, "Without going into details, what is the single most important lesson you have learned from Dr. Sha?"

Rulin smiled as she answered, "That's an easy question. Dr. Sha teaches the meaning of and serves as a catalyst to experience divine love. Divine love is the true basis of all reality, and once you understand the basis of divine love, you understand the true nature of not just who you are but why you are and how you can best interact with others."

"Are you saying this as a scientist or someone who has personally experienced Dr. Sha's soul miracles?" I asked.

"Both. I am still a scientist and have actually spent the last several years writing research papers on the science behind the efficacy of soul healing miracles, but there is no doubt that my continued interest in the scientific investigations of this healing phenomenon is influenced by my own personal experiences with Dr. Sha, his healing energies, and through the healing energies of the Divine itself," Rulin explained.

"Doesn't this level of personal involvement interfere with your scientific objectivity?" I queried.

"I don't think so. Science is changing. We already know that the observer is constantly impacting the outcome of scientific experiments. I am not doing actual experiments but investigating the physics behind soul healing miracles. The model from string theory and quantum physics is completely aligned with my own personal experiences. In fact, these personal experiences are enabling me to better understand the physics on both an intellectual and soul level. My work is showing that soul and mind are linked, and that the very nature of reality is based on the principles of soul that Dr. Sha teaches and uses in his healing. My goal is to develop the mathematical equations that will explain for scientists the connections between soul and matter. Up to now scientists have ignored soul in their attempts to measure the energies and universal laws that have created our universe and govern our existence," Rulin explained, warming to what clearly was a subject she enjoyed and had investigated in depth.

"Let's start at the beginning and keep this simple," I suggested. "Are you saying that as a scientist you can actually measure 'soul'?"

"As a scientist I can give soul a mathematical definition or formulation. From my mathematical formulation of soul, I can derive mathematically the relationships among soul, energy, matter, and information; I can use my mathematical formula of soul to explain the nature of our existence. From my mathematical formulation of soul, I can prove scientifically that soul, energy, and matter are one. Interestingly, this concept of soul, energy, and matter being one is the basis of the ancient beliefs in Tao, which are the basis not just for Dr. Sha's soul healing miracles but also for all energy medicine as developed by Chinese and other Asian masters over the last several thousand years," Rulin explained.

"Our mind is always processing information and energy. We are living in what has been called the information era. The reality is that what we call information is really contained within the soul. Every entity in the universe has information. This information is carried by matter and energy, and the ultimate information is contained in every being, both animate and inanimate. At first it may seem paradoxical to say that the soul of each being contains soul, energy, and matter but it is correct since the soul is primary to the other components of existence, and as I show in my scientific papers, the origin of all matter, information, and energy actually comes from what can best be described as the divine soul of creation. The theory of grand unification that Einstein and other physicists have contemplated is going to be revealed once we understand the true nature and properties of the divine soul. This reality is why karma cleansing is effective," Dr. Rulin asserted.

"This is a lot to comprehend. Let's take this one step at a time. What are the givens that readers must accept to understand your grand unification theory that the divine soul is the basis of reality and provides the scientific evidence that Dr. Sha's soul healing practices are based on sound scientific thinking and not wish fulfillment or the placebo effect?" I asked.

"The first given is to accept that every one of us in the universe comes from the same source. We are connected by the Source. Each one of us can tap into the infinite power, energy, and matter, infinite wisdom and knowledge, and infinite love when we connect with the Source," Dr. Rulin began.

"Well, that seems obvious to me though I am sure some scientists will disagree," I commented.

"Well, I can actually demonstrate from my mathematical formulation of soul that this statement is not just a faith or belief system. It can be scientifically proven. The next given is to understand that what we think, what we say, what we hear, what we taste, what we feel, and what we do create our karma. Our karma determines our individual soul. It determines the information, matter, energy, mind, and heart inside us. Our individual soul determines our reality. The reality we created through our karma separates us from the Source. When we clear our karma, we connect with the Source again. When we are connected with the Source or Divine soul, we are healed in every aspect. We restore our natural powerful, wise, healthy, and loving self.

"Soul healing is to remove karma. It is to change the information inside us. By changing our karma and the information inside us, we can be healed in every aspect of our lives.

"Soul healing is based on the fact that all souls are connected and beyond space-time. Soul healing may happen over distances, and also instantly. A soul healer can give healings to one person or simultaneously to many people anywhere in the universe."

"I have seen the reality of what you are suggesting but many scientists do not believe in karma," I opined.

Dr. Rulin eagerly explained, "In my research paper, I give karma a mathematical formulation using quantum physics. From my mathematical formulation of soul and karma, I show that karma determines our individual soul, which in turn determines our reality. To clear karma is to heal our soul. When we heal our soul, we heal our mind, our heart, our body, and every aspect of our reality."

"Okay. Let's accept that karma affects our soul. What additional givens must readers accept?" I asked.

"The final and perhaps most important given is to accept that our soul determines our mind and heart. In my scientific paper, I also give a mathematical formulation for the mind, heart, and consciousness. I show that mind and heart are two aspects of our soul. Our mind is the aspect of the soul that processes information. The heart is the aspect of the soul that perceives and is aware of the possibilities and different vibrations inside the soul. Our consciousness is the awareness of our mind activities. It takes both mind and heart to have consciousness. Soul, mind, heart, and consciousness are one."

"Well, this is where I am afraid you are going to lose most mainstream scientists. Even those who believe in karma and the soul will not necessarily believe that soul is primary to matter. Scientists like to measure time, space, and matter. When you introduce the concepts of the vacuum, zero-point energy, and the primacy of the soul above all other elements, I think we drift from hard science to belief-based science. But, of course, I could be wrong. Explain to me again the relationship between the zero-point energy and Tao, as my understanding of Tao is that Tao is emptiness," I asked.

"Tao is where everything comes from. Tao is the Source. Tao is the emptiness in the sense that it does not depend on personal likes or dislikes. But Tao has its own soul, energy, and matter. It is not equal to complete emptiness. The soul, energy, and matter of Tao is not zero. In this sense, our grand unification theory is different from the popular zero-point energy theory out there. In fact, I have calculated the total energy of vacuum energy of our universe, and it is not zero. It is equal to the critical energy, which can explain why our universe is observed to be flat for the most part," Dr. Rulin explained.

"This seems quite complex. What are the keys to your findings?" I asked.

"Most likely this will be explained by the nature of negative entropy and the principle of Tao creation and balance throughout the universe. Soul, energy, and matter are constantly created out of Tao. There are no limits to the spacetime, energy, matter, and information of Tao. Although on the level of human awareness there is constant change moment to moment, at the level of the Tao there is perfect balance and harmony in every moment. What we experience as change is change in form, thought, and substance, but not change at the level of Tao energy. This is why soul healing miracles work. They are grounded in the infinite and deeper reality of Tao, which actually governs all human experience and all creation," Dr. Rulin further explained.

"I am not sure all readers will be able to follow this line of scientific conjecture. Let's just discuss the basic concepts of soul, mind, and body. Before moving to the concept of soul healing miracles, Dr. Sha introduced the concept of body, mind, and soul healing. Please define each of these terms as used by Dr. Sha," I suggested.

"Soul is the essence of everything. Every human being, every animal, and every animate and inanimate entity in the universe has a soul. According to quantum physics, everything is made of vibration. Therefore, in essence everything is soul. Body is the physical measurement of soul by senses and detecting equipment of measurements such as length, width, height, weight, spin, electric current. Energy is part of the body because the measurement of energy is part of the measurement by our senses and equipment. Mind is the system that processes information. Mind is part of the soul. Everything is part of the soul. The three components—body, mind, and spirit—are all part of the soul," were the definitions Dr. Rulin provided.

"Okay. I think I understand these principles. Earlier you discussed the importance of information and energy in the healing practices. Explain the difference between energy and information."

"Energy is a physical quantity that is defined as how much work an object or system can do. Information consists of two aspects: one is the amount of possibilities in a system, the other is the choice made by the system. Once you understand these principles you can begin to understand why karma cleansing is effective. Each individual has access to infinite energy. The information that Dr. Sha and other miracle soul healers bring to each individual during a healing allows the individual to choose what aspects of their soul connection they choose to send energy to. It is this choice and sending of energy which has the ability to alter the soul imprint. The soul exists outside of time, so healing past imperfections in the soul can have immediate impact on the present situation of any individual. The soul directs the experience of the body and accounts for what are being called 'miracle healings' by medical doctors and the patients themselves. Someday, I predict, when everyday people have a better understanding of the true nature of the universe, there will be no need to call these healings soul healing miracles. They will just be accepted as the most logical way to take advantage of the knowledge we are developing of the interconnections between the past, present, and future," Dr. Rulin explained confidently and from her perspective as simply as she could.

I was not sure I was totally satisfied with the scientific explanation of why karma cleansings work, but I was certainly intrigued. I thanked Dr. Rulin for the interview and thought I should explore what other researchers and scholars have considered "miracle healings" and what we mean when we contemplate the notion of miracles in our lives.

For those scientists among you who wish to explore scientific concepts I strongly recommend you purchase a copy of Dr. and Master Sha and Dr. Rulin Xiu's co-authored books *Soul Mind Body Science System* (BenBella Books, 2014) and *Tao Science*.

Miracles

THROUGHOUT RECORDED HISTORY, the concept of miracles has been at the core of both religious and political movements. The claim of miracles has been essential to the establishment of many religions and has been used to gain and exert political power. As many scholars have been adamant that miracles cannot exist as those who have "sworn" they do.

In common usage, the term *miracle* is applied to any event that is not explainable through natural observable laws. Even critics of miracles will accept that unusual events can occur that seem miraculous, but they are certain that upon further investigation, natural laws could be uncovered that would explain the miracle. The belief of those who accept miracles is that a divine force exists that can override natural laws at any time, creating unexplainable outcomes or at least outcomes unexplainable by any evidence other than the existence of the Divine.

Miracles are sometimes attributed to technological developments that were unimagined prior to their existence. Four hundred years ago, the concept of jumbo jets flying hundreds of thousands of people around the world on a daily basis would have seemed a claim that could only be realized through a "miracle." A colorful example of this is the ad by Xerox of monks discovering that ancient texts that took months and years to be created one at a time by artist calligraphers could be reproduced instantly with a Xerox copy machine. The monks look at each other at the end of the commercial and then look upward as they exclaim, "It's a miracle!"

This lighthearted dismissal of the possibility of true miracles and the reliance on the laws of science, nature, and human genius to create once-in-a-lifetime achievements is important to our discussion of Dr. Sha and his claims of soul healing miracles. It is also important to an examination of other miracle healers as we attempt not only to document the possibility of true medical miracles but also to understand if the laws of nature and the laws of the Divine are actually working together to create these miracles. My early conclusion is that we do not need to create an either/or scenario. The laws of nature do in fact determine all that we observe. The reason we have had recorded miracles for centuries is that we have never completely understood the relationship between the Divine and natural laws. I would go even further and suggest that the ability to fully understand the Divine will in the future reveal that true miracles from past prophets and saints were based on a deeper understanding of the true nature of reality, a reality that is created at a level that transcends our everyday perception of time and space and that incorporates the concept of divine and individual "soul" as explained and theorized by Dr. and Master Sha, Dr. Rulin Xiu, and others who have been making scientific investigations into the nature of soul healing miracles.

But before we explore the possible scientific explanations for miracles, let's consider some of the ways in which miracles have shaped human history and present world culture. For those who have no belief whatsoever in the possibility of divine intervention or the Divine itself even existing, I encourage you to explore the nature of string theory and quantum mechanics, as within the realm of science we can recreate the scenarios, circumstances, and qualities that those who believe in the divine attribute to the divine causation of miracles. Since the majority of readers are open to the possibility of the Divine, for simplicity and clarity I will invoke the belief in divine intervention in discussing the following miracles. I do not personally believe in the Divine in the sense that followers of Jesus, Muhammad, or Buddha believe, but I do believe in an all-knowing, self-organizing principle that governs all creation, including events both human and nonhuman on planet Earth.

The second most famous miracle of Western civilization is the birth of Jesus. Jesus was said to have been conceived of a virgin. There is no scientific explanation that would explain this birth. Those who believe in the immaculate conception accept that a divine creator God engineered this conception. Those who do not believe in Jesus just assume that the immaculate conception is a story and not based on fact. The greatest miracle attributed to Jesus is the belief in his resurrection. The belief that Jesus was killed on the cross and then emerged three days later fully alive is the basis for Christian faith, a religion that inspires and governs more than a billion individuals on planet earth at this time. In addition to these two major miracles Jesus is said to have turned water into wine, walked on water, healed the sick, given sight to the blind, and in the case of Lazarus, raised the dead. Those who believe, believe. Those who don't, don't. There were no video cameras on earth at the time of Jesus. There were no scientific studies of his healings. Did they take place or didn't they? Scientists for the most part assume they did not and could not. Scientists who believe in Jesus explain away the miracles as metaphors or illustrative stories that are not to be accepted literally. Jesus himself throughout the New Testament is reported to have explained to his followers that ordinary mortals can perform miracles. All that is necessary is faith in God. To quote the Gospel of Matthew 17:20, Jesus says, "If you have faith as small as a mustard seed, you can say to this mountain, 'move from here to there,' and it will move." Dr. Sha, when he tells people that he can do soul healing miracles and that they can do soul healing miracles, is echoing a similar belief, though in the case of Dr. Sha, his claim is that, based on natural laws rather than belief, you can achieve these results. We will save for a later chapter the discussion of whether or not faith in the Divine is in fact, as I believe thus far in my investigation, necessary to achieve soul healing miracles.

After the death of Jesus, many reports of miracles continued to be reported, all related to matters of Catholic faith. In fact, the number of miracles reported has been so extensive that the Catholic Church has created protocols for the investigation of reported miracles and even requires evidence of posthumously performed miracles to elevate former popes such as Pope John Paul II to beatification, as was done by Pope

Benedict XVI on January 12, 2011, and his canonization by Pope Francis on April 27, 2014. In addition to official church confirmations of miracles at sites such as Lourdes in France and Fatima in Portugal, there are many unofficial reports of miracles on record at small churches and chapels throughout Europe dating back hundreds of years. While studying cultural anthropology at Harvard University, I was presented with an undergraduate final thesis on the topic of reported miracles in Spain from 1500 to 1800. The author, William Christian, had investigated authenticated official church reports of miracles in many small towns throughout Spain, which reported that prayers, in most cases to the Virgin Mary, had overcome myriad illnesses ranging from the recovery of sight and hearing to the use of arms and legs that had been badly damaged through accidents. In Spain this investigator uncovered what had become known as "the Cult of the Virgin Mary," which was the strong belief that praying to Mary was the most effective way to achieve medical miracles. Entire towns (mostly the women, as the men left the miracles to the women) would pray for the end of droughts and other "miracles." In many cases the townspeople were absolutely certain that it was divine intervention by God through Mother Mary that brought rain and saved them from famine.

The Catholic Church was concerned with the growth of the Cult of Mary and the possibility of direct entreaties requesting miracles that did not require official church supervision. Although not limited to the Catholic Church, many women who reported "miracle healings" were considered to be working with the devil or to be witches and were often tortured and put to death. It is interesting to note that the performance of "miracles" or the appearance of performing miracles created such violent reprisals. Although much toned down today, there are still many medical doctors and scientists who, when presented with healing miracles whether performed by Dr. Sha, John of God, or other miracle healers, are outraged that such claims are made, as they violate the scientific dogma and are as blasphemous to modern science and medicine as the gifted peasant healers were to the Church centuries ago.

Turning from the Catholic Church, we can find documented reports of miracles from a wide range of historical and present-day figures representing all major religions and all nations throughout our planet. Whether Jewish, Hindu, Sufi, Buddhist, Mormon, or from less-established religions, the concept of documenting actual miracles is universal. In all cases miracles are considered signs of divine intervention favoring those who have been able to entreat and connect with the Divine. There is no limit to the specific types of miracles reported. In Yogananda's *Autobiography of a Yogi*, he reports on the ability of his own great yogi teachers to bi-locate; that is, to be in two different places at the same time. As a casual believer in Yogananda and not a devout student, I find this claim unlikely, but Yogananda's devoted followers are certain this is just a factual report. Certainly, if true, this ability would be considered the manifestation of a miracle. We also have countless reports of psychic events that seem miraculous. My own mother had psychic abilities and once, on a trip in Paris when I was a young boy of nine, phoned our housekeeper and warned her to remove me and my brothers and sister from our house in Scarborough, New York. She had just woken up from a dream and in the dream saw the boiler in the basement exploding and setting the house on fire. I remember our caretaker calling the fire department and the fire chief telling her, "Good thing you called us. In another twenty minutes this boiler would have exploded." I am not sure I would consider this psychic dream a miracle, but certainly it indicates an extraordinary occurrence that some would characterize as miraculous.

In modern days, increasingly the focus has been on medical miracles. This focus on medical miracles may be in part due to the better reporting and measurement tools that we have due to advances in Western medicine. We can now measure blood counts and other phenomena associated with terminal conditions, and when healings reverse such measurements and patients return to balance and continued physical well-being for extended periods of time, it is appropriate from the perspective of today's scientific knowledge to call such events medical miracles.

Dr. Sha is not the only human being on planet Earth at this time performing healing miracles. I believe he is the only healer claiming he is capable of teaching others to perform healing miracles, but there are many others who have reported and continue to report astounding results from their healing practices. In most instances, these healing practices defy the logic of our present medical doctors and our Western medical paradigm. Not all of these practitioners call what they do "miracle healing," and many of them prefer to focus on the scientific principles that govern their abilities and their results, eschewing altogether any claims for a connection to the Divine or the ability to perform "miracles." I have had the opportunity to either directly or indirectly experience or interview some of these healers and I can attest to their effectiveness. Many of these healers, such as John of God of Brazil, do not have a specific scientific explanation for what they do and how they do it. Others, such as Braco, do not even speak when they sit and provide energetic "blessings" for thousands of people at a time. Many of those in attendance report remarkable healings and experiences. Of course, not all of those who attend report positive outcomes. Is it just a matter of self-delusion and playing the odds that there will be a significant number of "spontaneous" remissions, or in some cases are true healing miracles taking place?

I have also worked with other medical doctors who have developed their own unique healing systems. The fact that other practitioners are using similar techniques to those used by Dr. Sha was one of the reasons I wanted to do more research on exactly how Dr. Sha accomplishes soul healing miracles. My background as an anthropologist leads me to believe that the principles that govern one type of successful procedure are likely to be mirrored in other practices. The fact that this is the case encouraged me to interview actual patients who have received soul healing miracles from Dr. Sha and to also interview other healers whom Dr. Sha has trained to provide soul healing miracles.

I have a young client, Jake Ducey, who is a brilliant inspirational speaker and the author of his autobiography *Into the Wind*, written when Jake was just nineteen years old. Jake ends all of his e-mails with the quote "miracles are normal." By definition, miracles can never be normal or they would not be miracles. Evidence seems to be mounting that what we have considered to be miracles are not miraculous at all, but demonstrations of certain individuals such as Dr. Sha to utilize the emerging knowledge of the true nature of time, space, and physical reality to connect our everyday reality to soul reality. With our limited present knowledge, the healing results I am about to report are indeed healing miracles. When skeptics and believers can reconcile their views on spirit and science and how the two can work together, we will have achieved a true miracle, a miracle that is obtainable with just the slightest effort and the willingness to remain open to true knowledge.

The Evidence

"THIS IS REAL," stated the chief of police of New Brunswick, New Jersey, Don Bowling, after he received a five-minute soul operation from Dr. Sha. Police Chief Bowling had fallen down some stairs twenty-one months previously and fractured his ankle, hurt his knee and back, and had been using a cane since he was unable to pivot or walk normally. There were tears in his eyes as he thanked Dr. Sha for the healing.

Don Bowling is not the kind of man you would expect to even know about a healer such as Dr. Sha. Don Bowling does have faith and his own spiritual beliefs but is a typical police chief, focused on gathering evidence and only believing in what he can see with his own eyes and evidence that meets the requirements of his sharp mind. Don is over six feet six inches tall. The video that was taped of this healing is available at this link: youtube.com/watch?v=be-0N1HFT7U. Hopefully you will watch this healing and the others on which I report in this chapter. Each is incredible in and of itself, and together they are truly incredible as they include a police chief; a young mother and her baby in Vancouver, Canada; a major actress in India who had been deaf for more than twenty years; a nurse from Hawaii with a chronic knee injury; a former drug addict in Colorado; and a sixty-four-year-old man whose doctors believed he would die within a few months since he had multiple cancers that could not be removed with surgery or radiation or be treated with chemotherapy. Though we may still need additional proof that these are true miracle healings, my initial investigation is that these are extraordinary outcomes that scientists and medical researchers should investigate.

One of the more curious aspects of these healings is that at no time does Dr. Sha actually touch the individuals whom he heals. The video does show some slight physical acupuncture contact in the case of the Indian actress who had been deaf for more than twenty years, but for the rest there is no physical contact whatsoever. I think this is important as it establishes the principle that these are, as Dr. Sha explains, "soul operations." *Soul operation* means divine light goes through Master Sha's hands and spiritually opens the area that needs healing. Divine light removes soul mind body blockages in the area. This is the soul operation concept that Master Sha shared with me. Soul operations involve healing the soul with the belief that once the soul is healed, the energy will flow to the body and heal the aspect of the body that has been out of alignment with its soul. Dr. Sha believes that each body organ and body part has an individual soul and that the Divine has the ability to realign such out-of-kilter organs and body parts. If nothing else, the fact that Dr. Sha generally does not touch a patient should encourage those who are skeptical to allow themselves to experience a soul healing themselves. The soul operation is noninvasive and has no side effects.

Police Chief Don Bowling explained that he had not been able to walk normally for almost two years. The insurance company had determined that he was no longer eligible for any surgery or additional care. He had adopted a regimen of exercise to prevent further deterioration of his leg, ankle, and knee, but in his words, he had reached a state where his condition "was getting no worse, no better." Dr. Sha explained that he would perform a "soul operation and soul transplant" for both legs. Master Sha explained that during the soul transplant the Divine would create a new soul for an organ and transmit it to the recipient. The healing was taking place at the United Nations in New York City in front of an audience that had assembled to learn about Dr. Sha's soul healing techniques. Dr. Sha focused on Police Chief Bowling's leg. Dr. Sha made movements with his hands and arms and focused his attention with intensity that was noticeable. After just a minute, he asked Police Chief Bowling if he could feel anything. The police chief responded," I feel warmth in my left leg." This was the injured leg. Dr. Sha politely asked the police chief to hand him the cane he had been using to walk. Police

Chief Bowling handed Dr. Sha the cane and was asked to turn and walk. Much to the police chief's surprise, he could turn and walk effortlessly and without pain.

Don Bowling is a man with a good sense of humor, and when he was given back his cane, he asked the audience if anyone "wanted to buy his cane," as it was clear to him that he no longer needed it. He turned to the audience and explained that he was a man of faith and that he did not put up roadblocks that might prevent his recovery, for he believed everything is possible. He was clearly amazed and grateful for the healing he had just received. He had tears in his eyes briefly when first asked to speak. Choking back those tears, his comment "This is real" was clearly heartfelt and his honest assessment of what he had just experienced. To him and to those in the audience it certainly seemed a miracle.

An even more amazing miracle healing on this same video clip is that of Zakary. Zakary's mom was notified late in her pregnancy that her fetus had developed hydrocephalus, known in layman's language as water on the brain. The swelling was so severe that the prognosis was for a stillborn. Zakary's mom was encouraged to meet with Dr. Sha, and Dr. Sha performed a soul healing operation, major karma cleansing, and divine light body on the yet-unborn fetus. A divine light body means that the Divine creates a new soul for all systems, organs, and cells, and this was transmitted to Zakary. The baby was born alive but with severe challenges. The water around the brain was so great that the brain itself could not be detected. The swelling required a shunt and made Zakary look deformed. Zakary also had seizures and scarring on his eyes and lesions in his joints and throughout his body. The doctors were not sure what to do and warned that Zakary was unlikely to live more than a few weeks or months.

Zakary's mom continued to have treatments with Dr. Sha's students and followed the forgiveness regime that Dr. Sha had taught her. At the age of one, Zakary was still alive and received a second healing blessing from Dr. Sha. At this time Zakary was still feeding from a nose tube and had numerous challenges, but he was on the path to becoming a normal child. His mom was providing extensive care and love but was giving primary credit to the soul healing that Dr. Sha had performed a year earlier just before Zakary was born. On the video clip, Dr. Sha performs another soul healing with soul transplants and soul operations on many different organs in Zakary's body, including his central nervous system and his brain. At the end of the session, Dr. Sha's students join in a chant of "divine light being" addressed to Zakary. Zakary seems to comprehend and smiles as he is serenaded.

A year later via Skype, Zakary's mother reports back to Dr. Sha that now, almost two years old, Zakary can eat on his own, his seizures have stopped, the scarring on his eyes has healed, and he can see. His brain has grown so quickly that the doctors have had to remove the sutures, and Zakary can sit up on his own, recognizes colors, and can play with animals. Based on the video shown from the previous year, it seems to be a true miracle. The doctors who had been afraid to even touch Zakary have no explanation other than Zakary is "healing naturally." It seems odd for these doctors to fall back on "healing naturally" when they were the ones who prior to birth and in his first few months after birth had predicted that Zakary would not survive. If indeed Zakary is "healing naturally," it can only be because Dr. Sha's soul healing operation, karma cleansings, and many, many divine treasures have realigned Zakary with his true nature and the true nature of his soul and that of the universe. At a minimum, that is the explanation Zakary's mom believes.

When I spoke with Zakary's mom, Erica, I learned that she was living in Moose Jaw, Canada, and was finishing her degree with a concentration in special education. As a young girl she had been born on a small island in British Columbia, and since her mother was Polish, she spoke only Polish until she was seven years old when she moved to Moose Jaw. When she was sixteen years old, she befriended a deaf student, and it was at that time that she decided she wanted to work with the disabled. She worked part-time in Moose Jaw's Valley View Center for the mentally ill and developed an appreciation as well as compassion for those less fortunate. She resolved, in her words, "to dedicate my life to equality for all people." Erica is a strong-willed young woman. She met her future husband, Zakary's father Kevin Rimmer, when she was only seventeen at an A&W Root Beer stand in Moose Jaw. When Kevin came to her parents to ask if he could court her, they told him, "You probably can't afford her," as they had taken Erica on trips to Poland to visit family and accustomed her to a life that would include travel. Kevin at the time was working as an automobile mechanic and already had a child from a previous relationship. But Kevin was determined, and although it took him five years to complete his education so he could obtain a position as an instrumentation specialist with higher pay, he returned when he felt he could afford Erica and, with a one-carat diamond ring, announced his intention to marry her. Erica had been attracted to Kevin from the start and with her parents' blessing agreed to marry Kevin.

Their romance was interrupted by the gravity of her pregnancy going awry. She had been made aware of Dr. Sha by her mother, who had always pursued spiritual teachings. Desperate but without any real faith in Dr. Sha's abilities, Erica had an initial emergency phone consultation, followed after Zakary was born with a personal visit with Dr. Sha in Vancouver. Erica continued to have consultations with one of Dr. Sha's teachers, Master Sher, and was directed to do forgiveness practices and to listen to Dr. Sha's chants. She also played soul healing chants through her smartphone directly to Zakary, placing the music on his head. Even with the tremendous progress Zakary had made there was still worry that he may not totally heal. Erica had faith in Dr. Sha and felt that Dr. Sha's direct intervention was the most powerful healing possible. Just as this book was being completed, I received an e-mail from Erica stating that the most recent MRI on Zakary was all clear.

Addictions are almost impossible to "cure" medically. There are many wonderful treatment programs for the drug, alcohol, food, sex, gambling, and related addictions that are destroying tens of millions of lives daily in America and throughout the world. In another video clip, you meet twenty-five-year-old native Coloradan Steven Pointer, who reports that for the first time in years, he no longer has a craving for marijuana or alcohol after just a single group soul operation and single interaction onstage with Dr. Sha at a retreat held in Colorado in April 2013.

I caught up with Steven a year after the intervention to get details on his experience and his progress.

"It's been more than a year and I have not touched a drop of alcohol or smoked any marijuana since my healing with Dr. Sha. This amazes even me, as I was a hard-core stoner.

"For at least the previous five years I had smoked weed every day, sometimes four or five times a day. I had also been a daily beer and whisky drinker, often getting wasted three or four times a week. I was able to hold down a job waiting tables at P.F. Chang's, but my relationships and life were a mess. My aunt, who is a psychotherapist and into spirituality, had turned me on to Dr. Sha's books and in October of 2012 invited me to attend a two-day workshop. I was kind of into the I Ching and meditation, so the book did resonate with me, but that did not change my addictions. In fact, I was a skeptic, and the first time I heard Dr. Sha speak I felt he was 'far out' and hard to follow. At the same time, I believed in the general principle of forgiveness and the idea of karma, so when my aunt suggested that I go to that retreat in October of 2012, I was open to going.

"The October retreat was scheduled for a two-day weekend and I had already made plans to go to a concert the Saturday night, so I did. I got wasted as usual with both weed and alcohol at the concert, but even with a hangover felt positive energy from the Sunday session. I was still addicted after that first retreat but with my aunt's encouragement was motivated to attend the April retreat. Besides, I had consulted the I Ching and was given the strongest possible affirmation that I should attend. When Dr. Sha did a soul healing operation for the entire group the first day of the retreat, I felt dark energy leave my body. That night, for the first time in several years I slept soundly and did not crave either weed or alcohol before going to bed. The next day Dr. Sha asked me to go onstage. This was huge for me, as I had never wanted to admit I had drug and alcohol problems. I had gone to AA for an entire year off and on but had never stopped drinking and smoking weed for more than six weeks. That group soul operation did the trick. I am sure the karma cleansing with Dr. Sha the next day is why it stuck. I have not had any craving since and now realize that it was depression that was driving me to drink and smoke. With the help of Dr. Sha's exercises, I am getting a handle on my depression and intend to use what I have learned to help heal others. My former drinking buddies wonder what happened to me, and I am amazed myself, as alcohol was all around me at the sushi restaurant where I used to work but I have no cravings at all. Recently I have gotten a new job doing yard work and painting. Perhaps a year is too short a time to call this a miracle drug and alcohol addiction healing, but the experience continues to be a miracle for me. My life is now my own."

As a registered nurse, Brenda Gartner had received the best of care. She understood the medical profession and had access to the best doctors and hospitals. In 1999 she had had a sports injury that damaged her knee. She had been in constant pain for more than a decade. She could not even kneel down. With a single soul mind body transplant from Dr. Sha, she could for the first time in twelve years kneel again. For her it was a miracle healing that no traditional medical doctor or operation could have equaled. This is how she describes her experience:

My Miracle Healing to Left Knee by Master Sha

I had played softball most of my adult life, first in high school, then college, then through my work recreationally. In 1999 I was playing a game one evening and played my usual position on first base. A batter for the other team, a large-frame Hawaiian male, hit a swift ball up the third base line, where my teammate snagged it and whizzed it to me on first base, hoping to put the batter out. I jumped into the air to catch it, only to have the runner come and plow my legs out from under me. I dropped immediately to the ground in severe pain. Even though I worked in the ER at the time, I did not seek medical attention; instead, I was feeling better three weeks later and again went to play ball one evening. This time I was the batter, and immediately on hitting a homer way out into the field, during the twist to hit that ball I again felt instant pain to my left knee. This time my knee instantly filled with fluid and ballooned to twice its size. That night I went straight to the ER where I worked and was sent to see a specialist the next day who immediately scheduled me for surgery. The surgery proved not one but two significant injuries: a medial meniscus tear and a severe ACL (anterior cruciate ligament) tear. There was a complication following the surgery and three days later I had to return for a second operation, and within the next ten years, yet two more surgeries. It came to a point in 2009 where I was told that I had no more cartilage in my knee and that I would need a knee replacement but that I was too young and would have to tough it out until I was older. There were not many days when I was not in some kind of pain ... varying from irritating discomfort to limping because the knee would lock and grind from the result of bone on bone. I was also not able to bend that left knee anymore, making it very difficult and almost impossible to kneel in church each Sunday. In 2011 I was blessed to receive a soul mind body transplant and sphere for my knees from Master Sha, and immediately the pain was gone and I could kneel for the first time in twelve years! I did have a little locking over the next two days ... and so Master Sha gave me one more healing a couple days later since we had been attending a workshop he was giving in Honolulu, and by the third day—no more pain of any kind, which is the way it has remained to this very day. I am so thankful to Master Sha for this miraculous healing.

Shammi Aunty is a renowned Bollywood star in India. She suffered from deafness and wore hearing aids for more than twenty years. She lived in Mumbai. A few years ago, Dr. and Master Sha wrote ten weekly articles to introduce his soul healing for the Speaking Tree, a supplement to the *Times of India*. One day Shammi Aunty read Master Sha's article. The article introduced a sacred divine code, 3396815, offering soul healing. At that moment she had stomach pain and thought she would give the code a try. She said, "Dear 3396815, please heal my stomach pain. Thank you." This is the technique of Master Sha's teaching, the Say Hello technique. It is so simple. Shammi Aunty chanted "3396815, 3396815, 3396815, heal my stomach pain." In a few minutes, the pain suddenly disappeared. She was so surprised and said, "In my life, every time I have stomach pain I have to take pills. This is the first time the stomach pain disappeared without pills. San San Jiu Liu Ba Yao Wu

(3396815, pronounced *sahn sahn jeo leo bah yow woo*) removed my pain. I am extremely grateful."

Then she came to one of Master Sha's events. Master Sha gave her soul healing in addition to acupuncture. She recovered from twenty years of being deaf. Master Sha met with her two times more over the next few years. Her hearing was still in good condition.

In the video Dr. Sha is standing behind her and asks her how she is. She does not respond. She cannot hear a word. Dr. Sha stands in front of her so she can read his lips and has her lie down and keep her mouth open and shut her eyes. Dr. Sha does a powerful transmission that in this case includes the application of a single acupuncture to her ear. The entire process takes less than a minute. After it is complete Dr. Sha asks her while she still has her eyes shut and cannot read his lips, "How are you?" The actress responds, "I'm okay." Again, a miracle. After what she describes as "a very, very, very long time" she can hear again. She is joyful and grateful.

An amazing and well-documented indication of Dr. Sha's ability to perform miracle healings is the story of John Chitty. In 2010, John was diagnosed with stage four prostate cancer that had metastasized to his lungs and bone. His initial PSA (Prostate Specific Antigen, a primary marker of specialized inflammation; any score above 4 is considered to be a problem) score was sky-high at 266. The diagnosis was confirmed and documented by tests including biopsy, MRI, X-ray, and bone scan. His doctors said he was not a candidate for radiation, surgery, or chemotherapy because the cancer was too widespread. Cancer was frequent in John's family, including both parents and both grandmothers, further complicating the prognosis. The only medical approach available was hormone therapy, to try to buy time. Because of his beliefs about alternative health, John intentionally did not ask for or receive a prediction about longevity, but the doctors emphasized the extreme danger of the condition.

At the invitation of a friend who knew of Dr. Sha's work, he attended a free public meeting and received a soul healing session from Dr. Sha.

The next day his urinary symptoms were greatly reduced. He followed Dr. Sha's recommendations including practices described in the soul healing books and attended a ten-day retreat for additional care. A month after the retreat, just four months after the PSA 266 test result, his PSA score was down to 1.

When the next round of testing was performed six months later, X-rays showed that the lungs were clear; previously the images showed "nodules too numerous to count." A bone scan showed that the bone inflammation was minimal. An MRI showed that the prostate cancer had shrunk, both inside and outside the organ. The doctor reading the 2011 X-ray, comparing the image to ten months earlier, not knowing that chemotherapy had not been used, wrote on the report, "It appears that chemotherapy was effective."

I spoke with John and he explained some of his background. He graduated from Princeton University in 1971 and married Anna, also a Princeton graduate, in 1973. They raised two children, both now adults. They pursued careers as holistic therapists, focusing on the strong interdependence between mind and body. They became teachers of holistic health and in 1992 established a vocational school for alternative therapies that continues today. Three years after the start of his cancer adventure, John finished writing a book entitled *Dancing with Yin and Yang*, which describes how Taoist (from China) and Ayurvedic (from India) energy principles can be applied to psychotherapy. Dr. Sha is appreciatively cited several times in the book.

John was already a firm believer in esoteric health ideas (such as mindfulness, karma, and reincarnation) that are foundational in Dr. Sha's teachings and methods. He had studied meditation with a guru from India since the late 1970s and he found Dr. Sha's methods entirely supportive and compatible, as well as being immediately effective for cancer.

John describes his encounters with Dr. Sha with great enthusiasm and gratitude, as follows:

"I was in despair about my prospects when I went to that first meeting, involved both in intensive research about alternative cancer strategies as well as putting my affairs in order. I had no idea about what to expect, but my friend told me to raise my hand if Dr. Sha asked for volunteers for demonstrations. When the opportunity came, I responded immediately. First, he helped several others with various ailments, with good results each time. Finally, at almost midnight, he called me to the front. The treatment was entirely new to me, with chanting and hand gestures, apparently invoking resources from what I would call the invisible world. There was minimal actual physical contact but I could feel Dr. Sha's kindness, presence, and power as being extraordinary.

"That first night, I felt elevated by the treatment, but I didn't sense a specific effect until the next morning, when I discovered that my urinary symptoms of frequency and flow were greatly reduced. They never returned.

"During that first treatment, Dr. Sha encouraged me to come to his ten-day retreat the following week, and he graciously made it financially possible. He clearly understood the gravity of my situation, and I could feel his sincerity in wanting to help me.

"I received another treatment from Dr. Sha during the retreat on the last night at three in the morning. Maybe he was saving the toughest case for last! I benefitted enormously from that treatment and really from the entire ten days. In addition to Dr. Sha's daily teaching, all of his assistants were superb, each in their own way. That retreat changed my life.

"Now, almost four years later, I feel well and I have no symptoms. In retrospect, cancer has been a gift, a wake-up call to perform at a higher level in my life. I continue my many alternative anti-cancer strategies (including strict diet, herbs and supplements, oxygen therapy, hormone therapy, and others), and continue to have tests periodically, but clearly I am no longer near the edge. I am a better person because of Dr. Sha and his teachings. I credit Dr. Sha for the creation of my book, not only in that I survived to make it happen, but also in that his example emboldened me to expand to a higher level of service to my students and clients.

"My appreciation for Dr. Sha continues to grow. The kindness and generosity that he demonstrated are truly models of what the healing arts should be. His dedication to service and the consistency with which he practices what he preaches are profound inspirations. His mission is not just about health, it is about empowering us to truly reach our full potential by paying close attention to 'what we think, what we say, and what we do,' and to do our best to attain the high standards that he exemplifies.

"Dr. Sha is truly a potential miracle for anyone who is open to his message. His work is a serious endeavor, to be approached wholeheartedly. Tao practices require focus and commitment. With my life at stake, I had extra motivation. I still use his internet resources and books. I play his music at low volume in the space where I do my cancer therapies and in the area where I sleep, so that I am constantly immersed in his Tao wisdom. I take every opportunity to attend when he or his representatives come to town, and he has treated me additional times in these events. Every time I see him, my next PSA test scores are immediately and dramatically better.

"As a last comment, I am convinced that Dr. Sha's methods can be beneficial for anyone. My story may be more drastic in some ways, but I think that the essential common ground for healing is universal. Anyone who is willing to take responsibility and really follow the instructions he provides so abundantly can have the benefits."

What we realize in analyzing these miracle healings is that something very special is happening. Dr. Sha may have learned traditional Chinese energy healing, but what he is doing is simply beyond any recorded results from these traditional forms of healing. Other healers report similar successes, but none of them have been able to document their actual success rates to the extent that Dr. Sha has. Even more amazing is how Dr. Sha is able to include the patient and his students in the healings.

Zakary's mom acknowledged that the healings for Zakary included healings from Dr. Sha's disciple, Master Sher. Dr. Sha had provided an initial blessing before Zakary was born and had done additional remote soul operations, karma cleansings, and divine treasures when Zakary was one year old, but that was the extent of his direct contact. Zakary's mom followed through with forgiveness practices and working with Master Sher. John Chitty had two healing sessions with Dr. Sha but also took the responsibility to follow through with forgiveness practices that Dr. Sha feels are essential to long-term stability and maximum health.

Dr. Sha's emphasis on self-healing baffles the mind. What does he teach that is so special that the patient him- or herself can essentially become his or her own healer? I wanted to learn more. I wanted to know if Dr. Sha might ever have a case where a total skeptic had come to him and been healed despite a complete lack of belief in any spiritual connection of any kind, without a belief in even the existence of a soul, let alone a belief in the possibility that every cell in the body has a soul.

The Importance of
Belief and Emotion

ONE OF THE most notable characteristics of every healing I observed is the significant emotion demonstrated by all those who have been healed. I was also impressed with the emotion released by Dr. Sha himself, as well as by his student healers, during a healing. These practitioners really cared about helping those they healed. They were in a sense "getting off" on healing others. So was Dr. Sha. He giggled like a schoolboy whenever he healed someone. His smile when someone was healed was genuine and infectious. Normal doctors are pleased when they have positive results but they are taught to be reserved and not to show their emotions. There are exceptions, but this is often the case. Not so with Dr. Sha and his student healers. They come right out and tell you they love you and in the moment of healing they are present for you in a way that is unique. It really is in the moment of healing as if you are the only person in the universe. Everyone's attention is focused on you. Dr. Sha is communing with what he believes is the Divine, and magic happens. Miracles happen.

The other component that seems necessary for these miracle healings, despite Dr. Sha's protestations to the contrary, is that everyone involved does in fact believe in the Divine. Dr. Sha states that he has healed people who do not believe in the Divine but he confessed that with belief the healing is stronger. "Of course, for healings to be permanent, it is important that after the healing people study my books and practice the specific chants related to healing their condition. It depends upon their karma, but for those with very bad karma it is unlikely that a single heal-ing will resolve their condition unless they continue to do the for-giveness chants and express gratitude to the Divine for their healings." I do not think that the necessity of belief for maximum benefit negates the power of Dr. Sha's healings or the reality of them. My own studies of other treatment modalities as well as those of many anthropologists and some medical researchers have found strong correlations that the greater the belief a patient has in his or her healer or doctor, the greater the effectiveness of the therapy or operation. In the case of Dr. Sha and other energy healers, I suspect that this correlation is even higher. This is a hypothesis that can, and I hope, will one day be tested. The test would involve recruiting a significant number of patients who do not believe in karma or reincarnation and having them receive healings and then measuring the results. Hopefully someday medical researchers will undertake this research. In the meantime, we can continue to analyze why these soul healing miracles are occurring with ever-greater fre-quency, why Dr. Sha is able to train others to do them, and why scien-tists such as Dr. Rulin Xiu are convinced that these healings are supported by scientific analysis and scientific principles.

To help with this analysis, I organized a weekend meeting with my good friend and noted academic authority on healing and "spirit" communi-cation, Professor Gary Schwartz of the University of Arizona. Gary is an expert on what he calls the survival of consciousness after death. Gary is the first mainstream university scientist to carry out research with me-diums that demonstrates scientifically that there can be communication through mediums with entities no longer present in physical form. Many would call these entities souls, so it seemed an ideal fit to have Gary study Dr. Sha and the phenomenon of soul healing miracles. Also, Gary had investigated energy and spiritual healers as part of his NIH–funded Center for Frontier Medicine in Biofield Science as reported in his book, *The Energy Healing Experience*.

At the time I arranged for this meeting, Gary had just completed the first post-materialist science conference with the participation of noted au-thorities from around the world. Gary has a Ph.D. from Harvard Uni-versity and taught at Yale University before accepting his post at the

University of Arizona. He is connected with top scholars and research-ers at major universities, including one of the co-chairs of his conference, Lisa Miller, Ph.D., a professor of clinical psychology at Columbia University in New York.

To say Gary was intrigued with Dr. Sha is an understatement. Gary's most recent books have focused on the need for modern science to find a way to incorporate spirit and the wisdom of spirit into mainstream science and mainstream healing. Despite Gary's enthusiasm or perhaps because of it, Gary was careful throughout the weekend meeting to constantly press Dr. Sha for scientific facts and explanations of what Dr. Sha was doing during his healings. Gary was not willing to take anything for granted, and without insulting Dr. Sha pressed for basic explanations for every claim Dr. Sha was making and for details on the circumstances surrounding each and every healing. Gary stated many times throughout the weekend that he was held to the highest possible standards by his colleagues to ensure that all of his experiments met the stiff criteria that would result in the data revealing the truth and not the opinions or feelings of his research team. Those who have worked with Gary know that this is true. Gary lives to show that science, when pursued vigorously, can tackle any question and do so objectively.

Throughout the weekend, Dr. Sha constantly spoke of soul as the primary component in his healings, as the primary component in all aspects of reality. "The soul is the boss. *Heal the soul first; then healing of the mind and body will follow.* The cause of all sickness is blockages of soul mind body. The blockages of soul are negative karma. The blockages of mind include negative mind-sets, negative beliefs, negative attitudes, ego, and attachments. The blockages of the body include energy blockages and matter blockages. The key blockages for sickness are soul blockages, which are negative karma. Why have I created hundreds of thousands of soul healing miracles in the last ten years? Because I offer Divine Karma Cleansing for soul blockages and I also teach people how to self-clear negative karma by forgiveness practice and by other spiritual and energy practices," Dr. Sha explained. Gary responded as a good scientist should: "So where is the soul? How do you measure the soul? How do you know if the soul is wanting you to heal?" The questions kept coming, and Dr. Sha kept smiling and answering the questions with ever-greater details.

"Soul is a light being. A human being is made of jing qi shen (pronounced *jing chee shun*). Jing is *matter*. Qi is *energy*. Shen is *soul*. They are three elements but they are also one. Soul has matter also. Soul is not just a light being," Dr. Sha started to explain. As an observer I was not always able to follow the details of the discussion between Dr. Sha and Professor Schwartz. Some of the topics were quite specialized, full of paradoxical statements and seeming contradictions. Dr. Schwartz kept explaining the fundamental requirements he had for determining if what Dr. Sha did with his soul healing practices could be studied scientifically or not. By the end of the weekend, Dr. Schwartz concluded that it could and agreed to work with Dr. Sha to assist with large-scale studies that might someday not just authenticate Dr. Sha as a true miracle soul healer, but also discover the exact mechanisms that allow the participation of soul in the healings.

During the course of the weekend, I learned a great deal about what Dr. Sha means when he speaks of the soul. Understanding Dr. Sha's concept of the soul struck me as fundamental to penetrate the mystery of soul healing miracles and how Dr. Sha operates. Gary kept pushing Dr. Sha to explain the nature of the soul and Dr. Sha kept smiling as he gave long, detailed answers:

"Jing qi shen, matter, energy, and soul are three. People do not know they are one. Yin yang, Heaven and Mother Earth are two, but they are one. People forget that yin yang are two. The most important, however, is that they are also one. Jing qi shen are three but they are one. That is what I explain in my books. Energy means tiny matter. Soul is the tiniest matter. You cannot say soul without matter. Soul carries matter also. They are one. You cannot truly separate them. You are made of jing qi shen. The books you write are made of jing qi shen. Everything is made of jing qi shen."

Dr. Schwartz would step in to be sure he was understanding. "Let me rephrase. What you are saying is that everything has density. Everything is incorporated into the soul and the soul is the source of energy and everything has density. Then at the level of energy, there is an explosion or transformation from the physical and energy is less dense than matter in that it has been transformed. So even though soul has density, soul has less density than either body or energy. Theoretically then we should be able to measure the density and energy of the soul," Gary concluded at one point during the discussion.

"What I am suggesting is a way to integrate soul healing miracles with science. I believe scientific research could prove the effectiveness of soul healing. It takes time for scientists to realize soul healing. I am writing a new book, *Soul Mind Body Science System*, with Dr. Rulin Xiu, who is a physicist. We are explaining in scientific language about soul, mind, and body including soul healing, negative karma, and much more. It could serve the scientists and modern medicine to realize the importance of the soul for a human being's health and every aspect of life."

My head was spinning with the introduction of so many ancient Chinese concepts being reinterpreted by Dr. Schwartz and Dr. Sha in terms of modern science, and yet it became clear to me that with or without the arduous scientific experiments and studies that Gary was proposing to "prove" the reality of Dr. Sha's soul healing miracles, fundamentally it was going to come down to a matter of belief. If researchers were unwilling to believe in the concept of the soul, I was certain they would be unable to measure the energy of the soul. It was somewhat similar to the experiments that have been done showing that light is either a particle or a wave depending upon the perspective of the observer. Those who are unable to believe in the existence of a soul will never truly comprehend that a soul exists and that it is through soul energy that Dr. Sha is able to perform his soul healing miracles. And yet whether anyone believes in the soul or not, soul healing miracles will continue to take place. We have documented them in the previous chapter. They are real. Those who do not believe in the soul will have to come up with other explanations.

Each of us must find our own way to believe or not believe in the existence of the soul. My father on his deathbed was certain that there was no afterlife and no possibility of a soul. As a chemist under Nobel Prize winner Harold Clayton Urey, he had studied the elements that create life, and he was certain that upon his death those elements would just decompose and the atoms and molecules would transform and find ways to become part of other elements after his death. There would be no more Milton Gladstone. I believe that my father did have a soul and that his soul exists even now and is aware and pleased that I am investigating these soul healing miracles that prove his own beliefs were wrong.

My own beliefs, like those of many others, change over time. I believe that we are eternal beings and that we do have souls. I guess that without that belief I would not have come this far on my journey to understand and appreciate Dr. Sha. To some extent, my belief in the existence of souls is based on knowing rather than belief. I had my own near-death experience when I was just fifteen years old. I discuss this experience in my novel *The Twelve* and also in the film *Tapping the Source*. I was clinically dead for several minutes and experienced a kind of euphoria that I have never known while limited to my human body. As a young man I seldom discussed my near-death experience, as it seemed "too weird" to my friends and family and business colleagues. And yet I have "known" I have a soul and whenever possible sought to find confirmation throughout my life. Dr. Sha knows he has had communion with the Divine. He does not believe he has had and continues to have such communion. He *knows* he has. He knows exactly where in his body to locate his connection with the divine soul that provides him information necessary to perform soul healings. Dr. Sha described for us the exact location in the solar plexus where the soul resides within each of us. Dr. Sha showed us the hand gestures to use to access the energy of the soul. He has described these practices in his previous books. So for Dr. Sha, nothing in his practice of soul healing miracles is theoretical. It is just factual. This is how it is, this is how it works. And amazingly it does work, and not just for him, but for the thousands of patients he has healed and for the hundreds of students he has taught.

Dr. Sha speaks of his Master Teachers. He has certified over thirty Master Teachers thus far. He has over four hundred Master Teachers in training. He has created more than five thousand Tao Healing Hands Soul Healers. Dr. Sha views himself as a divine servant. He does not make the decisions on how he is best able to pursue his mission to heal the world. He knows it is through a combination of training others and healing others. He knows he is in partnership with the Divine. This is not his belief but his knowing.

When I observe Dr. Sha healing, training, or teaching I am struck by his sincerity, his integrity, his commitment, his intensity, and his joy. He is clearly exuding love for all humanity. His songs of healing and forgiveness allow others to participate in these genuine expressions of love and caring. Dr. Sha has such childlike joy when healing and teaching that it is infectious just observing. Perhaps this level of emotional commitment is part of the reason why he is successful and why his students have learned to adore him. It is almost as if through a contact high they too experience the joy of communion with the Divine that is at the center of Dr. Sha's practice. Whether based on belief or true knowing, those who are open to Dr. Sha's soul healing miracle system benefit. They feel the true emotion that Dr. Sha experiences and to some level they experience this emotion themselves. You can also see this level of emotion in many of the patients when they reflect back on their healings. They are truly grateful and overcome with emotion. It is the emotion of a connection with someone powerful and loving, with some force in the universe that has recognized and healed them. Some of them are grateful specifically to Dr. Sha, but Dr. Sha does not seek this gratitude. He tells everyone, "You can do soul healing miracles. You can heal yourself. Practice, practice, practice. Serve, serve, serve. That is all I do. That is all you need to do. We are all on this journey together."

But in addition to belief and emotion, there is the matter of purity. Dr. Sha is a very pure soul. He works at it daily. He keeps his karma clean. He believes that purity is the key. Purity is health.

are a good driver but our records indicate otherwise.... If you get another ticket your driver's privileges will be suspended. "

The problem I was having as I approached Encinitas was that I really wanted to get home, and going forty miles per hour was just a little too slow. As I rolled through the last of too many stop signs going through Encinitas, I breathed a sigh of relief. "Only a mile to go," I thought as I speeded up just a little bit down the final stretch along the San Elijo State Beach on Pacific Coast Highway. "Home free," I thought. Just then I heard a police siren and saw the flashing lights of a police car behind me. "Oh no, with so much work to do in the coming weeks this is not a good time for me to have my license suspended. What am I going to do?"

As is common in California for nighttime stops, the police officer took his time getting out of his patrol car before approaching me. It was probably only a minute or two, and during that brief moment I looked at the copy of Dr. Sha's *Soul Healing Miracles* on the seat beside me. For some reason I opened to the calligraphy pages and just sent out a thought, "Oh, please, Dr. Sha, if there is any healing power in this calligraphy, please use it to help me get out of this ticket." When the police officer rapped on my window asking for my license and registration, I was pleased to see that it was a female police officer. She had a stern but approachable look on her face when she asked me, "Do you know why I stopped you?"

"I guess I was going over the speed limit by five or ten miles. I really apologize, but my home is less than a mile away and I have been up almost eighteen hours after a long workday and just wanted to get home before I became too tired to drive," I started to explain.

"You were speeding a little, but that is not why I stopped you," the officer explained. "I was monitoring the last stop sign in Encinitas and you never came to a complete stop. There are lots of young people drinking at the bar on the corner and we have had accidents at that crossing. You need to come to a complete stop, especially at night. People could be injured." "I am so sorry. I rarely go to Encinitas at night and thought I came to a complete stop," I stammered.

"You slowed and almost stopped, but the law is you must come to a complete stop. We call those rolling almost stops 'California stops' but they are not legal stops, and we will ticket you if you ever do such an incomplete stop again. I am mainly here to arrest those who are drinking and driving, so just be careful going home and I will let you off this one time," the officer told me as she went back to her patrol car.

I will never know if my entreaty through Dr. Sha's calligraphy had anything to do with a police officer stopping me but not giving me a ticket for the first time in my life, but it made me think that perhaps the book *Soul Healing Miracles* might have some magic in it after all. I soon got a chance to find out.

I am an avid golfer. I am self-taught and my swing is far from ideal. I hit down on the ball with too much force and take huge divots on almost every shot. I have been told by golf pros that I have plenty of raw talent and that they could help me become a scratch golfer if I would be willing to work with them to change my swing. For me golf is just a game, and these golf pros have told me they would need to work with me for six months or more on the range and that during that time I would not be able to play matches with any positive results. I like playing matches and am fine keeping my 16 handicap and just having fun on the golf course. The downside is I can only play once or at most twice a week since my unconventional and violent swing creates sharp pain in my left elbow if I play more than twice a week. It's known as golfer's elbow and I have had this affliction three or four times in the last ten years when I have overindulged in golf, usually around end-of-year-tournament time. Every time I have had golfer's elbow it has taken me at least four to six weeks to heal before I could play golf again.

In December 2013, I was in contention to win the year-end golf tournament at my home course of Encinitas Ranch Golf Course. My birthday is also in December and my best buddies invite me to their clubs as birthday presents every December. I played Bel-Air, the Farms Golf Club in

Rancho Santa Fe, and some other nice courses the week before the final tournament. Unfortunately, I overdid things and woke up just three days before the year-end tournament with golfer's elbow. No way I would be able to play. But that was also the day of the birthday party at which Dr. Sha was giving healing blessings. I felt embarrassed that evening over dinner when I told Dr. Sha that I wanted a blessing for such a small ailment as golfer's elbow, but Dr. Sha just laughed and told me, "You do not need my blessing. You just need my book. Tonight, you recite one of the chants from the book and put the calligraphy on your elbow, and in the morning you do this again, and in two days you will be able to golf, no golfer's elbow."

I was in disbelief, but I did as Dr. Sha had told me, and to my surprise two days later my elbow was fine and although I only came in second in the final match of the year, I had no pain in my elbow. I am writing this chapter six months later and there has been no reoccurrence of my golfer's elbow despite a more active than usual golf schedule. I am reluctant to call this a miracle healing, but at least for me it was a minor miracle that has made my life more enjoyable. But even more remarkably, the book was useful with a more significant problem that I encountered just three months ago.

I had been driving from Sedona, Arizona, to Cardiff, California. This is a six-hour trip (seven if you stay below the speed limit, which I don't) and I was driving from 1 p.m. to 7 p.m., which included the last hour at dusk and sunset. Those last two hours I was driving west looking directly into the sun. As soon as I got to my home office I went to my computer, where I had six hundred e-mails waiting for me. Most of them were work related and as I had been out of the office for a week, I felt it important to go through as many of the e-mails as I possibly could. I completed my task around midnight, and by then my right eye was throbbing and my vision blurry. I had overdone it and stressed out my eye. Not knowing what to do, I took my copy of *Soul Healing Miracles* to bed with me that night, held the calligraphy images against my right eye, said a chant, and went to bed. The next morning, I repeated the process, holding the book to my eye, and since it was Saturday, I went to the beach for a walk. By the time I came back from the beach to check on my e-mail, my eye was totally healed. I had no pain and my eye has been fine ever since.

Again we might just say this is a coincidence or that the stress in my eye would have just gone away naturally. Perhaps that is the case, but then I started checking with other people who have been using their copies of *Soul Healing Miracles* to heal minor ailments and have found to my surprise that the book does actually seem to heal them as well. One woman reported that she was able to heal her digestive problems, another explained to me how she puts the book under her pillow at night and for the first time in twenty years she no longer suffers from insomnia. Can all these anecdotal reports just be coincidences or is this book itself actually a healing tool and not just a book?

Having had such positive experiences with the book myself, I decided to be bold when speaking at an Author 101 conference organized by Rick Frishman, who had been the person to introduce me to Dr. Sha. While onstage I held up a copy of *Soul Healing Miracles* and reported to the five hundred authors in the audience that I strongly recommended they purchase copies of the book. I explained that Dr. Sha had inserted calligraphy that had healing energy and that the book was not just a book but also a healing tool. I concluded my remarks with the comment, "From what I have observed, you do not even need to read the book to benefit from the book's healing energy, just hold the calligraphy next to the body part that is hurting and you may feel better."

When I got off the stage, I felt a little sheepish. Perhaps I had gone overboard. Just because the book had helped me and some of my friends did not mean I had any scientific proof of my assertion that you did not even need to read the book to experience the healing energy of the book. As I was walking away from the event room, a well-dressed woman in her mid-fifties approached me and asked me to let her examine the calligraphy in the copy of *Soul Healing Miracles* that I had had with me onstage. She opened the book to the calligraphy, put her hands on the calligraphy, and turned to me and said, "Wow, do you have any idea how much energy this calligraphy holds? I am a medical doctor and a medical intuitive. I deal with healing energy every day and this book is a powerful healing tool."

I was so shocked by this medical doctor's response that I did not think to get her name and address. I was not planning on writing this book at the time or I would have done so. I am still skeptical that *Soul Healing Miracles* is an actual healing tool and not just a book, but when credentialed people I have never met and who have no interest in promoting Dr. Sha give me such reports, it makes me think that it might be possible that even a book can be a healing agent.

Sample Self-Healing Exercise

WHAT WE HAVE learned and are continuing to learn about Dr. Sha and his ability to reach into the Divine to create healing miracles has extraordinary meaning for all of us. If you are not comfortable with the notion of the Divine, think of Dr. Sha's abilities as tapping into an invisible but real source of energy that is constantly present and constantly influencing our daily reality even if we are unaware of it. Perhaps this energy is like radio waves, constantly beaming but undetectable unless we have the right radio equipment to receive it.

Dr. Sha has fine-tuned his soul, heart, mind, and body so that he can receive this energy at will. I am sure that Dr. Sha would emphasize that for him, above all, he has fine-tuned his soul. Even if you do not believe you have a soul, you can use Dr. Sha's techniques to fine-tune your mind and body and essence so that you too can become a receiver for this energy. The basic premise seems too simple to be true, but it is.

Even more confounding from a skeptic's perspective is that the basic requirements for this fine-tuning are so simple. In what is perhaps the ultimate oversimplification of Dr. Sha's teachings, all that is required is to seek forgiveness for all the wrongs you have ever done to others and to express gratitude that you will be forgiven and your desire for optimal health granted. From an intellectual perspective it is really this simple. It seems too simple to be effective. But there is no reason not to try. Of course, to fully benefit from Dr. Sha's teaching requires constant practice and devotion with daily exercises and constant connecting to these principles.

I asked Dr. Sha if we could include one of his most simple exercises in this book just as an example for readers to get a sense of the practices he teaches. I have modified this exercise slightly to reduce to a minimum the use of Chinese terms and to create a version of this exercise that hopefully will resonate with those who do not necessarily believe in the Divine. The actual exercise itself was published in a special edition of *Self Healing with Dr. and Master Sha* published in December 2011 through Dr. Sha's Heaven's Library Publication Corp. in Toronto, Canada. The exercise comes from chapter four of that book, "Tao Oneness Practice." This is a basic practice that is part of Dr. Sha's Four Power Techniques®, which include Body Power, Soul Power, Mind Power, and Sound Power. In modified form the exercise is as follows:

You start by putting your mind power on your lower abdomen. It is within your lower abdomen that your essence resides. It is from your lower abdomen that you access power. There is a reason this part of the body is called the solar plexus. For those who believe in soul, this is where your soul resides. The great meditation teacher Charles Haanel in *The Master Key System* also told his students to always focus on the lower abdomen throughout all meditation practices. Dr. Sha believes you should always focus on the lower abdomen to stay connected to the Divine throughout the day and not just while meditating or doing forgiveness exercises.

So with your mind focusing on your lower abdomen, sit up straight.

Put the tip of your tongue as close as you can to the roof of your mouth without touching.

Contract your anus slightly. Interlock your hands and place them on your lower abdomen.

Say hello to your soul.

Repeat the following:

> *Dear Divine,*
> *Dear Oneness of the Universe,*

Dear Source of Energy,
Dear soul, mind, and body of all spiritual fathers and mothers in all layers
of Heaven and on Mother Earth,
Dear countless planets, stars, galaxies, and universes,
Dear all of the people, animals, and environments that I have ever hurt,
harmed, taken advantage of, or made any kind of mistake against in past
lifetimes and in this lifetime,
I love, honor, and appreciate all of you.
I sincerely apologize.
Please forgive me.

Dear all souls who have harmed me in past lifetimes and in this lifetime,
I love, honor, and appreciate all of you.
I forgive you totally.
Please turn on all my Divine and Tao treasures for healing life
transformation.
(Master Sha has downloaded more than ten permanent divine
treasures to all humanity and all souls, including countless
planets, stars, galaxies, and universes.)
Please form and expand my essence and source of energy.
Please heal my _____ (make a request to heal any aspect of your
mental, emotional, or physical body).
Please heal my relationship(s) with _____ (name the people you
choose).
Please bless my finances.
Please bless my intelligence. Please bless my success.
Please bless _____ (request any aspect of your life).
I am extremely grateful.
Thank you. Thank you. Thank you.

Now focus your mind on the bottom of your lower abdomen. Visualize
a bright golden light ball forming, expanding, and rotating in your
lower abdomen. This golden light ball is your Jin Dan or center of your
being, your awareness, and your soul. Jin means *gold*. Dan means *light
ball*. Jin Dan (pronounced *jeen dahn*) means *golden light ball*.

Once you connect with this center, you should chant for three to five minutes with whatever word is best for you to define this center.

For Dr. Sha and his students, this concept is Jin Dan and they either silently or aloud repeat this name for the entire time they chant, and they do this every day and often many times a day.

This is really all that is required to access the energies that will allow you to purify your body, mind, and soul and allow you to develop your own powers of self-healing. I strongly advise those interested to purchase copies of Dr. Sha's books to learn the proper hand positions and the fully developed exercise. But if you just do even this modified version and experience any energy in your body at all, you will capture the essence of what Dr. Sha is doing and training others to do. It seems too simple, but the evidence is overwhelming that this simple meditation technique is effective.

As someone who does not meditate on a regular basis and who does not believe in an anthropomorphic concept of God to whom we can pray, I have difficulty doing an exercise like this on a daily basis. I am willing to try almost anything once, and the first time I actually did this exercise was while I was writing it down just now. I have to admit that just doing the exercise has generated a tingling vibration throughout my body. It feels good and I feel connected with a source of energy that is both within and outside of my body. I hope you try this exercise and have a similar experience. It is a wonderful feeling and a feeling that you can create for yourself no matter the circumstances of your present everyday life.

In analyzing this exercise, there are several phrases that struck me as revealing the deeper truths with which Dr. Sha is connecting.

First, I was struck by the way the exercise was constructed.

Put your focus on the lower abdomen. The lower abdomen is the seat of power and at least figuratively the seat of the soul. It is not just Dr. Sha who believes this. Many great teachers from both Eastern and Western traditions place the lower abdomen as the power spot for their teachings as well.

The next salient point was Dr. Sha's willingness to entreat not just the Divine but Mother Earth, Heaven, and countless planets, stars, galaxies, and universes. Most prayers from other traditions limit themselves to God. Dr. Sha has no such limitations. He lives in a world that includes countless planets, stars, galaxies, and universes. Who would have the boldness to realize that all consciousness and all matter is infinite and interconnected and that only by including all that is can a prayer be truly effective? Dr. Sha calls this the outer souls, the souls that are connected outside of yourself and your own self-created world.

Then the next part of the exercise has you address not just the people you have hurt, but also animals and the environments in which you have interacted as well. Dr. Sha has you request forgiveness for mistakes not only in this lifetime but past lifetimes. I do not believe in past lifetimes but see no harm in asking for such forgiveness. It cannot hurt.

Then Dr. Sha has us recognize and honor all those we have hurt and express our appreciation for them as well. Remember, we are honoring not just people and animals but the countless planets, stars, galaxies, and universes. We rarely think of how our actions may be harming such distant planets and galaxies, but of course our thoughts and actions reach out infinitely and impact all elements in all universes. We need to apologize to all of these entities, not just the animals and people whom we may have harmed on planet Earth.

And then the key phrase—"please forgive me."

Forgiveness is the key to so many traditions both Western and Eastern. The Lord's Prayer in the Christian tradition includes "Forgive us our trespasses …" Forgiveness is a foundational principle in all world religions. Asking for forgiveness is an essential element in the ancient Hawaiian practice of Ho'oponopono and many other indigenous traditions. I suspect there is a reason asking for forgiveness has endured for millennia in so many traditions. It must be effective.

The rest of Dr. Sha's exercise has you forgive all those who may have harmed you in this or past lifetimes. You must not just forgive them totally, but you must honor and appreciate those who have harmed you. This may seem inappropriate if someone has truly violated you, but I can assure you from personal experience that forgiveness sets you free and also provides a blessing for whomever you may be forgiving. Growing up, I was severely beaten dozens of times by my schizophrenic older brother. He nearly killed me on several occasions. It was frightful and dreadful. I do not enjoy being around my brother even today, and I avoid him whenever possible. But I do not have any negative thoughts toward him and I truly forgive him and truly love him. We are all on this planet doing the best we can in every moment. Some of us do horrible things to each other. We need to punish or at least constrain those who do evil, but we also need to forgive them. We are ultimately all one, and even those doing evil among us are part of the divine energy of the universe that can and will heal all who seek such healing.

Once you have forgiven everyone and yourself, you ask for the divine treasures that will expand your Jin Dan. This is the good part. This is where you get your power. Your power to heal and transform. You are now ready to ask for specific healings for whatever is ailing, whether mental, emotional, or physical. This is the opportunity to ask that the universe support and bless your key relationships. You do not need to limit yourself to healing alone. You can ask that all aspects of your life be blessed, your finances, your intelligence, and your success in all your endeavors. It seems too good to be true, but it is not.

Now you end your exercise by expressing gratitude:

I am extremely grateful. Thank you. Thank you. Thank you.

It is not enough to just say you are grateful. You must verbalize your thanks, and saying "thank you" three times is the minimum. You can never say thank you enough. You are thanking the energy that has created you and the universe for your very existence. The greatest miracle of all is that you are alive and connected to all matter and energy in every moment. By recognizing this fact, you can create your own miracles. At least this is what Dr. Sha believes. I have to admit that as I observe and experience the divine gifts that Dr. Sha has brought to so many people, I am beginning to believe as well.

Am I losing my objectivity? Perhaps, but I do not think that that is the case. Dr. Sha's teachings are perhaps more powerful if you believe in his concepts of reincarnation and past lives, but such beliefs are not necessary. Do the above exercise and discover for yourself. Just keep an open mind and allow yourself to feel energy moving through you. You may be pleasantly surprised to learn that you have the ability to heal yourself and receive countless blessings.

Can Calligraphy Heal?

IF YOU HAD asked me this question a year ago, I would have emphatically said "no." Today I am not so sure. I am still somewhat in disbelief even though I have personally used Dr. Sha's calligraphy to heal my golfer's elbow and eye strain. I am unsure because I know that I also did the healing chant and I have a personal relationship with Dr. Sha. Perhaps the healing only worked because of the chants and my personal relationship with Dr. Sha. How can I be certain?

As I have previously admitted, I am not much of a meditator or chanter. I really just did the chants once or twice and without any real commitment to them, so my healings in my mind either have to do with my relationship with Dr. Sha or with the calligraphy or perhaps some combination of both. Dr. Sha is absolutely certain that his calligraphy can heal. Of course, it is better to do the chants as well.

In studying other miraculous events, there have been reports of miracle healings that have occurred just on the basis of contact with images and pictures of Jesus and Mary. I have never taken these reports seriously. Just cases of believers who hypnotized themselves into believing these artistic creations healed them. Really, how can a work of art heal us? Art is beautiful. It makes us feel good to look at it, but heal us? You've got to be kidding.

And yet it is becoming harder and harder for me to doubt Dr. Sha.

In his book *Soul Healing Miracles* Dr. Sha writes, "In June 2013 the Source gave me new power to create the Source Calligraphy for healing, blessing, and life transformation." Well, I guess a year ago this healing modality did not even exist. This is one of the qualities I so admire and enjoy in working with Dr. Sha. He is constantly evolving and improving as a healer and as a human being. With all the success he has already achieved with his energy medicine healing, who would have thought he would be motivated to learn an entirely new modality, an entirely new art? I have seen the video of Dr. Sha training with his calligraphy teacher (you can view the trailer here: drsha.com/soulhealingmiracles/soul-healing-miracles-and-the-source-ling-guang-calligraphies). Just learning how to do this level of artistic creation is not easy. To think there is also healing energy behind the effort boggles the mind. I could not imagine John of God or any other "natural miracle" healer having the drive to develop such a new talent.

In *Soul Healing Miracles* Dr. and Master Sha explains that on August 8, 2003, an era that had lasted 15,000 years ended and a new era began. The new era is called the Soul Light Era. The Soul Light Era will also last 15,000 years. In Dr. Sha's belief system there are a series of 15,000-year cycles for each era, and this new era is especially propitious, allowing human beings to connect with saints and countless soul treasures. These soul treasures are the reason he was able to create Soul Light Calligraphy that allows those who view and touch his calligraphy to receive divine blessings.

Although I highly respect Dr. Sha and his beliefs, I do not share his belief system. I am an expert on the Mayan calendar and believe that their system of 26,000-year cycles is more aligned with physical evidence than the idea of 15,000-year cycles. The precession in the orbit of our planet is 26,000 years, not 15,000 years. In other words, our planet takes 26,000 years to complete a cycle in which the wobble in the rotation of the earth comes to a completion. Most scientists do not think there is necessarily a connection between the precession cycle and human cycles, but many Mayan scholars do, including John Major Jenkins, who has written extensively about this phenomenon. In any event, for Dr. Sha the concept of 15,000-year cycles is important and the specific date of August 8, 2003, is the date on which our present cycle began. For the Mayans, our present cycle began on December 22, 2012, the day after the previous 26,000-year cycle ended on December 21, 2012. My novel *The Twelve* explains why December 21, 2012, was such a pivotal date and why the Mayans believe that we have entered a new cycle that will honor feminine rather than masculine spiritual principles.

I share this aside because it is not important whether or not we agree with Dr. Sha's concepts of reincarnation, karma cleansing, or the concept of 15,000-year cycles. All that matters is whether Dr. Sha's techniques and his calligraphy actually produce soul healing miracles and blessings to those who gaze upon them. Apparently, the answer remains yes. I do not expect every reader to just take my word for the powerful healing effects that this calligraphy has. Dr. Sha has graciously created a wonderful calligraphy image for this book.

On the back cover, you will see a special Soul Calligraphy image that Dr. Sha created on Saturday, April 19, 2014, especially for this book called *Ling Guang* (Soul Light) Calligraphy.

If you want a quick overview of how and why this calligraphy is able to help you heal and provide blessings, let's paraphrase how Dr. Sha explains the origin and use of his calligraphy in *Soul Healing Miracles*.

According to Dr. Sha this calligraphy:

> *Carries Source energy.*
> *Carries Source love, forgiveness, compassion, and light.*
> *Connects with countless saints both in Heaven and on Mother Earth.*
> *Carries countless Heaven's saints' animals.*
> *Carries countless treasures of Heaven, the Divine, Tao, and the Source.*

Dr. Sha provides precise exercises and instructions on how to use this calligraphy to heal spiritual, mental, emotional, and physical bodies. He recommends his Four Power Techniques of Body Power, Soul Power, Mind Power, and Sound Power.

We will only provide the example of Body Power. The basic instructions give three options:

- put one palm on the back cover with the Source Calligraphy. Put your other palm on any part of the body that needs healing; or,
- put the back cover with the Source Calligraphy on any part of your body that needs healing; or,
- meditate, looking at the Source Calligraphy, or just have the Source Calligraphy near you while you meditate.

Again, this is just one of the four techniques. Should you use this, be sure to end your session acknowledging that the calligraphy is healing you and thank the calligraphy for participating in your healing.

From Dr. Sha's perspective, every time you ask for healing, you must acknowledge the source of that healing and express gratitude for the healing. These are the two critical steps that you must never forget to do.

I have no idea if doing this exercise with the calligraphy in this book will have any immediate impact on your health or well-being. I do know that thousands of people have reported healings just by using the calligraphy in *Soul Healing Miracles*. I am not attempting to provide the benefits of Dr. Sha's soul healing miracles to you in this book. I just want to provide you with as much background as I can on what Dr. Sha does, how he does it, and how simple and non-invasive his techniques are. You do not need to change your own belief system to benefit from soul healing miracles. I continue to maintain my own beliefs regarding the nature of the universe and the relationships between my everyday reality and the unseen dimensions that clearly influence human beings and the evolution of health and wellness throughout our lives. I am intrigued by Dr. Sha's beliefs and impressed with how they work, not just for him but for thousands of people. I believe that his calligraphy does in fact offer healing properties, not just to those who follow his practices but even to those who, like me, just casually look upon the calligraphy as art. I do not understand how this calligraphy can actually heal people, but then I would have never believed that simple chants and exercises of gratitude and forgiveness could serve as healing agents either.

Can Sound and Music Heal?

ONE OF THE unique aspects of Dr. Sha's personality and his healings is his devotion to chanting and singing. Dr. Sha loves to sing, and he sings well. Famous singers such as Roberta Flack have said, "His voice is incredible and carries incredible power. ... His voice is like the voice of God singing. God's voice in his body is so unique that it is definitely a healing sound."

When Dr. Sha does his healing chants in Chinese, they sound to me like ancient Native American chants. There is a tone and vibrancy that is universal. According to Dr. Sha, one of his Four Power Techniques for healing is Sound Power. With Sound Power you take a phrase and you repeat the phrase out loud many times. If you are not able to sing or repeat the phrase out loud you can think the phrase to yourself, as even thoughts can have healing vibrations.

An example of Sound Power from *Soul Healing Miracles* is the following forgiveness practice: Chant silently:

Divine Forgiveness
Divine Forgiveness
Divine Forgiveness
Divine Forgiveness
Divine Forgiveness
Divine Forgiveness
Divine Forgiveness ...

Connect with all souls or, if you do not believe in reincarnation, with the idea of forgiving all your ancestors for any harm they have ever caused you or you them.

Then chant:

> *I forgive you.*
> *You forgive me.*
> *Bring love, peace, and harmony.*
>
> *I forgive you.*
> *You forgive me.*
> *Bring love, peace, and harmony.*
>
> *I forgive you.*
> *You forgive me.*
> *Bring love, peace, and harmony.*
>
> *I forgive you.*
> *You forgive me.*
> *Bring love, peace and harmony.*

Dr. Sha's instructions are: "Chant these phrases as often as you can. Chant for at least ten minutes per time. The more often and the longer you chant, the better."

Dr. Sha shared with me the following story of how chanting healed a clinically ill woman.

"A very prominent person's mother had serious leukemia. This family owned a few hospitals. The top oncologist said that this type of leukemia had no cure. The doctors had given her two weeks to live. She could hardly eat, her energy was depleted, and she was lying on the bed, unable to move. The family member asked me to do a remote healing on the telephone to the mother. I offered healing blessings, karma cleansings, and divine treasures. I then sang a Tao Song blessing. The recording file was sent to the family member. Within two weeks the mother was out of the hospital and she listened to the song day and night. Three months later she went for a checkup. Her leukemia was completely gone. She is still free of leukemia up to today. My Tao Song carries jing qi shen (matter, energy, soul) of the Source with love, forgiveness, compassion, and light of the Source. I always teach that the Source frequency and vibration can transform the frequency and vibration of our health, relationships, finances, and all life.

"I want you and all readers to remember:

> *Source love melts all blockages and transforms all life.*
> *Source forgiveness brings inner joy and inner peace of all life.*
> *Source compassion boosts energy, stamina, vitality, and immunity of all life.*
> *Source light heals, prevents sickness, purifies, and rejuvenates soul, heart, mind, and body; prolongs life; transforms relationships; transforms finances; and every aspect of life."*

This seems much too simple to be effective, but thousands of his students do these chants every day and claim extraordinary benefits. You can think of this simple forgiveness practice as chanting a forgiveness mantra. This mantra of forgiveness goes out to the universe and touches all the cells of the universe with healing energy. This healing energy comes back to you with unlimited abundance. This is Dr. Sha's belief. There certainly can be no harm in sending out this message of forgiveness. Try it.

If you are like me, you probably won't do this Sound Power exercise on a regular basis. I don't and doubt it will ever be part of my routine, but I do feel good when I do it.

In analyzing why and how sound and music can be healing, I researched the literature on sound and vibrational healing and learned that many mainstream doctors and researchers are exploring the power of sound and music to heal. Studies have been done that show that Gregorian chants, when repeated, can alter the energy of those who chant. New studies are showing that those who listen to chants over extended periods of time can go into alpha or theta brain states, greatly reducing stress. Chanting has been part of many world religions, including Hindu practices and those of indigenous peoples throughout the world. Again, I suggest that practices that have endured universally across different cultures for thousands of years are likely to have had positive results, or they would not have continued.

For those of you who would like to hear what Dr. Sha's chanting and singing sounds like, go to the following link to hear him: youtube.com/watch?v=2gFe-1uTcHY.

Whether music has specific healing properties or not, great music and great singing move us. We often speak of the music of the heavens, and almost all major religions have singing or chanting as part of their spiritual practices. There is a reason for this, and no doubt that reason is related to the deeper reality that the source of all energy and all matter is vibration. Harmonious vibrations are soothing. Cacophony and screeching sounds upset us. Choose positive vibrations in your life. Listen to Dr. Sha's singing and see how it makes you feel. If you resonate, you may find that just listening is one of the easiest healing practices you will ever have the joy to experience.

The Company We Keep

I HAVE EXPERIENCED as a businessman, anthropologist, literary agent, and author that we can learn a lot about people from observing the company they keep. Who are the people they spend time with, what motivates those people? As a young boy I would accompany my father as he visited printing companies and other vendors with whom he did business as a book publisher. I would ask my father why he wanted to visit these companies when he could just phone them. "I can tell a lot about a company by the way people act. Are they smiling? Are they busy? Is the warehouse clean? Those details tell me whether I want to do business with a company or not," he advised.

In the case of Dr. Sha, I have learned that he attracts highly intelligent people who are motivated by a sincere desire to heal and help others. Even the people who primarily help him in an administrative, legal, or financial advisory capacity are highly evolved souls dedicated to helping others. They are thoughtful, concerned with details and impeccable ethics, and want clarity and fairness in all they do. Perhaps this is due in part to the belief they share that karma will ultimately decide the fate of their souls, but whatever the reason, they go out of their way to acknowledge others, to be kind, and to treat potential business associates with respect and generosity. Dr. Sha sets the tone by always acknowledging how grateful he is to those who work with him and for him. He sets the model, and if there is a corporate identity around Dr. Sha's enterprises, it is about gratitude.

The corporate identity is also about hard work. Everyone associated with Dr. Sha seems to be a tireless worker. Dr. Sha often works nonstop for at least twelve hours at a time healing and teaching, and when he does, his close associates work those hours as well. No one seems to mind. They are on a mission to serve, and the act of healing energizes them as much as it energizes Dr. Sha. I think all of us have felt, at least occasionally, the euphoria of being in the middle of a meaningful task that is going well and feeling a sense of invincibility and high, limitless energy. This seems to happen all the time for Dr. Sha and his associates.

I thought it important to learn more about the character of some of Dr. Sha's longtime supporters, especially those playing key roles in bringing his message of self-healing and self-empowerment to the world. I decided to interview his director of global marketing, Master Ximena Gavino. This interview gives us greater insight into the company Dr. Sha keeps and the company he has created.

Master Ximena Gavino was born in Quito, Ecuador, nestled among seven active volcanoes in the Andean mountains. Her father's childhood was characterized by extreme poverty, motivating him to start working as a shoeshine boy when he was just four years old. Self-educated and a voracious reader by the time Master Ximena was born, he had become a government clerk, taking dictation from important government officials directly at his typewriter. This was quite an accomplishment for a poor boy who had never even graduated from the sixth grade, let alone high school. Master Ximena's mother was from a working-class family. Taking after her grandmother, Master Ximena's mother had studied and been certified as a teacher. When she married, she followed the tradition of the times in Quito and gave up pursuing a teaching career. She immediately started her life as a stay-at-home wife and shortly became pregnant with Master Ximena, and then over time with additional children. Master Ximena grew up in a modest neighborhood in Quito not far from her aunts, uncles, cousins, and grandparents. When Master Ximena was five years old, her father had an opportunity to migrate to the United States. He initially came alone to Chicago, where he traded his office job for that of a busboy at the International Club. A year later he sent for Master Ximena and his wife. Her siblings would come a year later with their uncle.

Master Ximena thrived in Chicago. She quickly learned to read, despite not speaking English and suffering from dyslexia. Since both her parents valued education highly, she found herself rewarded for her interest in reading. Her education began at a private Catholic elementary school but she switched to an inner-city high school, filled with tough street kids doing their best to survive in a big city and tough neighborhoods. Despite the challenges, Master Ximena thrived by focusing on academics, including advanced classes, and participating in after-school clubs. By her junior year in high school, her father and mother had progressed through hard work at factory jobs to working as a salesman in a furniture store and an office clerk, respectively. They moved the family to the northern suburbs of Chicago, known for the high quality of the schools. This was ideal for Master Ximena and her siblings, who excelled. At graduation time, Master Ximena's father handed her a packet with an application to the University of Illinois, Chicago Circle. His employer had suggested that she attend college through scholarships. She was the first of the five children to graduate from college, something she originally thought beyond the reach of immigrants. Her parents' lives kept improving, and soon Master Ximena's parents owned their own furniture store and were able to send all their children to college and to occasionally travel.

Coming from a background of poverty in which hard work and education were highly valued, Master Ximena chose to major in business and graduated with honors. She was the only Hispanic student in grade school, middle school, and high school, and it was only when she went to graduate school that she started to study with other Hispanic students. When she applied for jobs, she was hired for the sales team of one of the largest beverage companies in the United States. She traveled extensively, attending conferences, especially those that related to Hispanic markets, such as the Hispanic Chamber of Commerce and the League of United Latin American Citizens. After three years, she decided to apply to the MBA program at the Ross School of Business in Ann Arbor, Michigan. She was accepted, and upon graduation worked for some of the top consumer product companies in America. After nine successful years Master Ximena began her consulting career as an independent consultant before joining a prestigious consulting firm in San Francisco that was starting a global branding practice. Within a few years, she formed her own boutique consulting practice.

It was at this juncture in 2001 that Ximena became quite ill. Initially her search for a diagnosis from the medical community yielded limited results. Unable to work and becoming increasingly weak and hopeless, she turned to alternative and complementary medicine, where she finally received a diagnosis of Crohn's disease, celiac, which had created a condition called leaky gut and an ulcer. A good friend who was a medical doctor herself recommended Dr. Sha and his healing groups with stage four cancer patients. Her friend did not have cancer, but the groups had helped her tremendously to regain her energy. She encouraged Master Ximena to attend one of Master Sha's workshops.

Master Ximena's first workshop with Dr. Sha was held in what was then the Crowne Plaza Hotel in Union Square with about twenty people in attendance. Steeped in Western medicine since the age of five, she was highly skeptical of alternative medicine. As an A student who had studied chemistry, biology, and physics in high school and college, she was certain that chanting and other vague healing modalities could not change the internal malfunctions of her digestive system that had been causing her such discomfort and stress. But skepticism notwithstanding, in that very first encounter with Dr. Sha, Master Ximena had a life-changing experience. She describes it thus:

"I was so weak that day I barely had the energy to walk to the workshop, which was only three blocks from my house. That evening Dr. Sha changed my life forever. He gave me hope at a time when I was very hopeless. He started the evening by telling us, 'I have the power to heal myself. You have the power to heal yourself. Together, we have the power to heal the world.' My skepticism faded with his explanation of the causes of illnesses and the methods for healing, I knew he was speaking 'truth.' For the first time in my life, I understood how the body worked. It was so simple. Next Dr. Sha asked us to line up to receive a qi gong healing from him. Dr. Sha asked me to stand up and tell him what was wrong. I started to talk about my symptoms, but before I finished Dr. Sha said he was a medical intuitive and he could see that the main energy blockage was in my middle abdomen. He asked me to close my eyes and put my hands at my side while one of his students stood behind me with her hands on my shoulders to stabilize me. Dr. Sha shouted something that sounded like 'ye ye ye' and I felt this intense heat in my middle abdomen and something being pulled out. He then asked me to walk back and forth. That was it. A brief three-minute qi gong healing changed my life. As I prepared to leave, I gathered a flyer of upcoming events. My insides were vibrating uncontrollably, but I didn't know if that was good or bad, so I walked home slowly and headed straight to bed. The next morning, I woke up feeling better than I had in more than a dozen years. I could not explain to anyone what had occurred for me, only that I needed and wanted more of whatever Dr. Sha was offering. For the first time in years, I had hope. I started going to every Dr. Sha event and workshop I could attend. Every time I went, I felt better and better. I asked if I could attend the healing groups for stage four cancer patients. I did not have cancer but I needed to attend something with Master Sha every two to three days in order to keep my energy high. What was occurring in the groups was astonishing. Using five-thousand-year-old ancient Chinese healing secrets, people were not only getting better, but being healed of stage four cancer. Every week, people would give an update on their medical progress, and inevitably someone would share their latest medical report that the number of tumors was declining, they were responding better to some of the traditional medical treatments or had decided to forgo those treatments altogether. This was before Dr. Sha became a Divine Channel and Divine Soul Healer. He was teaching people to heal themselves by applying the Four Power Techniques: Body Power—the use of hand and body positions to promote healing and transformation; Mind Power—creative visualization to promote healing and transformation; Sound Power—the use of sacred mantras and sounds to promote healing and transformation; Soul Power—to Say Hello to invoke the power of the inner souls and outer souls to support your healing and transformation. Each technique was powerful alone, but the power increased exponentially when used in combination. The real key to healing, according to Dr. Sha, was service. He would say, 'Chant for others, do not chant for yourself. Forget about yourself. Don't think about *me*.' Inspired by Dr. Sha's teaching, I approached a woman who had stage four renal (kidney) cancer that had metastasized in her lungs and bones about chanting together by phone. At first she said no, but I kept attending the healing groups, and several weeks later she said we could chant together. We set up a schedule and I would go to her home and chant for an hour in the mornings. We would also chant together over the phone for another half or full hour in the evening. I was not prepared to support anyone with cancer. I knew nothing about it, but with Master Sha's techniques, it was so easy. We simply followed the guidance he had given us in the healing groups. Although she had been told she had only three months to live, she lived another nine months. During that time, she made peace with her very, very large community of friends. She moved into her sister's home, where she remained until her transition. She ate regular food and her only life support was an oxygen tube. She transitioned peacefully one week after celebrating her birthday surrounded by her family and friends. I am sure it was Dr. Sha's techniques that helped keep her alive and gave her such a high quality of life. Many cancer patients are in so much pain that they are often given strong narcotics. That was not the case for her. She was lucid and at peace.

"I will always be grateful to her for awakening in me the calling to be a healer. Through this experience I realized that I had the power not only to heal myself, but to help heal others. By this time, I was in the care of a board-certified gastroenterologist who was one of the best on the West Coast. He had done a series of tests and confirmed that at a minimum, I had an ulcer. When the final set of tests was completed, he was amazed that all of my symptoms, as well as the underlying illnesses relating to Crohn's, leaky gut, and my ulcer, had disappeared. 'I have never made a mistake in diagnosing these illnesses in my career,' he said. 'Don't worry. We took extra biopsies to make sure we get to the bottom of this,' he continued. At the follow-up visit, he asked me what I had done, and when I explained some chanting and changes to my diet, he dismissed it completely. 'It is not medically possible that these illnesses have disappeared from chanting alone.' But it was true. I knew when the Crohn's was gone because the burning just stopped in the middle of chanting. The same occurred for the celiac and the ulcer. For the first time in twenty-five years, I was no longer dependent on Western medicine and on my way to truly healing. In these twelve years, my health has improved dramatically. I no longer take any medication and rarely even vitamins. Although I'm in my mid-fifties, I am definitely a high-energy individual.

"I have also been incredibly fortunate to have learned about healing directly from Dr. Sha and in 2011 to have been chosen as one of his Master Teachers. My life before meeting Dr. Sha was successful by all outward appearances, but I was physically sick and terribly unhappy. Now I have purpose in my life and have received through Dr. Sha incredible healing abilities to help people with life-threatening conditions and often extremely challenging situations. There are no words to fully express my gratitude to Dr. Sha. It is my deepest desire to serve as fully and unconditionally as Dr. Sha serves humanity. I started volunteering for Dr. Sha, and over the years served as general manager, manager of the Teaching and Training Department, Events, and Marketing. This was at the very beginning of his mission to serve as a soul healer. Dr. Sha had had a very successful practice as an acupuncturist, qi gong healer, and medical intuitive. He had been earning more than one million dollars a year as an acupuncturist in Canada, where he had two clinics, one in Vancouver and another in Toronto. He would see about seventy clients a day. Dr. Sha gained his reputation as a power healer in the Philippines where he was training Western doctors in traditional Chinese medicine and acupuncture for the WHO (World Health Organization) while also attending graduate school for hospital administration. He was under the supervision of the medical doctor for the Chinese ambassador. One day the doctor received a call from the embassy that the ambassador's driver had thrown out his back and could not move. During the house call, Dr. Sha applied Sha's Acupuncture and with just two points had the man back on his feet. After that, Dr. Sha was serving the highest government, military, and business officials in the Philippines and in China, where he had started his healing practices. But when the Divine told him in 2003 that he had to give up all of his acupuncture and related healing techniques and rely solely upon the Divine to heal, he had to give up the highly rewarding financial opportunities and was earning less than $30,000 a year. He did this despite protests from those around him and his advisors. Dr. Sha was clear that he had to, to serve the Divine, and listened on a daily basis to whatever the Divine asked him to do. The Divine was asking him to create an entirely new form of healing. I was his general manager and marketing manager, and I would advise him, 'Dr. Sha, you should not let the audience know that you are a Divine Channel offering divine soul healing. Most people are not ready to hear that message.' One day Dr. Sha responded with a smile, 'Ximena, what about me? Do you think I was ready? It took me several weeks to accept what the Divine was asking of me.' Over the years, Dr. Sha has been unwavering in his commitment to God. To his credit, he has followed Divine Guidance for everything, even when it meant going completely against all his advisors. Everything he does must be in alignment with Divine Guidance or he will not do it. That meant at times watching people walk out before he could demonstrate his healing power, but he persevered."

As the interview was coming to an end, I asked Master Ximena how Dr. Sha had changed in the twelve plus years she had known and worked with him.

"That is a wonderful question. When I met Dr. Sha, he was a powerful acupuncturist and qi gong master; in fact, he was named Qigong Master of the Year in 2002 at the Fourth World Congress on Qigong in San Francisco. He has been tested heavily by humanity and the Divine. Dr. Sha's only motivation is to serve humanity. He has very deep compassion for humanity and wants only to alleviate suffering. Over the years, Dr. Sha has transformed from a powerful acupuncturist and qi gong healer to a truly humble, selfless, and unconditionally loving Divine being. Dr. Sha was never motivated by money or fame. He only wants to serve the Divine and help humanity. Whether one person or one thousand people attend his event, he gives them the same teachings and healings with a completely open heart. I have been very honored to watch Dr. Sha transform from a powerful, noble, and kind healer when I met him twelve years ago to an extraordinary spiritual being who truly represents the love, forgiveness, compassion, and light of the Divine in its purest form. His commitment to healing all beings and being a source of love, compassion, and joy is limitless."

An Enlightening Conversation

Henderson Tan Ong: From High-Six-Figure Graphic Designer to Soul Healer Volunteer

HENDERSON TAN ONG was born in Manila in 1971 to Chinese parents. At the time of his birth his father was an importer/exporter and his mother was an assistant. He was the youngest of four children. His childhood was traditional, with very strict discipline and conformance to the goals of his parents. He did not enjoy school as a young man and was considered the black sheep of the family.

As it turned out, Henderson was extremely gifted as a graphic artist, and at the age of nineteen he moved to the United States and studied at the Academy of Art University in San Francisco. Upon graduation he worked for a small local advertising agency. His superior skills were soon noted, and within ten years he was the International Art Director for TMP Worldwide, the largest recruitment advertising agency in the world.

When I met Henderson, he explained to me that three years previously he walked away from his high-six-figure salary to follow and learn from Dr. and Master Sha. I asked him:

"Henderson, most people would think twice before walking away from such a prestigious position, so what were you thinking walking away from such a prestigious and high-paying career?"

Henderson: I was born and raised a Catholic. I truly believe in God. I prayed for many things in my life and God answered me. The answers come in different forms and shapes. I was very grateful that I was able to see it. Everything that I have ever asked for from God, He has granted me. One day I asked of God, "What is it that You would want me to do next for my life?" He then showed me the spiritual path.

Bill: How did God show you the spiritual path? How did you find Dr. Sha?

Henderson: Have I mentioned I was a dancer?

Bill: No, you have not.

Henderson: Dancing was an integral part of my life. At a young age I would do street dancing and break dancing. As a teenager I had an opportunity to dance for a formal event to take place at the cultural center in Manila where I lived. Unfortunately, I pulled a muscle doing backflips and was in a lot of pain. My parents brought me to a Chinese traditional doctor who had recently come from China. People called him Sha Da Shi. Sha means *family name.* Da Shi means *grandmaster.* This was my first encounter with Grandmaster Sha.

Sha Da Shi used qi gong and acupuncture to heal me. I was healed immediately and was able to perform at the cultural center. His techniques were unique. People lined up to see him. He did not charge me or other people who could not pay. I was moved by his actions and when I was older, I asked my mother if I could go to China to learn traditional Chinese medicine. My mother said no and instead my life's journey brought me to America to study art.

I had always wondered about Dr. Sha and where he might be, but this was the late 1980s and early 1990s and there was no e-mail and no way to make a phone call to him. I just focused on my studies and did not pursue my interest in Grandmaster Sha.

Bill: So, many years passed before you reconnected with Dr. Sha?

Henderson: Yes. It was not until 2010 that I thought to reconnect with Dr. Sha and it was through what I view as a divine "accident."

Bill: Please explain.

Henderson: I had pulled a muscle in my back. It was the same muscle I had pulled years before as a young street dancer in Manila. I was in a great deal of pain but instead of being angry or disappointed I was grateful. I was grateful because I realized that God was telling me to search for Dr. Sha. It was the busiest month of the year for me at work but I had a legitimate excuse to take the day off. I stayed in bed and pulled out my laptop and did a search for Dr. Sha. To my surprise I learned that Dr. Sha was now a spiritual teacher based in Toronto, Canada with a center not far from me in San Francisco. I started reading about him on his website and discovered that he was teaching that the way to heal yourself and others is to raise your frequency. The very next day a friend of mine posted a video on YouTube about frequency that explained that low frequency draws matter together and high frequency repels matter. This explained to me why Dr. Sha's techniques of raising frequency could dissipate cancer cells in patients. I was intrigued and purchased Dr. Sha's tapes and CDs. I started playing them quietly every day in my office. Within three months I noticed enormous changes. My relationship with my boss improved and the happiest and most productive people in the office were drawn to my office.

Bill: You felt the tapes and music from Dr. Sha were raising the frequency of your office and attracting more positive energy?

Henderson: Absolutely.

Bill: What happened next?

Henderson: Well, one day my boss came to me and told me I couldn't take the vacation days I had coming to me because there was too much work to do. I told him I was ready to leave anyway and arranged, after a suitable adjustment period, to resign and follow Dr. Sha full time.

Bill: Had you decided that you would become a full-time student that quickly?

Henderson: No, I had not decided whether or not I would become a student. I just knew I wanted to explore what Dr. Sha was teaching. I had plenty of money in the bank and good stock options, so at my own expense I just started going to all of Dr. Sha's retreats all over the world and volunteering to help him in any way I could.

Bill: Your business friends and colleagues must have thought your decision strange.

Henderson: Most of them did, but they were also supportive when they learned that I considered this my spiritual journey. One of my best friends decided he needed to check out Dr. Sha for himself. He warned me that if he saw anything phony about Dr. Sha he would be the first one to knock me on the head and bring me back to my senses. He accompanied me on a trip with Dr. Sha to Taiwan. By the time we returned he acknowledged the integrity of Dr. Sha and my journey and no longer questioned my decision to abandon my career as a graphic designer.

Bill: In my encounters with other spiritual seekers, they have all felt that their spiritual master was best for them. In your case as a devout Catholic, how have you resolved your potential conflict between your belief in Jesus and your belief in Master Sha?

Henderson: I believe in the miracles of Christ and I believe in the miracles that Dr. and Master Sha has performed. When

Dr. Sha explains his miracles, he teaches his students about Tao. Tao means the way. Christ also taught, "I am the Way, the Truth and the Light." Fundamentally, the teachings are the same. By the time I was in the fifth grade I had read and studied the Bible at least twice. Jesus showed love and forgiveness to all people. Jesus forgave all who approached him. Dr. and Master Sha demonstrates the same truth and practice.

For me Jesus will always be the most high. Jesus is the son of God. Dr. Sha is not the son of God but what he teaches is pure and true.

Bill: Dr. Sha mentioned to me that he chose you to be one of his disciples and Master Teachers. What does this mean?

Henderson: I was honored and blessed to be chosen to be a Master Teacher in November 2013. I was humbled and grateful for such an honor.

Bill: Does this mean as a Master Teacher that you are able to do soul healing miracles?

Henderson: Yes. I have done more than a dozen. Even before I was a Master Teacher I was doing healings, and some of those I have healed had stage four cancers and other severe challenges.

Bill: So Dr. Sha has actually taught you how to do healings of such severe challenges? How can this be? I have never encountered in any literature information about any other healer who had the ability to train others to perform healings of such severe illnesses. The common belief among scientists and researchers is that even if miracle healers exist, they have unique abilities and qualities that account for their miraculous results and that these qualities cannot be imparted to others. Can you please explain what you do, how you do it, and how Dr. Sha was able to teach you these unique skills.

Henderson: First off, there is nothing really unique about me and other Master Teachers and miracle soul healers. We are ordinary people. We have studied Dr. Sha's forgiveness techniques and learned from him how to perform karma cleansings and soul transplants and how to help individuals access their own treasures. We work hard to purify ourselves and to be of unconditional service to humanity. Our practices raise our own vibration, and the higher our vibration, the better we can serve. We do not actually do the healing at all. We serve as channels for the Divine. The Divine does the healing.

Bill: What do you mean? This makes no sense to me.

Henderson: The healer is the channel. The healer channels down the frequency from Heaven to the receiver (patient) and that will change the vibration of the receiver. As a result, the patient will be healed. Let me give you an example that is close to my heart. My father has bone cancer. When I first reconnected with Dr. Sha, I would request a blessing for my father every time his PSA count went up. Dr. Sha would give him a blessing and his PSA count would go down. My father does not believe in soul healing miracles and yet I learned firsthand that Dr. Sha's ability to raise my father's vibration resulted in healing my father's bone cancer. I think my father would heal and hold his healing faster if he believed in Dr. Sha and would do some of the forgiveness practices but even without my father's participation, my father's condition is not getting worse.

Bill: What makes for a successful soul healing intervention?

Henderson: There are many factors. It is not just the purity of the Master Teacher or healer. No matter what the vibration of the individual healer, Heaven's frequency is going to be a million times more powerful. When Heaven comes down to Mother Earth, miracles happen.

Bill: Once you learn to allow the frequency of the Divine to come through you and to those you hope to heal, are you guaranteed success?

Henderson: Neither I nor Dr. Sha nor any other miracle soul healer can guarantee results. You must remember karma. In the end the results will be determined by how much negative karma an individual brings to the moment and how much of that karma can be removed and how quickly.

Bill: Well this has been a most enlightening conversation. Thank you so much.

Preliminary Conclusions

I HAVE ALWAYS warned my clients and friends that if something sounds too good to be true, be careful, as it probably literally is too good to be true and is in fact false. I was quite prepared when I started writing this book to prove Dr. Sha was illogical and that his soul healing miracles could not possibly be true. Guess what? I lose. This is the one time when something that seems too good to be true actually is true.

I am probably one of the most fortunate people on Earth. My life has always been blessed, but having had the opportunity to spend intensive days with Dr. Sha and his disciples, students, and "case studies" has been a blessing beyond any of the numerous blessings I have already received. My encounters with Eckhart Tolle, the Dalai Lama, Sri Sri Ravi Shankar, leaders of some of the largest corporations in the world, billionaires, visionaries, religious leaders from all major world religions, sports heroes, Hollywood celebrities, and of course hundreds of brilliant authors I have represented, many of whom have been essential contributors to the founding of companies such as Google, Apple, and Microsoft, pale in comparison to the blessing of working closely with Dr. Sha.

Dr. Sha will always be Dr. Sha for me. I am not intending to become his student or disciple. My golf and tennis buddies would never understand if I altered my highly joyful lifestyle. I have a full and wonderful life. I have a business to run. I have more books to write. I have obligations to my wonderful author clients such as Thom Hartmann, Jean Houston, Barbara De Angelis, Barbara Marx Hubbard, Neale Donald Walsch, and so many others whose books and life commitments I admire and enjoy. But Dr. Sha is likely to become much more than just a client. He already is. I have learned so much from observing him, and I am a better person for investigating the principles and experiences that have led him to become Dr. and Master Sha: World-renowned Miracle Soul Healer.

After investigating his claims, seeing him in practice, debating his beliefs, and talking with dozens of his students and advocates, there is no denying that Dr. Sha is indeed a miracle soul healer bringing health and happiness to all with whom he interacts. His goal is to bring this health and happiness to millions through his books, videos, and retreats. He hopes to hold large conferences at which he could serve all those in the audience, rich or poor, who have similar illnesses, whether they be sports injuries, pain, inflammation, growths, addictions, relationship or financial challenges. Dr. Sha offers his services to people from all walks of life, whether they can pay for soul healing miracles or not. Dr. Sha has a history of great compassion for anyone coming into his presence and never concerns himself with the economic status of those he heals. Of course, he needs for those who can afford his healings to contribute to the economic stability of his mission, but so do all medical doctors and establishments. I have never seen any spiritual organization offer free healing like Master Sha's organization offers. If you visit drsha.com, you will discover that Master Sha and his Master Healers are offering many low-cost and even free soul healing services. While writing this book, I have observed and felt Dr. Sha's commitment to serve humanity and all souls unconditionally. His love, forgiveness, compassion, and care have moved me deeply.

Is this a religion? I say no. Dr. Sha does believe in the Divine, as do his students, but his students represent all major religions and they are encouraged to maintain their religious beliefs and affiliations. After all, the Divine is at the basis of all world religions, and Dr. Sha chooses to focus on what unites world religions, not what separates them. His goal is to increase love, peace, and harmony on our planet. How can any of us not embrace this goal? How fortunate are we all that Dr. Sha has tireless energy and never hesitates whatever the obstacles or personal inconvenience to give healings to all who need them.

So if not a religion, what is this phenomenon? It is truly a healing practice available to all, open to those of all beliefs who wish to heal themselves and others? Do you need to believe in karma and reincarnation to be healed? The answer is clearly no. Does it help if you do? I believe the answer is yes, and Dr. Sha has made it clear that he could never accept a disciple who does not believe in the power of past-life karma cleansings. After all, karma cleansings are at the root of the healing practice.

Since I do not intend to become a healer myself, it hardly matters to me whether I believe in reincarnation and past-life karma. I was quite certain when I started this journey that such concepts were unscientific and based on ungrounded evidence. Now, at the end of my journey with Dr. Sha, I am less certain. The logic of Dr. Sha's argument in favor of past karma, and the power and effectiveness of his karma cleansings have forced me to shift my own thinking. I need more time to sort out this mystery, but unless I discover illogic in Dr. Sha's premise, I may in the end relent and agree that reincarnation is possible. Once I open that door, karma cleansings may seem logical as well.

Time will tell where my own journey takes me, but I encourage all readers to follow Dr. Sha's advice: "If you want to know if a pear is sweet, taste it." I have tasted the pear of Dr. Sha's friendship and his soul healing practices, and it has indeed been sweet. May you find such sweetness in your own lives as well.

PART TWO

Exploring Master Sha's Service

My Current Journey
with Dr. and Master Sha

Reintroducing Dr. Sha

W HEN I INITIALLY sat down to write this book, my goal was to discover the science behind soul healing miracles. Were these legitimate healing miracles, and if so, what might be the explanation? What meaning, if successful, do these soul healing miracles have for the medical profession and society as a whole? The journey has taken me far beyond these initial questions. I now question some of my basic assumptions about the nature of reality itself. What you have read in Part One was originally the complete book as I had imagined it. But so many questions were raised in my personal journey of self-discovery that I requested to spend an additional week with Dr. Sha to discuss in greater detail his core beliefs.

During this wonderful week of research, we shared every breakfast, lunch, and dinner together and I was with him sixteen to eighteen hours a day. We found that we enjoyed the same foods, and that once we found something we enjoyed, we were creatures of habit. We went to the same Japanese restaurant for lunch five days in a row and ordered the same meal every day. We discovered that we both really enjoy noodle soup. Every night we went to a wonderful French restaurant where I introduced Dr. Sha to more exotic fare. I was pleased he enjoyed my selections. We laughed and became and are good friends. My wife Gayle and Dr. Sha's assistant, Master Cynthia, were with us for every meal and every discussion as well.

Master Cynthia took dictation of every conversation. I do not know how she was able to keep up, as both Dr. Sha and I are fast talkers, especially when we had heated discussions and even arguments about the science behind soul healing miracles. Like any good friends, our disagreements, once resolved, only made our friendship more lasting and more real.

I am truly grateful for the access and friendship that Dr. Sha has given me. I am one of very few people for whom Dr. Sha in addition to being a healer and a spiritual teacher is able to just be a friend. Dr. Sha is a very private person. He has a wife, three children, and a dog. He does not get a chance to spend much time with his family, but they love him and support him and his mission in every way they can as long as they can stay out of the limelight themselves. Dr. Sha's children are grown and successful in their own lives. His daughter and my daughter are both getting married this summer, my daughter in Europe, his in Canada. We shared how happy these events make us and we both look forward to grandchildren in the coming years. I would not say that Dr. Sha is a "regular guy," but as a human being he is just like any of us, concerned about family and enjoying the small moments of his life. Fortunately, Dr. Sha loves to perform and is okay with the responsibilities and lack of privacy that comes with being a "spiritual rock star." Dr. Sha is always on call. He never refuses to give healings, and even during our lengthy discussions would have to break to give remote healings sometimes to people in Europe or Australia. Dr. Sha with modern technology is literally on call 24/7. Fortunately, like me, he does not enjoy computers or cell phones and Master Cynthia screens all of his calls and e-mail. Were this not the case he would not get a moment's peace. I did all the driving while we were in Palm Springs where these conversations took place. Dr. Sha confessed he has not driven a car in ten years, and his wife does not think he is a good driver. It was fun driving with the top down with just Dr. Sha and me in the car down the main drag of Palm Springs. We could have been just two friends out for a ride, and on one level we were, but of course we were in every moment focused on discovering the mysteries behind soul healing miracles and the mystery that is the human being Dr. and Master Sha. To say I felt privileged is an understatement.

In addition to these conversations, Dr. Sha connected me to his Master Teachers and asked them to provide me with explanations of who they are, why or how they became channels, and to describe in some cases specific trainings or experiences they have had. I was close to the deadline already for submitting the final manuscript, so I asked these Master Teachers to provide no more than five to ten pages each. They had less than a week to submit their material, and I was pleased at the high quality of their stories. In the chapter "The Company We Keep," I introduced Master Ximena.

You were also introduced in chapter nineteen to Master Henderson. They are both Master Teachers and could have been included in Part Three, but as I had interviewed both of them personally, I felt they should be presented as I already have. The stories show how intelligent, dedicated, caring, and loving Dr. Sha's Master Teachers are. The stories are powerful and give foundation to the reality that Dr. Sha is creating an organization that will ground these soul healing miracles in a way that will reach millions of human souls. Dr. Sha is unambiguous about this goal and tireless in working toward it. So are his Master Teachers. Everyone involved with what they call "the mission" is dedicated on both a human and soul level to this work. They are here to heal themselves and others and to progress on their individual spiritual paths. How fortunate for humanity that their own spiritual growth provides such blessings and healings for so many.

Even though I have yet to meet face-to-face most of the people who you will read about in Part Three: Stories from Master Teachers and Divine Soul Healers, I feel that I already know them well just from reading their stories. I thank them and I am sure that any remaining doubts you might have about the integrity and effectiveness of soul healing miracles will be considerably lessened once you read these inspiring and fascinating vignettes of their personal soul healing journeys.

But before we share these stories, let's resume our conversation with Dr. Sha. Dr. Sha cannot help himself when explaining his work. He is a born teacher and healer, and that is what he does in every moment. During our conversation Dr. Sha adds additional examples of his soul healing miracle successes with exercises and examples so readers can learn in greater detail how they can immediately participate in their own soul healing. Enjoy these bonus chapters and be sure to read the wonderful stories in Part Three of the Master Teachers themselves. The stories will bring you light, if not enlighten you.

Further Conversations with Dr. and Master Sha

AFTER SPEAKING WITH some of Dr. Sha's student teachers and observing those he has healed firsthand, I became more interested in the science and history of soul healing miracles. I was fortunate to have a second opportunity to have an in-depth interview with Dr. Sha.

Bill:	Dr. Sha, what is the highest teaching you offer to humanity?
Master Sha:	I am delighted to answer you. The highest teaching that I offer to humanity is the teaching of Tao.
Bill:	What is the Tao, Dr. Sha?
Master Sha:	Millions of people in history, including non-Chinese have heard about Tao. Many people have felt that Tao is so sacred that it is a mystery. It is very hard to understand Tao. Many foreigners think that Tao is the way. That is correct, but let me explain the essence of Tao.
	Lao Zi, the author of *Dao De Jing*, said: *Dao Ke Tao, Fei Chang Dao*.
	Pronounced *dow kuh dow, fay chahng dow*, this means *the Tao that is explained in words and comprehended by thoughts is not the true Tao*.
Bill:	This is a book. How am I going to explain in a book if words and thoughts are not adequate?

Master Sha: Lao Zi said, *Shang Shan Ruo Shui.* Shang Shan means *highest kindness.* It refers to Tao. Ruo means *just like.* Shui means *water.* Shang Shan Ruo Shui (pronounced *shahng shahn rwaw shway*) means *highest kindness (Tao) is just like water.* You are asking me if Tao can be explained in words. How can I share with your readers? That is what Lao Zi taught in the *Dao De Jing.* Tao cannot be explained by words. Lao Zi also said that Tao cannot be seen, cannot be heard, cannot be touched. Tao is the Source that cannot use any words. Lao Zi said, "I name the Source as Tao. The nature of water is close to Tao. What is the nature of water?" Lao Zi continued, "Water stays in the lowest part of the mountain or earth. Water holds all dirty things without complaining." The humility and big heart of water are just like Tao.

Bill: Do you access Tao when you do soul healing miracles?

Master Sha: That is the point. That is the top secret of soul healing miracles.

Bill: Okay, Dr. Sha, we have the secret. It is still going to be confusing for the readers. It is even confusing for me. I have heard that the Tao is all and the Tao is nothing. How can the Tao be all and nothing?

Master Sha: Follow the teaching of Lao Zi. Let me try to explain in a simple way about Tao.

- Tao is the Source of Heaven, Mother Earth, and countless planets, stars, galaxies, and universes.
- Tao is The Way of all life.
- Tao is the universal principles and laws.
- Tao is emptiness and nothingness.

Bill: Is the Tao truly nothingness?

Master Sha: That is the point. Many people study Tao and think Tao is nothingness. But in fact, Lao Zi in one chapter of *Dao De Jing* explained that Tao is in the blurred condition; no time, no space. Please make certain that every reader understands that the universe is made of space and time. Tao has no space or time. Lao Zi said, "Within the blurred condition, there is matter, energy, and message." I explain Lao Zi's teaching, *Tao is made of Tao jing qi shen. Jing means matter. Qi means energy. Shen means soul.*

Bill: I want to move from theoretical to practical. When you do karma cleansing for a person, do you read the Akashic Records? Are the Akashic Records part of the Tao because they have no space or time?

Master Sha: Akashic Records are not within the Tao.

Bill: If it is not within the Tao, where is it?

Master Sha: Let me explain the profound secrets that Lao Zi offered in *Dao De Jing* for humanity.

Tao Sheng Yi (pronounced *dow shung yee*)
Yi Sheng Er (pronounced *yee shung ur*)
Er Sheng San (pronounced *ur shung sahn*)
San Sheng Wan Wu (pronounced *sahn shung wahn woo*)

Tao literally means *the Source*. Sheng means *creates* or *produces*. Yi means *one*. Er means *two*. San means *three*. Wan Wu means *countless things*. Tao Sheng Yi, Yi Sheng Er, Er Sheng San, San Sheng Wan Wu means *Tao creates One, One creates Two, Two creates Three, Three creates All Things*.

Bill: I love that explanation, and it resonates with me as a mathematician. Tao creates One, One creates Two, Two creates Three, Three creates All Things and infinite beings. Dr. Sha, can you explain further in simpler terms why this is a profound teaching and what is the actual process and not just the abstract equation?

Master Sha: Tao is the Source. Tao has its own jing qi shen, which means *Tao matter, energy, and soul*. Tao creates One. One means *the Hun Dun condition*. Hun Dun (pronounced *hwun dwun*) condition means *blurred condition with no shape, no images, no time, and no space.* This condition has waited for qi (energy) transformation. It has taken a long, long time. Within this condition, there are two kinds of energy. One is named Qing Qi. Qing means *light.* Qi means *energy.* Qing Qi (pronounced *ching chee*) means *light energy.* The other is Zhuo Qi (pronounced *jwaw chee*). Zhuo means *disturbed* or *heavy.* Qi means *energy.* When the qi transformation happens, Qing Qi rises to form Heaven. Zhuo Qi falls to form Mother Earth. This is how oneness, the Hun Dun condition, creates Heaven and Mother Earth. This is One creates Two.

Two creates Three. Three means the Hun Dun condition, which is One. Heaven and Mother Earth are two. Hun Dun plus Heaven and Mother Earth are three. Three creates all things and all beings. Hun Dun, oneness, plus Heaven and Mother Earth join together to create all beings and all things. This is Three creates all beings and All Things. This is the process and how Tao creates One. One creates Two. Two creates Three. Three creates All Things. This is Tao Normal Creation. I wrote *Tao I: The Way of All Life* and *Tao II: The Way of Healing, Rejuvenation, Longevity, and Immortality.* I have explained much deeper and in detail about this Tao Normal Creation.

Bill: Does this explanation explain where and how you access the Akashic Records?

Master Sha: I explained earlier the Akashic Records are not within the Tao. Akashic Records only works for the two levels of Heaven and Mother Earth. Tao and oneness is before Heaven and Mother Earth. Karma does not work on that level. Karma only works on Heaven and Mother Earth level.

Bill: Now we are getting somewhere. Other medical doctors suggest health is a matter of balance. Is the purpose of karma cleansing to balance an individual's relationship between Heaven and Mother Earth? You do bad things and have lessons. You do good things and be of service to others and your karma is healed. It seems we are speaking about balance. Can you comment?

Master Sha: Karma law is the law in Heaven and Mother Earth. In the two levels Heaven and Mother Earth, karma is one of the most important laws. You do good things for others, you make others happier and healthier, and you are rewarded with health, relationships, finances, children, descendants, intelligence, and in every aspect of life. If a person harmed others including killing, taking advantage of others, cheating, stealing, and more, the person will learn lessons, including in health, relationships, finances, children, intelligence, and every aspect of life.

Bill: When you say lessons, do you mean suffering?

Master Sha: Lessons are the blockages of life and suffering of humanity and animals.

Bill: The Buddha has said that life is suffering. Do you agree?

Master Sha: Buddha has not said that word. Buddha said that everything is made of karma.

Bill: Buddha's teaching as I understand is attachment and desires are the reason for suffering.

Master Sha: I completely agree. Human beings have too many desires. They want to be famous. They want to be millionaires and billionaires. They want to travel all over the world. They want a big vacation house. Two biggest desires of a human being are materialism and fame. Many people may think that is the purpose of their life. They want to have a lot of money and want to be famous. Buddha's teaching is that this kind of desire will affect their spiritual journey.

Bill: What is the way out of suffering? You have written in your book *Soul Healing Miracles* that it is to be of service to others. To be of service to others you can escape suffering.

Master Sha: Yes, unconditional service is the key to escaping karma.

Even those who seek simple things such as their own health and wellness, if they are attached to their health and wellness more than serving, they can create karma and suffering. The key that goes beyond Buddha is unconditional service.

Bill: I think I am beginning to understand. The Akashic Records are important, but not the most important for soul healing. The most important is to access Tao. How do you access Tao when you do a soul healing miracle?

Master Sha: I appreciate you, Bill. You have brought such deep questions. They cannot be answered in a few sentences. You have brought another deep question.

In my teaching, karma is the root cause for success and failure in every aspect of life. You do great service and you receive a reward. You harm others and you learn lessons. In the Western world, "What goes around comes around." Humanity carries the negative karma. I have offered Divine Karma Cleansing from July 2003. Now it is 2014. It has been about eleven years. I have not seen one person who is free of negative karma.

Bill: What about you?

Master Sha: I also carry karma. Because humanity carries karma, if you want to receive soul healing miracles you have to clear negative karma first. Karma is on two levels, which means Heaven and Mother Earth levels. Every person has to clear negative karma first then your soul journey can go beyond Heaven and Mother Earth back to the Tao. For a human being to go beyond Heaven and Mother Earth, which means go beyond Two, return to One, and return to Tao, that is the final achievement of one's spiritual journey. To reach Tao is to reach immortality. For a human being, remember the earlier formula. A human being is on the Wan Wu level. In order to reach Tao, Wan Wu, all things have to go back to Three, go back to Two, go back to One, and then return to Tao. From Wan Wu to Tao is Tao Reverse Creation. This is the task of all spiritual beings, regardless of religion, nonreligion. This is the highest spiritual journey. It is the highest path.

Bill: To reach Tao and become a Buddha, are they the same thing?

Master Sha: To reach Tao and to become a Buddha are the same thing. To reach Tao is the highest achievement of the spiritual journey. To become a Buddha is the highest achievement of the spiritual journey. At the highest level, Tao teaching and Buddhist teaching, holy teaching and all spiritual teachings, the highest level is to reach the highest enlightenment. The highest enlightenment is to meld with Tao, the Source. Then you become the Source. You are the Source. The Source is you. That is the highest achievement.

Bill: In your knowledge, has any human being achieved this?

Master Sha: Yes.

Bill: Can a normal human being, even someone reading this book, living today on Mother Earth reach this state of Tao?

Master Sha: A human being can reach Tao. Normally to reach Tao could take thousands of lifetimes of effort. One lifetime means from birth to death. To reach Tao is a long, long process. If one person can reach Tao in this lifetime it is the effort of thousands of lifetimes before. This lifetime a person will receive huge upliftment. My answer is "yes," but a rare human being can reach Tao.

Bill: Out of seven billion people, how many people in this lifetime do you think will reach Tao?

Master Sha: Bill, you pose difficult questions, so I connected with Divine and Tao just now and have been told that of the seven billion people currently alive, there are only fourteen people on Mother Earth who might reach Tao.

Bill: I actually find this very positive. Of course, the other seven billion people will have other lifetimes to reach Tao. The other aspect I find positive in the negative situation of our planet is that it makes it very difficult to reach Tao.

Master Sha: No, it is the greatest opportunity to reach Tao because chaos and disorder create greater opportunities to serve. In chaos there is an opportunity for a pure and unconditional servant to be uplifted to Tao.

Bill: Ultimately, Dr. Sha, if I have understood the importance of your teachings, it is not just for individual wellness, but for spiritual enlightenment.

Master Sha: The wellness is the first step. People are suffering with challenges of the physical body, emotional body, mental body, and spiritual body. People are suffering with challenges of relationships and finances, children, and every aspect of life. To have wellness is to reach balance and happiness, health. That is not enough. It is the first step.

Bill: Great. I understand the highest achievement is to reach Tao. We have to start from the beginning. Let us give the readers a simple exercise to start their journey.

Say Hello

I N READING *SOUL Healing Miracles* I came across an exercise that was called Say Hello. I almost laughed when I read this. It seemed so simple and infantile. I could not believe a serious book about soul healing would start with a technique that was so simple and called Say Hello. I must admit, however, now that I have had a chance to interview Dr. Sha, even though the Say Hello technique is so simple, it may be the most important technique and the best place to start on your own journey of self-healing. I asked Dr. Sha to explain the purpose and practice of the Say Hello exercise.

Bill:	What is Say Hello?
Master Sha:	Say Hello technique means to *say hello* to invoke with inner souls and outer souls to self-heal and heal others and to transform all life.
Bill:	Give us an example of a Say Hello technique that someone who has not read any of your other books can do right now.
Master Sha:	I will give an example. I am delighted to share one story first.
	In India there was a physician who came to the stage in front of one thousand people, and he shared he had a lady client who suffered seventeen years with psoriasis. The condition was so severe that her skin would fall to the floor from her whole body. This lady tried modern medicine, Ayurvedic medicine, spiritual chanting, and

many other ways without success. This physician told her that Master Sha teaches the Say Hello technique. In five sentences, please do it:

Dear soul mind body of my skin,
I love you.
You have the power to heal yourself.
Do a good job.
Thank you.

The physician told the woman that Master Sha shared in his book that for chronic conditions—this means a person who suffers an unhealthy condition for one year—to practice two hours per day. You can practice a few minutes here and a few minutes there. Add all of the practices to reach two hours per day. The woman started to practice after the physician told her. She repeatedly said again and again:

Dear soul mind body of my skin,
I love you.
You have the power to heal yourself.
Do a good job.
Thank you.

She practiced day and night with these simple phrases. The first day her itchiness was better. The second day the redness of the skin was better. She practiced nonstop, and within eight days her whole body was clear. The physician said, "Wow, how powerful this Say Hello technique is. I went to Amazon.com to purchase all of Master Sha's books. I am so eager and thirsty to learn Master Sha's techniques. I wish all of the people in India could study Master Sha's techniques."

There are thousands of soul healing miracles just from people using the Say Hello technique.

Millions of people suffer from knee pain. I will use the knees as an example.

Dear soul mind body of my knees,
I love you.
You have the power to heal yourself.
Do a good job.
Thank you.

Practice for about ten minutes per time, a few times a day. This could bring heart-touching results for your healing.

I am delighted to share one more story.

A woman fell in her garden. Both of her knees were on the ground and she was in excruciating pain. She cried and could not move. She thought that she may have fractured her knees. Suddenly she remembered her son taught her the Say Hello technique. She started:

Dear soul mind body of my knees,
I really love you.
You can heal yourself.
Do a good job.
Thank you.

She repeated these phrases of the Say Hello technique. Within less than two minutes, her pain was suddenly gone. She stood up and walked like a normal person. She could not believe the power of the Say Hello technique.

Bill: Dr. Sha, is this all we need to know about the Say Hello technique?

Master Sha: This is one part of the Say Hello technique. This is called say hello to inner souls. The second part of the Say Hello technique is to say hello to outer souls. Outer souls include countless healing angels, archangels, Ascended Masters, gurus, lamas, kahunas, holy saints, Taoist saints, Buddha, bodhisattvas, and all kinds of spiritual fathers and mothers, as well as the souls of the sun, moon, solar system, galaxies, and universes, which I call "countless planets, stars, galaxies, and universes." They have power beyond a human's comprehension. This is the way to do it:

Dear Divine,

Dear Tao, the Source,

Dear countless healing angels, archangels, Ascended Masters, gurus, lamas, kahunas, holy saints, Taoist saints, Buddha, bodhisattvas, and all kinds of spiritual fathers and mothers,

Dear countless planets, stars, galaxies, and universes,

Please forgive all of the mistakes that my ancestors and I have made in all lifetimes.

In order to be forgiven I have to serve unconditionally.

There are all kinds of services, including chanting and meditating.

To serve is to make others happier and healthier.

I will chant Ling Guang as much as I can.

Ling means *soul*. Guang means *light*. You can chant:

Ling Guang, Ling Guang, Ling Guang (pronounced *ling gwahng*)

or

Soul Light, Soul Light, Soul Light

I have written a Ling Guang calligraphy for this book. It is on the back cover for you.

Bill: Thank you, Dr. Sha. I am sure readers who do this exercise will want to learn more and pick up a copy of *Soul Healing Miracles*.

Energy, Matter, and Soul

E VEN THOUGH WE have discussed concepts of energy, matter, and
soul earlier, my further conversation with Dr. Sha revealed to me
that a deeper understanding of these principles is necessary for any scientist or serious reader interested in determining the scientific validity
of Dr. Sha's soul healing miracle practices.

> Bill: Dr. Sha, explain as simply as you can the relationship
> between energy, matter, and soul.
>
> Master Sha: I am delighted to share. I am writing *Soul Mind Body Sci-
> ence System* with Dr. Rulin Xiu, a physicist. We are ex-
> plaining the relationship of matter, energy, and soul in
> a spiritual way and in a scientific way. Here I would
> only like to explain the spiritual wisdom. You can study
> the scientific formula and scientific explanation in *Soul
> Mind Body Science System*, which will be published in
> November 2014.
>
> This is the simplest explanation. There are three sen-
> tences:
>
> 1. Qi Dao Xue Dao—Qi means *energy*. Dao means *ar-
> rive*. Xue means *blood*. This is one of the highest prin-
> ciples in five-thousand-year-old traditional Chinese
> medicine's history. Qi Dao Xue Dao (pronounced
> *chee dow shooeh dow*) means *qi arrives, blood arrives*. Qi
> has the leading position. Qi is the boss of blood.

Blood is matter. The relationship of energy and matter is energy leads matter.

2. Yi Dao Qi Dao—Yi means *thinking*. Yi Dao Qi Dao (pronounced *yee dow chee dow*) means *if you think or focus on a part of the body, then energy arrives*. This is the key principle of countless meditations throughout history. Yi means *mind*. Mind means *consciousness*.

3. Ling Dao Yi Dao—Ling means *soul*. Ling Dao Yi Dao (pronounced *ling dow yee dow*) means *soul* (which is *message*) *arrives, consciousness arrives*.

    This summarizes the relationship of soul, mind, energy, and matter. The sacred process is soul → mind → energy → matter.

Bill: Dr. Sha, this may be oversimplifying, but if I understand correctly, what you say is, soul is the boss of thinking, thinking is the boss of energy, energy is the boss of matter, which is the blood. So, your basic principle is if you start with the soul, you will heal the body more effectively than any other way.

Master Sha: Bill, you got it.

Bill: For the readers, please explain how they can use this knowledge for self-healing.

Master Sha: For example, I created a calligraphy for this book, *Ling Guang* or *Soul Light*.

> *Dear Source Calligraphy, Ling Guang, Soul Light,*
> *Please give me a healing to heal my back, to heal my*
>   *hypertension, to heal my hip pain, to heal my*
>   *depression and so much more.*
> *Thank you.*

Then constantly chant:

> *Ling Guang* (pronounced *ling gwahng*)

or

> *Soul Light*

Soul Light is the message, which is the soul message. Then the mind will follow. Then energy will follow. Then blood will follow. Therefore, just chant *Soul Light* and the miracle could happen very quickly. Some people may take longer.

Bill: But, Dr. Sha, not everyone believes in the soul. Will they still benefit? If not, can they at least benefit with the relationship of thought, energy, and matter?

Master Sha: Yes.

Bill: I understand starting with the soul is the best way, but not everyone can do that yet. For those who are not ready to accept Soul Light as a mantra, is there another chant that will help them?

Master Sha: One of the most powerful mantras is *Da Ai* (pronounced *dah eye*). Da means *greatest*. Ai means *love*. I have introduced this Source mantra in my book *Soul Healing Miracles* and I have a Source Ling Guang calligraphy called *Da Ai* in that book. Just remember to chant *Da Ai, Da Ai, Da Ai, Da Ai* or *Greatest Love, Greatest Love, Greatest Love, Greatest Love*. Greatest Love. This is the soul message. If you give a soul message to one part of the body to heal one condition, the consciousness will follow, the energy will follow, the blood will follow, and the healing will follow.

Bill: When you were a medical doctor, were you aware of the role of the soul?

Master Sha: No.

Bill: When you developed your practice of acupuncture, were you aware of the importance of soul in healing?

Master Sha: No.

Bill: When you were involved with qi gong and other ancient techniques, were you aware of the importance of soul?

Master Sha: No.

Bill: When were you aware of the soul in your healing?

Master Sha: It happened in 1994 when I met my beloved spiritual mentor and adoptive father, Dr. and Master Zhi Chen Guo. I went to China to see that he had twenty thousand people daily in the courtyard. He stood on a stage and offered soul healing. I did not know at that moment how to do soul healing, but I learned Soul Language. I had seen so many soul healing miracles through Soul Language and then I realized the importance of the soul.

Bill: As a medical anthropologist, I have studied traditional Western doctors. I have studied indigenous shamans. I have studied unique individuals such as John of God. One of the reasons I have been intrigued to explore the mystery behind your soul healings is because you are the first healer that I have met who has combined all of these traditions: Western medicine, traditional Chinese medicine, energy healing, and spiritual healing. What do you think of these different modalities, and how can they work together to improve the health of humanity?

Master Sha: Thank you for the question. This question is so important to serve humanity in a better way. Modern medicine focuses on matter. When you are sick, you go to see your physician. The doctor will do blood tests. The blood tests are to see the biochemical changes within the cells. A person may have to also do ultrasounds, CT scans, MRIs, and more to find the cysts, tumors, or cancer in different organs or parts of the body. Surgery cuts the matter. Pills are to adjust the biochemical changes within the cells. Therefore, modern medicine focuses on matter issues. In the book *Soul Mind Body Science System,* I have shared with humanity deep wisdom based on ancient wisdom. This wisdom is that a human being has three bodies: jing body, which is matter body; qi body, which is energy body; shen body, which is soul body.

Let me explain traditional Chinese medicine, Ayurveda, which comes from India, Reiki, and thousands of other healing modalities which focus on qi or energy. Traditional Chinese medicine has renowned secrets that I just shared: *If qi flows, blood follows. If qi is blocked, blood is stagnant.* In traditional Chinese medicine the key reason for all sickness is qi blockages. Therefore, traditional Chinese medicine and thousands of healing modalities focus on the qi body. Qi flows between the cells and organs and through the meridian system. Some may know about the acupuncture chart. Some may know about the meridian chart in traditional Chinese medicine. Meridians are the pathway of qi, but they cannot be found by modern science. There are only one or two meridians that scientific researchers can measure. In anatomy and surgery, meridians cannot be found. For Western doctors, meridians are invisible.

Modern medicine is starting to recognize qi now. There are millions and billions of dollars that have been given to the study of qi in the scientific field. Qi principles, qi knowledge, practice, and healing started five thousand years ago. Now modern medicine is aware and is starting to study qi. Thousands of MDs have joined conferences to learn acupuncture. Acupuncture is one of the key treatments of traditional Chinese medicine. Acupuncture promotes qi flow. If qi flows, blood follows. Therefore, traditional Chinese medicine and many healing modalities focus on qi body.

What is *Soul Mind Body Medicine* that Divine and Tao Guided me to create? What is *Soul Mind Body Science System* that Dr. Rulin Xiu and I are writing now? What are soul healing miracles? We are focusing on soul. What is the soul? Soul is the light being. Soul is the essence of life. We are teaching the soul system. The energy channel is invisible. The soul channel is also invisible. Normal eyes cannot see the soul. Modern science cannot find the soul. Modern medicine does not believe in the soul. Therefore, modern medicine separates the body and the soul.

In my teaching, a body has a soul. The deeper wisdom is a system has a soul. An organ has a soul. A cell has a soul. DNA/RNA have souls. Even the smallest matter like a quark has a soul. A space has a soul. Everything has a soul.

The wisdom I shared earlier is *soul leads the mind*, which is consciousness. *Mind leads energy. Energy leads blood.* There are hundreds of thousands of soul healing miracles just with the Say Hello technique. There will be millions of soul healing miracles that will come by applying the Say Hello technique. The Say Hello technique is the practical technique of the process of "Soul leads mind, Mind leads energy, Energy leads matter." That is the relationship of soul, mind, energy, and matter.

Bill: Based on my observations, you may be correct. There is no doubt your technique is successful. You have made a logical argument for the existence of soul. You have also explained the basic principles of soul from your teacher, Dr. Guo. Were there precursors or teachers who came before Dr. Guo, or is there any evidence of any time in recorded history that there was anyone else who taught about soul?

Master Sha: Yes. In Buddhist teaching they chant Buddha for their entire life. There are countless soul healing miracles that occur just by chanting the Buddha mantra. People with stage four cancer or other hopeless cases have recovered, one after another. For example, millions of people in history who have followed Buddhist teaching chant *Na Mo A Mi Tuo Fo*. Na Mo (pronounced *nah maw*) means *respect*. A Mi Tuo Fo (pronounced *ah mee twaw faw*) is a Buddha's name. Millions of people in the Buddhist realm have chanted Na Mo A Mi Tuo Fo for their entire life. There are countless miracles. When people chant *Na Mo A Mi Tuo Fo* they connect with the soul of A Mi Tuo Fo. A Mi Tuo Fo's soul will come to offer healing to the person. This is the chanting practice.

Bill: As an anthropologist I agree with you. I know that chanting the names of Jesus and Mother Mary have produced healing miracles. From a scientific perspective, these are considered anecdotal evidence rather than scientific evidence. You may be correct. But what you are asking modern medicine to do is combine modern medical practices with spiritual practices. Perhaps this is the appropriate direction for humanity. But I know from speaking with many medical doctors that there is great resistance from the medical community to this approach. What if any advice can you give to well-intentioned, brilliant medical doctors who have been taught that spiritual practices are not a part of their training as doctors?

Master Sha: My words to modern medicine and scientific researchers are to open your heart and soul. The scientist Galileo said that the Earth follows the sun, and he received huge resistance from the public. Finally, it became truth.

The relationship of matter, energy, and soul, the process and leading relationship of soul, mind, energy, and matter will take time for scientists, modern medicine, and humanity to realize. We have created so many soul healing miracles in the last ten years. We are writing *Soul Mind Body Science System*. My advice is to open the heart and soul and observe more. We are literally doing scientific studies now to document soul healing miracle cases. I would like to say that it takes time for humanity, the scientific field, and the medical field to realize this ancient wisdom.

An author in China shared in his book *Tao Medicine* that 139 Nobel Prize recipients have agreed in writing that if scientists do not study ancient Confucian wisdom, science will find it hard to move forward. I was very impressed and very happy that so many Nobel Prize recipients are paying attention to ancient wisdom. This chapter and other chapters in your and my books share ancient spiritual and energy healing wisdom. In *Soul Healing Miracles: Ancient and New Sacred Wisdom, Knowledge, and Practical Techniques for Healing the Spiritual, Mental, Emotional, and Physical Bodies*, the message for soul healing miracles is:

> *I have the power to create soul healing miracles to transform all of my life.*
>
> *You have the power to create soul healing miracles to transform all of your life.*
>
> *Together we have the power to create soul healing miracles to transform all life of humanity and all souls in Mother Earth and countless planets, stars, galaxies, and universes.*

Bill: Thank you, Dr. Sha. What an inspiring and awesome vision.

Scientific Evidence

B ASED ON MY personal observations of so many healing miracles, I
have no doubt as to the effectiveness of Dr. Sha's techniques. However, my personal observations do not make for hard scientific proof. Professor Gary Schwartz had shared with me his enthusiasm for conducting
scientific investigations and case studies that would prove the efficacy of
Dr. Sha's healing practices. These studies hopefully will be undertaken in
the near future. They will cost hundreds of thousands of dollars and take
a year or more to carry out once funded. In the meantime, I continued to
search for hard scientific evidence. In my search Dr. Sha introduced me to
his first disciple, Dr. Peter Hudoba. You will learn more about Peter, including his background as an award-winning neurosurgeon trained initially in the Czech Republic and then in Canada. I asked Peter if any case
studies have already been done documenting from a medical and scientific perspective the efficacy of Dr. Sha's soul healing miracles.

"I am just in the process of organizing a large-scale case study project to
document Dr. Sha's results," Peter told me. "I already have two cases
that have been well documented and presented to physicians in Canada
and India. Let me give you my preliminary report on these two cases.
They are quite enlightening and should satisfy the medically oriented
among your readers that Dr. Sha's results are being verified by medical
doctors and others with the strictest protocols."

Below is Peter's initial report on these two case studies. The conclusions
are edifying and will lead, I hope, to more scientific and medical investigations of Dr. Sha and his miracle soul healings.

Dr. Peter Hudoba's Scientific Evidence of Two Case Studies

I'm delighted to present two research cases that I've compiled as a member of the research team at the Sha Research Foundation. I personally reviewed all relevant medical documentation, letters from attending physicians, reports of tests, MRI or CT scans, and pathology reports.

I presented these cases in 2012 at Albright College in Reading, Pennsylvania, and at Hiranandani Hospital in India, and in both situations the physicians attending the talks were impressed with the effectiveness of Master Sha's techniques.

The first case is of an almost fifty-year-old psychologist from the United States who became ill in 2009. She developed initial pain in her abdomen, becoming constipated and very tired, and losing a lot of weight as well. Because she felt unwell, she went to the emergency services at the hospital, where she had a CT scan done on her abdomen. The CT scan showed a large tumor in her stomach, with spreading of the tumor to her lymph nodes, spleen, and liver. The physicians did a biopsy of the bone marrow and it showed a stage four lymphoma.

This is a very serious illness. This was diagnosed in October 2009. She received the medication Rituxan (B cells antibody) eight times and was offered the option to receive chemotherapy. She refused to undergo chemotherapy.

She decided that she would treat herself solely with the system of Master Sha. Through 2010 she received several karma cleansings and started to receive some spiritual downloads and transmissions. All her treatment from then on consisted only of chanting classes with Master and Dr. Sha on the phone.

Over time, she started to improve, slowly gaining weight, and became stronger over the course of 2010. In 2011 she was constantly improving and by the end of 2011 a CT scan was done showing she was stable with no change in her condition. Technically, there was no worsening, nor any improvement. The tumor growth was simply arrested.

By January 2012, her illness from lymphoma had remarkably improved to the degree where she no longer had difficulty with digestion, nausea, and fatigue. Due to her health situation, she was unable to find a job and consequently she was not able to pay for follow-up CT scans or other investigations. Nonetheless, she continued to chant and meditate, and she continued to recover.

When I met her at the end of 2013, she had gained weight back and had wonderful skin color, and looked much, much better than when I saw her early in 2012. She told me at that time that she was completely symptom-free, was eating with a good appetite, and that she felt to be in very good health.

As I said, she hadn't seen a physician since early 2010 and never had a follow-up by CT scan, so she did not know what the situation was with her abdomen, but she feels excellent.

She is very grateful to Master Sha for whatever has been done for her, and she is one of the great examples of what Master Sha can offer to people, and especially how people can benefit when practicing daily. I visited her in 2012, and I personally observed that she practiced several hours a day. There are very few students who have that type of determination and zeal for the practice, and obviously that showed on her results. I am very happy for her.

The second case I am delighted to present to the readers of this book lives in Australia, and is in her fifties. I know her personally, also, and as in the first case, I had the opportunity to review her relevant medical documentation.

This woman was first diagnosed with MS in 2003, which progressively became worse. In 2007 she started to have difficulty speaking, which is common for the advanced stages of multiple sclerosis, and so she started to take speech therapy.

She progressively became weaker in both legs, had difficulty walking, with numbness in her palms and feet, and spasms in her right leg. These spasms came and went but became increasingly disruptive.

Later on, she developed urinary incontinence, and on occasion she was not able to empty her bladder. Because of this, she had to start using a catheter to empty her bladder, and later developed a chronic infection of the bladder from this catheterization.

On December 31, 2008, she had an MRI done on her brain, and it showed that she had findings consistent with multiple sclerosis in different parts of the brain. Fortunately, her spinal cord was normal.

She was diagnosed to have multiple sclerosis of the brain and started taking interferon. This did not help her, and her situation became worse.

Out of desperation she had started to seek alternative treatments, and in October 2009 she met Master Sha in person when she traveled to Sydney and where she received a healing and karma cleansing for her multiple sclerosis.

She told me that a few days after her karma cleansing, her walking started to improve and her infection of the bladder completely resolved in a short time. She was booked for surgery to have a permanent catheter inserted by the end of October. But when she returned from Sydney, she went to see the urologist before surgery, and it was found that her bladder had become normal, and therefore the surgery was canceled. She hasn't had any problem with her bladder since.

In June 2011, two years after she had the treatment with Master Sha, except for some urinary urgency, where if she has to go to the washroom to urinate, she has to do it a little faster than usual, otherwise all her symptoms had completely resolved. The weakness in the legs was completely resolved. Her numbness in the palms and feet completely resolved. Her incontinence completely resolved. Her neurological examination was completely normal, and there were no signs of multiple sclerosis anymore.

We exchanged e-mails in early 2014, and I found that all has remained as before. She feels perfectly healthy, five years later.

These two cases are completely documented. I personally viewed the MRI reports and the reports from the physicians who are treating the patients, the laboratory investigations, and in the case of the patient with cancer, I also personally saw the pathology report of confirmation of the original cancer.

Peter's report pleased me on multiple levels. I was pleased not only that these patients had major successes, but also that medical observations were made and recorded, providing realistic scientific analysis that these healings were in fact successful. Complete scientific proof will require many more cases, including an investigation of those cases where outcomes are not as favorable. I know that Dr. Sha desires to see these studies done and is confident that once hundreds of patients are subjected to this same level of medical scrutiny, he will be proven correct in his belief that soul healing miracles are an effective, safe, and important modality to be used to supplement traditional Western medical care. Dr. Sha is humble when I ask him to provide statistics on the number of patients for whom soul healing miracles are effective. He tells me that he can never guarantee results, that if a patient has very heavy negative karma, his treatments may not be effective. I respect Dr. Sha for being conservative, but as I explore more and more successful cases, I am willing to wager that Dr. Sha's effectiveness equals or betters that of the best medical doctors and hospitals in the world. Time will tell if I am correct, but in the meantime, I encourage all readers, especially those who are natural skeptics like me, to explore the evidence before making your decision as to whether you would utilize or encourage other family members to utilize Dr. Sha's techniques for your own medical needs. I have begun to use these techniques personally and am recommending them to friends and family. After all, as Dr. Sha states, "If you want to know if a pear is sweet, taste it." If you want to know if these techniques can work for you, try them.

Part Three of this book includes reports from practitioners of Dr. Sha's soul healing miracle techniques. Some of these healers have become fulltime members of Dr. Sha's mission and been designated Master Teachers and Divine Soul Healers. Others retain their everyday occupations but have been given Tao Healing Hands and instructions on how to use their natural healing gifts to heal themselves and others. Do not be put off by these "Divine" titles. These are everyday people who, except for their commitment to learning how to heal, are normal people just like you and me. The reality is that anyone can learn these techniques. Of course, some people will be more effective than others, but as you read these accounts from people, some of whom were faced with severe, life-threatening medical challenges, think about your own life, your own needs, and how you may directly benefit from the information in this book and the books written by Dr. and Master Sha.

PART THREE

Stories from Master Teachers and Tao Soul Healers

Master Richard Shunya Barton

From AIDS Victim to Master Teacher

IN EARLY 1984, I was studying for a degree in musical theater at San Francisco State University. In the weeks leading up to my twenty-third birthday, I developed a persistent sore throat, fevers, and swollen lymph nodes. I went to the school doctors. They tried to treat it with antibiotics; nothing happened. They sent me to my private doctor. He ran more tests but couldn't find any cause. I was sent to a specialist, who ran more tests. In the end, he called me into his office. He was probably fifty-something, with a heavy build, a serious face, and an immaculately white lab coat. He sat behind a large, heavy desk. He looked up from my charts and told me, "I have good news and bad news. The bad news is that you seem to have whatever it is that the guys here and in New York are dying from. The good news is, the guys here don't seem to be dying as fast."

This experience would come to be known as acute HIV infection. I had contracted the virus that leads to AIDS.

It would be another year before a test was developed to conclusively determine HIV infection. It would be two more years before there was even one drug for treatment, AZT. It took another couple of years to find out the hard way that AZT alone didn't work. It would take nine more years to find a combination of drugs that did work.

For more than twelve years, I watched friends, loved ones, acquaintances wither away to nothing and die. I watched them lose their strength, their jobs, their minds, their lives. By the late 1980s, I was going to a funeral about every month. Always at the back of my mind, the question was there: "Am I next?"

But there was also another conversation going on within me, a conversation of hope and possibility.

A few days after my diagnosis, I was passing by a metaphysical bookstore. It was the eighties in California, so unless you lived under a rock, you probably knew something about the "New Age." I suppose I may have had more exposure than most. Through high school, my parents would take me to Unity Church. My mom had completed the Course in Miracles. I had been going to lectures with a woman named Betty Bethards, who was known as "the Common Sense Guru" and "the Dream Lady," because of her down-to-earth style and teachings about dream interpretation. She described herself as a conscious channel, like the famous seer Edgar Cayce, only she was fully awake when messages came through her. I practiced the "white light" meditation she taught. I searched my dreams for messages from Heaven. I practiced positive affirmations.

So, I was walking by the bookstore, and I thought to myself, "Well, I guess this is where the rubber hits the road! I guess this is the time to fully put all my spiritual beliefs into practice and see if it really works!" Would it be possible to beat this new disease with spiritual practice? I made a conscious decision to find out.

I changed a lot in my life. I stopped drinking alcohol and using recreational drugs, both a common part of social life in San Francisco at the time. I changed what I ate and eventually became a vegetarian. I became more consistent with my meditation practice.

When I graduated from college, I found myself in Colorado, where I joined a weekly meeting for people living with HIV/AIDS, their friends and loved ones. It was known as the Circle of Love and Healing and was based on the work of Louise Hay. It focused on the power of positive thinking. Louise Hay had been diagnosed with cancer and was introduced to the ideas of the New Thought Movement, which began in the

1800s. The basic principles of the New Thought Movement teach that our thoughts have power for good or for ill, and that by changing our thoughts, we can restore health and well-being to our lives. Religious Science, Christian Science, and Unity Church all evolved from the New Thought Movement. Today, we see these teachings in popular books like *The Secret*. Louise used these principles in her recovery from cancer. She became very popular among those living with HIV/AIDS, creating a feeling of compassion, love, and hope when medical science had little to offer.

Other powerful influences for me at the time were Dr. Bernie Siegel's *Love, Medicine & Miracles* and Dr. Gerald Jampolsky's *Teach Only Love: The Twelve Principles of Attitudinal Healing*. My doctor was one of the founding directors of AIDS, Medicine and Miracles, an organization that served people living with HIV/AIDS who wanted to take this kind of a spiritual approach to their healing. I began studying to become a minister of Religious Science.

I continued to develop a way of looking at life that I had begun to explore in college. More and more, I was looking at life as a series of lessons to be learned. I began to live my life as though everything that happened in life was happening for a reason. As though I created everything in my life, either consciously or unconsciously, in order to learn and grow. I developed a belief in reincarnation and that we were here lifetime after lifetime, in a kind of a school, to develop our soul wisdom. I would think to myself, "What if this is true? What if I have created this experience in my life in order to learn something? What would it be that this experience is trying to teach me?" In this way, even negative experiences became opportunities to learn and to grow. Even the experience of HIV, the fear, the pain, all of it, became something from which I could learn and grow.

About this time, I literally became a "poster boy" for AIDS. The Colorado United Way was doing a fund-raising campaign and wanted to highlight the work that they were doing to fight AIDS. They asked me if I would be willing to participate. They created a poster and television campaign focusing on my story. It showed me working out and read something like this: "When you find out you have HIV, you want to scream. You want to cry. You want to give up. Years ago, Shunya was diagnosed with HIV. That's when he started living!"

But it was much more complicated than it sounds. I knew many people who did "all the right things" but died. I knew many people who did "all the wrong things" who lived. And all the while, my T-cell count, the marker of the health of the immune system, continued to steadily decline. My quality of life was good, but my blood work was telling a very different story.

I will never forget the day my diagnosis transitioned from HIV-positive to AIDS. In order to make sure that people living with HIV received appropriate care, the medical community and the government agreed that even if you did not have AIDS-defining symptoms, if an HIV-positive person's T-cell count were to go below 200, he or she would automatically be considered to have moved to AIDS. And that's what happened to me. A normal person's T-cell count is around 700–1200, depending on the test used. Mine had been steadily declining, until the day when they went below 200, and I was then considered to have AIDS. I had thought of myself, actually defined myself, as "only" HIV-positive. It was a point of pride. As long as I was "just" positive, I was beating the game. I was doing all the right things and I could say I was winning. But now that was over. Now I had "full-blown" AIDS. I had crossed a line, and there was no turning back. I would forever more be diagnosed with AIDS. It was devastating.

I wanted to give up. I wanted to lie down and die. I was tired of fighting. I was tired of living in a world where so many people would just as soon have homosexuals just disappear, and who seemed to believe that if it took something like AIDS to make that happen, well then "maybe that was just God's plan." I made plans to move back to San Francisco, essentially to give up and go home.

By this point, I was doing work with another spiritual teacher, a very heart-centered and caring woman named Amritam. It was around this time that Amritam pulled me aside and spoke to me very directly, very honestly from her heart. "What's happening with you?" she asked. "Where is the fighter I have known?" She said to me, "I'm mad at you for giving up. I'm mad at me for not speaking up sooner. I want you back the way you were. I don't want to lose you!"

I was really shook up. I didn't know what to do. But I saw it clearly. I saw that she was right, that I was giving up. I saw clearly where I was heading. I would have moved back to San Francisco. I would have been surrounded by well-meaning people who would have held my hand and comforted me. They would have agreed with me that this was a terrible world. They would have been very loving while I quietly gave up and slowly died. I had watched so many friends do just that. And I was given a clear vision of my fate if I chose that road.

Instead, I stayed in Colorado. I kept doing more spiritual work, purifying more and more, doing more and more practice, continuing the fight to stay alive. Through Amritam, I was introduced to about a dozen spiritual masters from all around the world and practically every tradition. I did practices from Tibetan Buddhism. I chanted Hindu mantras. I did Native American ceremonies. I maintained relatively stable health for some time. And then a big shift happened. I moved to Hawaii. And shortly after moving there, I became very, very ill. I had no job. I had no medical insurance. I was quickly running out of money. Again, Amritam stepped in. She directed some of my spiritual community to take me to the doctor, saying she didn't care if she had to pay for it herself, I needed to go. The doctor took one look at me and said, "I need to run a couple of tests, but I think I am putting you right into the hospital." I had developed AIDS-related pneumonia. My T-cell count had reached an all-time low of seven. Not a normal seven hundred, just seven. I had almost nothing left in my immune system to fight disease.

When I was in the hospital, I got a call from Amritam. She said, "You don't have to die, you know. You have a choice." I thought, "Is that what I am doing? Am I dying?" I thought dying would feel a lot worse than that! But yes, I was on the brink of dying. And I had a choice to make: did I want to stay, or did I want to go? I knew that the antibiotics that were being dripped into my arm were combatting the pneumonia. But my situation was touch and go. The doctors were asking me if it became necessary, would I want them to put me on life support or just let me go. I decided I wanted to live. I lay in my hospital bed chanting, meditating, and doing spiritual practice. And little by little, I got better. I became well enough to leave the hospital.

I went home and did even more practice. My friend Craig, from the Circle of Love, who had opened a yoga studio, sent me instructions for restorative yoga. I chanted. I prayed. I meditated. I spent at least four hours every day on my own healing. Slowly I got stronger. I remember going to the ocean to swim laps at a popular beach. The first day, I could only make one-half of a lap before having to drag myself, bleeding over the coral, to get out of the water. But I didn't let that stop me, I got stronger and went back and swam a full lap. For several months, I kept recovering. But a few months after leaving the hospital, something else went wrong. I was starting to have seizures. We still don't really know what these were. Some doctors think they were small strokes common to people living with AIDS. Some doctors think they were neurological episodes. All I knew was that they were something I had seen in many of my friends when the end was getting near, when they only had about six months to live. I started to panic. How long did I have?

Then I found myself doing something that I do every once in a while. I sat myself down and I had a long talk with myself. I thought, "Well, Shunya, one of two things is happening: either you are dying, or you aren't dying! So, if you are dying, then what?" And I thought, "Well, if I am dying, then I want to do it as consciously as possible. And I want to enjoy what time I have left. I want to spend it focusing on the love that I have in my life. That's all that really matters!" So then, I thought, "Well, if I am not dying, that seems like a pretty good approach to the time I have left anyway! So maybe it doesn't matter whether I am dying or not. Maybe I want to live my life as though I were anyway!"

And so I got better again. I kept swimming and grew stronger. I kept doing yoga and got healthier. I kept meditating and chanting and kept purifying. I kept focusing on the love.

The next year, the clinical trials for combination therapy for HIV/AIDS concluded. There was strong evidence that the drugs they had used one by one before, like AZT, used in combination could actually work for people like me. I talked to my doctor and chose the strongest combination they had. I began taking these pills diligently—day in and day out. Pills that had to be taken on an empty stomach. Pills that had to be taken on a full stomach. Pills that had to be taken in the morning. Pills that had to be taken in the night. Pills that caused horrible diarrhea. Pills that caused neuropathy. Pills that caused weight loss. Pills that caused weight gain. Even one liquid medicine that had such a horrible taste that they tried to cover it up with, of all combinations, peppermint and caramel. It was vile, and I am one of the few people in Hawaii who was actually able to gag it down every day for months until it could be replaced with something easier to take.

But for all the challenges and side effects, the pills actually worked. The virus in my blood went below the levels where it could be measured, a very positive clinical sign. My T-cells, the good cells that fight disease, climbed slowly back to 300 and over several years kept climbing and hit a plateau in the 500 range. Not normal, but for someone with my history, very, very good!

Nearly ten years later, I met Master Sha. I wasn't looking for a spiritual teacher, as I was still working with Amritam and two different gurus from India. But there was one area in which I knew I wanted a teacher. Ever since I was a boy, I had always had the sense that healing miracles can happen. It even seemed to me that we actually should be able to create them. It seemed to me that this was part of our natural way of being, and that somehow, we had gotten lost. For about a year before meeting Master Sha, I had been saying that I really wanted to meet someone who could teach how to perform actual miracles.

At this point in time, I was doing massage and energy work, both at a spa and at a healing clinic at the local Unity Church in Honolulu. I had heard there was some kind of Chinese medicine guy coming to do a talk at Unity who was supposed to be highly respected, but I really didn't know anything about him or about what he did and didn't have any strong desire to go see him. I mentioned it in passing to my roommate, and then just let it go. When the evening of the talk came around, I happened to be flipping through my e-mail and found the flyer for Master Sha's talk. Again, I mentioned it to my roommate, but with little or no expectation that we would be going. Next thing I knew, Robert was standing in the doorway saying, "Come on! Let's go!" So we went. That night, Master Sha performed a Soul Mind Body Healing and Transmission System blessing for a woman who had virtually no cartilage in her knees. She could barely walk with a cane. Master Sha offered her spiritual blessings. Within a couple of hours, she had put her cane aside and was walking up and down the church sobbing what appeared to be tears of gratitude. I had a strong feeling that I had found the teacher who could teach me about creating miracle healings.

I continued to study with Master Sha. I have learned so much about the energy centers and pathways of the body. My awareness of how healing actually happens has deepened tremendously. I have received countless transmissions to further my healing. I have received blessings, transmissions, and practices to boost my energy, stamina, and vitality. This has been one of the most notable outcomes of knowing Master Sha. I serve as the event manager for many of Master Sha's events. I am the business manager for Master Sha's Soul Healing Center in San Francisco. It is not unusual for me to work until one, two, or three o'clock in the morning. For someone who has been through what I have been through, I am amazed that my body can keep up as it does. When we have retreats, both I and another staff person with AIDS are usually there before most of the participants get there in the morning and after they leave at night. And many, or most, of those are people with no health challenges. The blessings and practical techniques from Master Sha work! Without them, I am sure I would not be able to keep up.

I am also so grateful to be one of Master Sha's Master Teachers and Worldwide Representatives. As such, I am able to offer Soul Healing Miracle Blessings to others to clear their karma and help reduce their suffering. I am so humbled to be able to do this, to be used by the Divine in this way. All I have ever wanted is to share my heart and soul with others in love. Being a Master Teacher allows me to do so in a very special way.

Master Sha once asked me what full healing of my condition would look like. To date, there are almost no cases in medical literature of someone who has had AIDS for as long as I have, where HIV has been completely cleared from his or her body. Many who have started treatment right after infection have cleared it. This is known as post-exposure prophylaxis. One patient, known as the Berlin patient, was seen to have cleared HIV from his system as a result of doing a bone marrow transplant. Part of the bone marrow transplant is to use immune suppression therapy. This effectively destroys the host's immune system and replaces it with the immune system of the donor. In this case, the donor also had the benefit of having a rare gene mutation that renders resistance to HIV infection. The bone marrow transplant procedure is so invasive and risky; however, it is not even being considered as a general treatment. There are other men living with HIV who have also had bone marrow transplants for other conditions and are continuing on HIV treatment. Given this, I told Master Sha that the first indicator would be my T-cell count going back to normal. My count was "stalled" in the 500 range. Recently, my doctor told me that my T-cell count was in the normal range, above 700. This is incredibly good news, for which I am very grateful. We will keep looking for other health markers and we both have great hope that a full healing will be accomplished.

Master Sabine Parlow

From Successful Insurance Broker to Master Teacher

I WAS BORN on a Sunday in November. During my childhood I was told many times that it is something special, being a Sunday child. At that time I did not understand it: my childhood was special, as very often I had been very sick and I was much too thin and too small.

I grew up in a small village in the north of Germany together with my mother, my three brothers, and two sisters. We lived a simple life and I learned early to integrate all the household work and the work in the garden into my life. In this way we could jointly contribute to our livelihood and we learned to appreciate nature, herbs, the countryside, and also animals.

At about seven years of age, I started going to school, but was immediately taken to a hospital for two months as I had a contagious disease. No visitors and no contact with the outside world. Only once a month I was allowed to see my mother behind a glass panel. I think I learned very early to have inner strength and to believe in myself.

At the age of eight I joined religious classes held in our village. I was able to learn from a Catholic priest much about the Bible, about God, and about the Ten Commandments, which I still carry in my heart today. In many sick and lonesome hours, I have called upon God and the saints for protection.

I went to school for ten years. Financial reasons prevented me from going to university. This often distressed me, and the wish to study one day always remained.

I learned to be a professional office clerk in a large company. I had the good fortune to be surrounded by wonderful colleagues who trusted me. I wasn't measured according to my social standing, but by my personality and my engagement. This built my self-confidence, and at the age of thirty I started a four-year university education program and received a business degree.

At that time I already had two wonderful daughters and my husband, who supported me fully. I should have been satisfied; however, a strong desire and restlessness prevented me from experiencing the inner peace that I had been seeking.

Since the days of my childhood, I knew that something special exists in life, although I could not name it, nor did I have an idea of what it could be. So, I was restless and searching for this inner fulfillment. In my early childhood I often had a certain image in my dreams: that I would meet a special Asian man. I thought it was absurd, as I grew up in the former German Democratic Republic and traveling to other parts of the world was impossible. Nevertheless, this picture and thought returned again and again.

At an early stage of my life, I became interested in alternative healing methods, as a man in our village was healing through his words. I witnessed myself how he helped some of our village inhabitants in a most mysterious way when modern medicine was at its wit's end. I admired this form of healing and I wished to learn more. However, this path was not encouraged and one would only speak secretively about it.

So, I was over thirty and still searching for this unknown wisdom, the teachings and secrets. I had just gone through an operation on my lower abdomen and my breast and been told that if I had waited longer cancer could have developed. Many people are shaken when hearing these words. I have also wondered, why me? We were looking forward to having another child. I would experience two more pregnancies; however, both babies transitioned directly after birth. I was in a very delicate situation with myself and my environment. At the time, I was full of self-pity.

I kept asking myself why all this was happening to me. I searched for inner peace, which was still missing. I wanted to learn something, something special, and yet did not know what it could be. No idea, no words, no clue. However, I knew it was to be found somewhere, but where? What could it be?

Then a stroke of fate hit me that it took me years to recover from. My favorite brother transitioned due to a car accident and my world broke apart. My brother and I had been best friends, trusting each other, and had been fighters in the business world and had enjoyed so many little things together. We had achieved success beyond our very simple world into which we had been born. We had jointly cared for our mother. She had moved into our village and had left the village community that she had known for fifty years. We wanted to care for her together, however eight months later, this dream came to an end.

So I took over my brother's business and led it for several years. At that time I had my own business and operated out of two offices in the city. Every night I prayed that my life should end. I did not want to live on without my brother. He always needed me ... and I needed him.

God heard my prayers and I developed cancer. It was already in an advanced state when I got notice of it. I was prepared to leave Mother Earth. The doctors gave me little hope for a long life.

However, by then my daughter had given me my first grandchild, and my daughter reminded me that both of them now needed me.

So one night I made a promise and asked the Divine to gift my life back to me. I promised to spend my further life in service to others, although I did not know how. I asked again that this path be shown to me, and it was.

On July 7, 2007, I received the wonderful opportunity to meet Master and Dr. Zhi Gang Sha. He was touring Germany for the first time and I took the chance to participate in his workshop in Hamburg. A couple of weeks earlier I had received the recommendation to read his book *Soul Mind Body Medicine*. I was fascinated, my heart was touched, and I could not understand how a human being was able to write a book with so much love and devotion. Only some years later when I read the German version of the book again did I fully understand it.

From the first moment I saw Dr. and Master Zhi Gang Sha I absorbed his teachings and wisdom. I knew I had found my teacher and Master. It was love and compassion for all souls that emanated from him. There were so many new aspects, so much hope, so much curiosity, and the feeling of coming home.

Since that first workshop, I have been his student in Total GOLD and on the same weekend I handed in my application for further training. I heard words like *karma cleansing* or *Akashic Records* for the first time, nevertheless, everything was clear to me, very important and familiar.

At that time, I had a full-time job and was successful as a freelancer for a large insurance company with operations in Europe and worldwide. My profession was fun for me, I was successful and I enjoyed many amenities.

However, the more I integrated the teachings, knowledge, and wisdom of Dr. and Master Zhi Gang Sha into my life, the greater the distance to the commercial world became. I got to know other things that were important to me and that enriched my life.

This situation has lasted for approximately seven years now.

In 2010 a special situation occurred within my family. My daughter happened to have strong pain throughout her whole body. She could hardly move or get up from bed. This situation had lasted already for several days. No medical doctor could help her, no clear diagnosis could be given. I was once again on my way to a retreat in Toronto called Divine Transformation. I had the opportunity to speak to Master Sha about my daughter. At that time he was offering for the first time the karma cleansing for the emotional and mental body. He took my daughter as a demo person and transmitted the karma cleansing via webcast from Canada to Germany. A little later I had my daughter on the phone and she could get up again, could walk upright, and her pain was gone. This was an extraordinary miracle.

Master Sha offered me the great honor to become his Disciple, his Worldwide Representative and Master Teacher.

I have received this honor beginning February 2011. This meant to progress rapidly on my soul journey and resulted in new challenges in my business life, my private life, and for my whole family. Everything turned upside down, everything was renewed, challenging, and beautiful. Things that were important for me before turned stale. The unknown and the new became interesting. The more I learned, the less I knew. The world and the wisdom that opened up to me were endless and fascinating.

In June 2012 Dr. and Master Zhi Gang Sha gave me the responsibility over the European business. This meant to restructure all of the business processes, to find appropriate and competent business partners to put the European mission onto a solid and powerful foundation. I found out that managing both businesses was not in alignment for me anymore. So I decided to give up my profession as an insurance and finance agent and to fully concentrate on the business aspects as well as on the teaching and the spreading of the mission.

I am so happy to have made this decision, as living a double life before did not fulfill me. To find inner peace and inner joy, one has to follow the soul and to listen and pay attention to her wishes. On January 1, 2014, a very big wish came true and I could end my exclusive contract with the insurance company prior to its official ending date.

Now I only serve one company.

Today I feel this fascination and I enjoy all of my tasks. I am grateful for all the challenges, as I know it is God's plan. He is the creator and the motto is "Follow nature's way." When I follow this path, much is possible and can be achieved and fulfilled. During all of the years that I have known Dr. and Master Zhi Gang Sha, I have experienced that he dedicates his heart to humanity and all souls to spread love, peace, and harmony. The quiet aspiration that all souls carry within will become reality one day. Master Sha pursues this unique goal with indescribable devotion, love, forgiveness, compassion, and purity, and we all take part in it.

We are able to learn, to experience, and be amazed. We can purify and further grow on our spiritual journey. Each day gifts us new blessings and offers us new challenges. Each day is a new beginning on our soul journey.

I am full of appreciation and gratitude for all these experiences. I am so grateful that I have met Dr. and Master Zhi Gang Sha and that I may be part of this soul family. I thank all who prepared this path for me. I am so grateful for the opportunity to share this with all of you. Thank you. Thank you. Thank you.

In love and gratitude,
Master Sabine Parlow

Master Lynne Nusyna

From Business Executive to Master Teacher

MY NAME IS Lynne Frances Nusyna. I have the honor to be a Master Teacher, Disciple, and Worldwide Representative of Dr. and Master Zhi Gang Sha. Through Master Sha I have been given the privilege of the title of Master. This is beyond my greatest dreams in this life. I did not envision that any of these honors would be given to me. I feel very privileged to be able to serve in this way.

I would like to share with you some of the events and circumstances of my life, my soul journey, my healing journey, and how I came to work with Master Sha.

I was born in Toronto, Canada, in 1948. My parents, Ruth and Morris, had both come through the Second World War without harm and were living with my maternal grandparents at the time of my birth. My mother was born in Canada. My father, his mother and father and sisters, had come from Poland when he was eight years old. My family is Jewish. The extended family in Poland was large and very close. It was not easy for my grandparents to make the decision to leave.

Before the war my grandmother went back to visit her family and urged them to come to North America. She was quite "psychic" and feared for their future. A few of her brothers did come. She had nine siblings. When the Russians and then the Germans invaded the country, many were caught in the firestorm that became the Holocaust. My great-grandparents, great-uncles, aunts, and cousins were all lost. We learned of their fate after the war.

The pain that this brought to my grandparents and to my father was incalculable and left its mark on me and all of our family members. To this day there is a feeling that there are many empty seats at our table on religious holidays, and there is a well of grief that has affected us all.

Some of those who survived came to Canada after the war and arrived just before my birth. So, I was the focus of a lot of hopes and dreams ... and love ... for many people. I was the first grandchild in my father's family and the first girl in my mother's. My grandparents lived next door to each other, so you can imagine how much attention I received.

Both families had their own businesses, and my father worked in his parents' furniture and appliance stores in downtown Toronto. My mother was a bookkeeper and worked outside of the home on a part-time basis.

Soon after my birth I became quite ill. A high fever and seizures. My life was in jeopardy. I was in the hospital for some time receiving medication intravenously. I survived, but there was no definitive diagnosis, so a pall of concern fell over my family. They were quite adamant that I always "take care of myself" and they shared the story of this life-threatening experience many, many times. It became the first of many illnesses that I experienced and continue to experience to this day.

Growing up I had a fierce need to achieve. Whether it was in school or in sports, I tried to do well. For the most part I succeeded. I got good grades and often I was selected for leadership roles at school, like the student council or captain of a sports team. Also, I received a religious education, attending Hebrew school twice a week and religious school on the weekends. My parents were Reform Jews, so women could partake equally in all aspects of religious life and education. I took piano lessons and dance lessons too. I was a very well-rounded, normal existence for a middle-class, North American Jewish girl. I was very fortunate.

The religious part of my upbringing instilled "scholarly" qualities in me. Judaism is a religion that encourages "questioning." Formulating a good question is more important than the answer. One has to think it through well before asking. I learned this at a young age because I was very curious about everything, particularly about the big questions of life. What is the purpose of life? Why do people fight with each other? Why do people worship differently? Is there more than one God? Why do people suffer? How could something like the Holocaust take place in the modern world? These were just a few of the questions. Most of all I couldn't grasp why ethnic groups, racial groups, and religious groups were so divided. It seemed wrong to me.

When I was old enough to do things on my own, I went out to explore. I went to churches and Buddhist temples. I went with my mother to one of the first yoga classes that was held in Toronto. We learned about meditation. I was seventeen. My father, also very curious, became the leader of a Christian/Jewish dialogue group, and I had a similar dialogue that I organized with my Christian and Jewish friends in high school. I became an active spiritual "seeker" looking for answers.

One other constant in my young life was that I was often quite sick. Despite the best efforts of my family and me, I developed respiratory issues and had pneumonia and bronchitis many times. I suffered from digestive problems that caused a lot of pain in my abdomen. Though I was quite athletic, I was really not very strong. When it came to my immune system, I seemed to pick up every virus there was. So, I spent quite a lot of time in bed, and I used that time to read a lot. I also wrote plays and poetry. I had a diary where I recorded my thoughts about life, religion, and relationships. I explored myself inwardly and tried at the same time to answer those big questions.

As to the illnesses, I wasn't diagnosed with any specific condition until much later in life. My parents always said I had allergies, that my constitution was weak, and that many people in my family suffered from similar maladies. I just learned to accept this and take it as an opportunity to develop in other ways.

When I completed high school, I moved on to university. Most of my friends joined me at the University of Toronto.

I loved learning so it was difficult to choose a major because so many things interested me. I decided to focus on two instead of one and studied both psychology and English literature and drama. My career goal was to be both a teacher and a psychologist. I was hoping to find a way to combine the two.

While at school I also did volunteer work in the downtown core. I was at a street hostel helping kids deal with drugs and life on the streets. I got training on how to counsel and support them. This confirmed for me how much I wanted to serve people, to help them. I had been doing some form of volunteer work since my early teens, so that impulse to serve had been evident for a long time.

When I graduated with an Honors B.A., I was ready to move on and become a teacher. I had already started to teach religious studies at my parents' synagogue and I liked it. The volunteer work showed me I could be a good counselor too. I applied to the College of Education and took both the English teaching program and the counseling program, thinking I would be working in both capacities in a high school in about a year.

The year in college was great because I knew very quickly that I was not suited for life in a public high school. It was just too confining. With some good coaching from the head of the counseling program, I decided to go out to work and apply to graduate school, intending to be a part-time student there. I got a job working for a social agency doing rehabilitation work with people with disabilities. I divided my time between doing public relations for them, which I knew very little about, and some counseling. They were both great learning experiences because my boss in the public relations end of things was an experienced newspaper man, writer, and editor. He introduced me to the world of media, and later on in my career I did quite a lot of work with newspapers and television companies. I also got to venture out into the business world because part of my duties was to do fundraising, which meant connecting

with companies who could donate financially to our agency. A very ec-
lectic job but great preparation for the future.

Meanwhile, I was accepted to graduate school in a combined master's
degree program of adult education and counseling psychology. I became well versed in all of the latest counseling modalities, as therapy
and "self-actualization" were huge in the seventies. Gestalt Therapy,
Bio-energetics, Transpersonal Psychology, Client-Centered Therapy,
Cognitive Behavioral Therapy, just to name a few.

Eventually I gave up my job and became a full-time student. I also was
actively involved in studying meditation, kundalini yoga, and alternative forms of health treatments. I still suffered from bouts of illness with
my lungs and my digestive system, so looking for ways to deal with
these naturally was of real interest to me.

At graduate school I got to do an internship at the Addiction Research
Foundation in Toronto, which meant I was seeing actual clients and
counseling under the supervision of a resident psychiatrist. While I was
in graduate school, I was approached to do a short workshop on com-
munications skills. During my internship I did a lot of counseling, but
because we were also being trained as adult educators, I developed and
delivered programs for clients on how to communicate effectively in relationships and on the job. The workshop I was asked to do was for a
professional association of people doing training in the corporate and
government world. I didn't know anything about this kind of work, but
always open to a challenge, I took it on. It was a success and one of the
participants asked me to deliver a similar course in her company, a multi-
national insurance corporation. I agreed. So without much knowledge
of the business world, I became a part-time corporate trainer. A new
door had opened.

When I left school, I decided to become an independent consultant and
did many different projects in all kinds of organizations. Change management, leadership development, strategic planning, team building,
executive coaching, sales training—I became quite expert in many areas.
At one point I took on the challenge of becoming a senior manager in a

large corporation and helped facilitate a major shift in their business. I managed the Organizational Development and Training Department and worked across Canada and in the U.S. with the executive team. I enjoyed it all, learned so much, and got an inside perspective of how organizations function and what constitutes success and failure there.

I continued to do counseling too and secured contracts with an employee assistance firm whose clients included police officers, health professionals, teachers, and corporate executives. I kept my practice active and saw clients in the evening, on weekends ... whenever I could.

I did get to do it all, just as I had hoped. Moreover, I became a wife and mother too. On a personal note, my family was still a great support and I enjoyed motherhood immensely. If you want to really learn about yourself, look at your children and you will see yourself reflected there. I got that insight early on and it still holds true.

My spiritual journey did not stop either. I became a student of a very powerful spiritual teacher who was also a psychiatrist. He taught me about new modalities like rebirthing, spiritual attunement, and therapeutic touch. I learned special breathing techniques that brought people to a very deep inner connection and stimulated past-life experiences. Some people would call this regression therapy.

It was of immense assistance to me. I always felt in my counseling work that the missing element was the spiritual. People tended to repeat the same patterns of behavior, of thinking, of relationships over and over again. I knew intuitively that we were somehow recreating our past-life experiences in our current life. I was sure that I was, but I didn't know how to access this information or how to apply it. This teacher helped me see it, but clearly the role of karma was important and the teachings didn't adequately explain how we acquired karma and how we could release it.

I was still feeling the effects of the physical conditions I had and was finally diagnosed with asthma in my thirties. The abdominal issues escalated and at one point I had to have surgery to remove my gallbladder. I avoided this for a very long time by working with a naturopath, but one day I suffered a major attack and was hospitalized. When I saw the picture of my gallbladder and all the stones, I agreed to have the surgery. Because of the effects of the anesthetic, I suffered a minor stroke afterward and had some nerve damage. The stroke itself was to become a vehicle for a big leap in my spiritual journey.

When the stroke occurred, I was working with another spiritual teacher and was asking the question out loud: how can I know unequivocally that I am more than my mind and my body? When the stroke occurred, I had no control over my body, my speech, nothing. I was helpless yet I ... my soul ... was intact and functioning well. I let my soul take over my mind and body and overall I was very calm, centered, and positive. I meditated as the ambulance crew and then emergency room doctor worked on me ... and through this "peace" I was able to focus and re-align everything inside. It was the proof I was asking for. There was a soul ... another being that existed outside of my physical body and my mind. My teacher said, "Lynne, be careful what you ask for." I wanted proof, and it came through having a stroke. Wow. I saw when the soul is engaged more fully there is great power.

I worked with this teacher for a few years more intensely. He had deep wisdom, mostly gathered through his own life and death experiences. I meditated and I learned how to access more directly my own soul's wisdom. I trained in different forms of energy healing like Reiki. Eventually we moved apart when he informed me that he could take me no further and that I would meet a very special man who was a powerful spiritual teacher and healer. He would take me where I needed to go.

My health began to deteriorate again and I was hospitalized with acute pain and bleeding in the colon area. I was eventually diagnosed with Crohn's disease. So now I had two chronic conditions. The asthma was still a large factor in my life too.

I decided to not take any medical treatment because essentially that would include surgery and large amounts of medication. I did acupuncture treatments and herbs, which helped me to manage both conditions so I could continue to work, study, and be a mom.

One day a friend called me and said that he and his wife had just heard a spiritual master and healer offering healing over the radio. He said that Dr. Sha was the real deal because they had both experienced relief from pain during the broadcast. They encouraged me to come with them to meet him at a workshop he was offering in the city. My heart skipped a beat when I heard his name because somehow it sounded familiar.

In March 2003 I went to the workshop, not knowing anything about Dr. and Master Zhi Gang Sha except that he had impressed my friends with his healing ability. I also had never met a "master," so I didn't know what to expect. When he was introduced, I saw a tall Asian man in a sports jacket get up. There were no robes, no special crystals or amulets, just a man.

As he began to speak, I realized very quickly that he was an incredibly powerful teacher. His presence emanated strength and certainty. He said that the purpose of life is to serve. He spoke about the power of the soul. He said everything and everyone has a soul. He said souls can communicate and souls can heal. Every word resonated deeply within me. It all sounded very right. When he said that one has to heal the soul first before the mind and body can be healed, I became excited. This was something I had contemplated because of my own physical conditions. I was still suffering. Right away I thought about what my former teacher had said and that maybe Master Sha was that special teacher. When the student is ready, the teacher will appear. I was ready.

I continued to listen, and when he described soul communication and that every soul has its own unique language, a huge light bulb went on within me. For years, whenever I was doing healing—and I had by then learned many healing modalities—a voice started to come through me that was not my regular speaking voice. It sounded like another language. This must be Soul Language, I thought. My soul was trying to engage in the healing I was offering. Wow, that explained a lot.

During that one afternoon I publicly spoke my Soul Language out loud. I translated other people's Soul Language and I learned about the nature of karma. That was a significant day for me.

After the workshop Master Sha offered to clear people's karma. I was overjoyed. *At last there is a way to actually do this.* I proceeded to the parking lot, where I received my first karma cleansing. There would be more to follow. I was literally knocked out. When Master Sha said that he was about to start two new classes on the telephone, I jumped up and applied. These were a Soul Study class and a Soul Language class.

I was really happy. I knew that I had met my teacher, and my soul was singing with gratitude.

Within a few days I was on the telephone two nights a week with Master Sha. Often these calls went well into the early hours of the morning, but I was so enveloped in the teaching that it didn't seem to matter that I had a business meeting a few hours later. I loved everything we were doing and it was useful. I could actually apply the practices to my own life, do self-healing, and share this with others.

The telephone classes were quite small, perhaps twenty people total. Most of the students were from the San Francisco area, where Master Sha had gone to spread the teaching. Once a month Master Sha taught a workshop in person on the weekend in Toronto, and I always attended. I met other local students and we met regularly to practice and support each other.

In July 2003 I had my first private appointment with Master Sha. I went to his small office and immediately he began to teach me how to bow down and honor Divine. He told me this was very important for my soul journey. This was new to me and not what I had expected at all. I thought he would ask me some questions or ... ? I didn't know. He shared with me that at a retreat a few days earlier, which I wasn't able to attend, he had received some remarkable teachings and special treasures. He called them Soul Software. When he explained that these were treasures from Divine, that he was a Master Teacher and they had been given to humanity through him to help us to heal and transform, I jumped at the chance to receive them. So, I became the recipient of Soul Software for my Lower Dan Tian and Snow Mountain Areas. These would strengthen my foundation centers and give me a stronger base physically and spiritually. He then taught me how to practice. It was a very special time. I didn't really understand then that I was witnessing a major step forward for humanity and all souls, but I knew that these tools were what I needed. I trusted Master Sha then and I trust him now.

I shared with Master Sha that I had some chronic conditions and he seemed to know this already. He gave me special software for my lungs, for my colon, for my intestines, and for my gallbladder, and I practiced with them. I had some relief and was able to get on very well without having to use a "puffer" for the asthma. As I grew older the condition had worsened, and when I was really, really struggling I had begun to use pharmaceuticals to get me through.

All this time I was still working in the corporate world and offering private counseling. I had taken on a major project in a public organization, and though I functioned as a senior manager, I was a contractor and was able to maintain some flexibility. It included a lot of business traveling, and often I did the evening courses from hotel rooms and airports.

Whenever I could, I traveled to be part of Master Sha's yearly Soul Enlightenment Retreats and other events and finally got to meet those voices I had been hearing on the telephone. I became a Power Healer and then a Soul Mind Body Medicine Healer and started to offer soul healing to my clients. I also saw that my soul communication abilities were growing and advancing. I didn't know that my Third Eye was open ... though I had seen images all my life but never took them as more than the outworking of my very creative imagination. When Master Sha asked me to do some readings and share my Third Eye images at a public event, I was quite surprised ... but I did. He told me afterward that what I had shared was correct. I was very happy, as I had never anticipated that I would be able to do this. This was an incredible blessing because I knew that I could serve people even more with this ability. Since studying in the Soul Language course, I had also become quite good at translating Soul Language and "flowing" messages through direct soul communication with other souls. Now with these wonderful tools I could see people's past lives, see blockages in their bodies, communicate with their body soul and the souls of their system and organs, and apply soul healing to help them get well. I felt, and still feel, incredibly blessed. Everything I had hoped to learn was coming to me through Master Sha.

In 2005 I traveled to China with other students to meet and study with Master Sha's teacher, Master Guo. He had great wisdom, and his clinic was a haven for people who were considered untreatable. Many of them had advanced cancer and other terminal illnesses. His work in Body Space Medicine and the wisdom teachings he shared with this group from the West was very, very special. I became quite sick when I was there and received herbs from Master Guo. He also did a reading and told me that I was going through a process called "tui bing" (pronounced *tway bing*), where my body was reexperiencing all of the illnesses from this life and probably past lives as well. I had a high fever, trouble breathing, and abdominal pain, and he gave me herbs and Master Sha gave me soul healing blessings. Clearly there was a lot of purification taking place and I could see blockages clearing within my soul, mind, and body. I also learned that we retain things at the deepest levels, even the illnesses we have experienced.

I continued to learn from Master Sha, and in 2007 I was honored to be appointed as one of his Assistant Teachers. I was still working in the corporate world, but I managed to attend all the workshops and retreats with him and I started to teach some of the teleconferences. He was passing on these responsibilities to his assistants. We taught the new soul healers and soul communicators and offered support at the bigger events that were now happening around the world. Master Sha had broadened his teaching to locations in Europe and Australia.

My health seemed to be stabilizing. I still had occasional bouts of abdominal pain and breathing issues, but nothing that couldn't be managed through the self-healing practices. I received many new treasures as Master Sha was now offering Soul Mind Body Transplants for all kinds of conditions, organs, and systems. These very high-level treasures were bringing relief to thousands of people, and I was one of them.

In 2009 I was even more honored to become a Master Teacher, Disciple, and Worldwide Representative of Master Sha. With this came the authority to offer karma cleansing. I was truly taken aback by this. I had never dreamed that this was possible for me, but I had never dreamed that my karma could be cleared or that my Third Eye would be open. It was all very exciting and I felt humbled to be in such a position. I had the sense of having come home. I was serving in an incredibly powerful way. I was working with the most powerful teacher and healer on the planet. It was truly a dream come true.

In 2010 I left the corporate world and was asked by Master Sha to open a Healing Centre in Toronto. I saw this as a great opportunity. We could help so many more people by having a physical center.

At the same time that I was coming out of the business world and more fully into the healing world, I started to experience health problems again. Shortness of breath, abdominal pain, bouts of bleeding internally. I was never incapacitated, but it was obvious to me that the more I was trying to serve, the more layers of karma were starting to manifest. I had lots of karma cleared but I could see that as Master Sha advanced and evolved and as we, his Disciples, evolved, our karma, previously unseen, was being activated. This was new wisdom for all of us, and I was not the only one experiencing blockages. They could be physical, emotional, or mental. Sometimes I also felt depressed and anxious. No traditional psychotherapy methods could help this kind of experience, it was too deep. I knew it was karmic.

Master Sha continued to help me when I sought his help and I thought things were fairly balanced until the spring of 2011. I had a major Crohn's attack and respiratory issues. The pain was excruciating and I started to bleed profusely. My breathing was very shallow and difficult. I thought about going to the hospital but I did a reading myself and knew that it was a higher level of karma manifesting. I also knew very quickly that I was going to die. I could literally feel the life force leaving my body. Unless you have experienced this it is hard to describe. It was all happening very, very quickly. I was able to contact Master Sha, who was in Europe at the time. When I spoke with him, I was alone, on the floor of my bedroom, crawling to get to the washroom. I was that weak. I had begun to prepare myself to die. I asked for forgiveness over and over. I was very sad to leave my family, but most of all I was sad because I would not be able to complete my soul journey. I knew I still had tasks to perform ... people to serve.

Master Sha gave me his love and I felt his determination to save my life. There were other Master Teachers there with him, and they did readings so that we could understand what was happening to me. There was a huge amount of karma, and the dark souls who were present were committed to take my life.

He cleared the blockages quickly and I could see myself that there was great resistance. He gave me many Soul Mind Body Transplants for all the damaged systems and organs. I was still weak. I was told that my life force—my qi and jing (energy and matter)—had depleted to almost zero. At that point Master Sha offered his own life force from what is called the Jin Dan. I felt the power come in immediately. Then I was able to sit up and move a little. The Master Teachers on the phone said my voice changed and I knew clearly that I was saved.

This is miraculous. I was going to die, I have absolutely no doubt about this. Master Sha put himself at risk to save me. I had seen over the years that karma was darkness, yes, but this darkness was full of souls whose express purpose was to exact retribution for the harm we had done to others in past lives. They do not like to be thwarted. This is their task. When Master Sha cleared the karma for me, they became very angry. They resisted and they tried to attack him as well. He did it all anyway. That is his love, his generosity ... it has no bounds. I felt this in my heart and cannot, even now, think about it without tears coming.

I recovered well that time but since then the karma has manifested again at higher levels. Without any hesitation Master Sha saved my life. This is true service. This is amazing.

In 2012 and 2013 I suffered two more powerful karmic attacks. I was taken aback at how quickly they came upon me, and other people witnessed this. I was literally fine and healthy one minute and the next I was flat-out writhing in pain, not able to breathe and bleeding. They saw me sinking. My sister tried to help me during one attack, realized that I was close to death and she was helpless. We are all helpless when the karma comes. That is why soul healing ... Master Sha ... is the greatest healing power on Mother Earth.

He didn't hesitate to help me again and again. Every time he did, I was literally just hours away from death. He brought me back. He risked his own life to do it.

I am not alone. Many people have experienced this power. Master Sha is a generous and most loving divine servant.

When I was a young girl and became ill so many times, I knew in my heart I would not have a long life. Probably that is why I tried to pack so much in and experience everything I could. Above and beyond it all has been the knowledge that this human life is truly only the vehicle for the soul journey. Without this body I can't learn what I have to learn and do what I have to do so I can move forward. I have carried a lot of karma from one human lifetime to another. So have we all. The reason that my family suffered in the Holocaust is clear to me now. The fact that so many people are suffering—good people—is clear to me now. It is all about karma.

Without Master Sha I would not understand the depths of this profound wisdom. Karma truly is the root cause of everything—success and failure, physical conditions, financial blockages, relationship issues ... everything. I am so blessed to have his teachings.

Without Master Sha I would not be here at all. Because of him I am able to continue serving as a Master Teacher. I can teach and offer soul healing. I can work with people in every walk of life and with all kinds of issues. I can see how karma is affecting their lives, their businesses, their families.

When I saw how selfless Master Sha was and how willing to sacrifice even his own life for me, I finally got the biggest teaching. It is one that he had shared many times but I really, really saw it when I got up off the floor where I had been moments away from death. Love truly heals all blockages and transforms all life. Master Sha's love has healed me and I now am offering my love and my life to heal others.

Thank you, Master Sha. I truly cannot thank you enough.

That is my journey. Thank you.

Master Lynne Nusyna

Master Mirva Inkeri

From Corporate Leader to Master Teacher

HELLO. MY NAME is Master Mirva Inkeri. I was born in Helsinki, Finland. When I was born, my father was a young police officer, very early in his career. He had switched from being a radio engineer to becoming a policeman. My mother was working in retail, in different aspects of retail. They were earning a decent living, working hard to make a good life for themselves and for their children. They loved to travel, see the world, and experience different cultures and different perspectives. I studied languages and also traveled and moved overseas.

I had been on a spiritual journey for fifteen years when I met Master Sha on March 29, 2008, in Sydney, Australia. He came for a one-day workshop, which was followed by private consultations, one of which I was very fortunate to secure. I can say that this meeting with Master Sha changed my life for good. Good in two ways, i.e., for the better as well as permanently. I started studying with Master Sha immediately. I discovered that his teachings took nothing away from all the previous spiritual teachings as well as alternative medicine disciplines that I had learnt earlier. On the contrary, Dr. Sha's techniques enhanced and deepened all of my previous learning greatly. I was amazed. Every single teaching Master Sha offered was a new revelation. He taught topics I had never heard anyone else teach before, and the depth and detail he went into was completely amazing. I experienced my consciousness expanding by the minute. He moved from one topic to another in an amazingly rapid flow. I had been looking for a spiritual teacher for a long time, and when he told me in my private appointment that my soul wanted to learn and study, I was listening. He told me he'd send one of his top teachers to Sydney to continue to teach us and asked me to study everything he was going to teach. This I did. Master Peter Hudoba was the first teacher to accompany Master Sha in Sydney, and he returned several times. I learned everything that was presented. My soul was hungry, and everything was so fresh and produced immediate and rapid results. Every day I would study *Soul Mind Body Medicine* and learn the practices from the book.

I was in the corporate world. I had studied travel and tourism, but I also was a certified executive coach. I was a certified administrator of different psychometric personality assessment tools as well as a Certified Master Black Belt in Six Sigma business and process transformation methodologies. I worked in different aspects of the corporate world with some of the largest international corporations as an internal consultant, helping different aspects of companies to function better, more effectively, more efficiently, serving their customers better, producing better-quality work. I often found myself dealing with deep interpersonal issues and deep human-being-related issues. Master Sha teaches that your soul is your best counselor and you can tap into the experiences, wisdom, and knowledge from all of your lifetimes by communicating with your soul. This was highly appealing to me. Once I learned to open my Soul Language and how to translate it, every morning as part of my morning practice, I would ask my soul for guidance on deep, complex, and challenging business situations. Then I'd translate my Soul Language. This was so unbelievable. I would be moved to tears; I would have huge revelations. I experienced joy, delight, and freedom. I received incredibly deep wisdom that I could have never thought of with my mind. Then I would leave for the office with incredible inspiration and grounding, as I knew I had received solutions and answers that were one of a kind. I could see before my eyes how by applying the answers I had received, I was resolving situations in different ways than I had done before. Things were much easier! It was amazing.

Two years after I started to study with Master Sha and he started to formally teach the Tao, I came to realize that the purpose of life is to serve.

To serve is to make others happier and healthier. Master Sha said this to me in my private consultation with him but I didn't realize it fully at the time. I didn't really or truly know what it meant or how it would translate practically into life situations. Early in 2010 when I did the very first Tao retreat with Master Sha, I came back from this retreat realizing I had no need to climb the ladder any further. I had no need for my own agenda. I realized I was there to serve my leaders, my boss, my customers, my stakeholders, whatever agenda they had for me. I was fully in service. This was a very freeing experience. This was my first experience of freedom from the ego.

I now work for Master Sha as the business coordinator of his mission. I have been in Canada working for the mission for the last two years, first as the director of customer services, then moving into overall operational management, and now coordinating every department, every aspect of the mission for Master Sha. This is a unique organization. All that I have learned in the corporate world has served me well and continues to do so. Yet there is a different dimension, different way, and different element to how this mission, how the Institute operates. There is a higher-level agenda beyond the logical agenda. Everything is done with both the yin and yang aspect, i.e., the logical rationalization as well as the soul level guidance. Master Sha teaches to heal and transform the soul of the company first, then the consciousness, and the physical level, will transform.

In my leadership position, every day I do what is called soul conferencing and soul marketing. It is just like in the physical world, except this takes place on the soul level. It is called soul-to-soul connection. I speak to the soul of humanity and different teams. Every meeting we start, we speak to the soul of the different teams, employees on all levels, first to bring them into alignment, to work together as one, to be guided and to be shown the ways in which to work in love, peace, and harmony so as to transform all aspects of our own agenda, any aspect of the ego to become humble servants. This is Master Sha's teaching. In this mission we deflate job titles. This provides the platform to have no attachment to what your role is called. You just serve.

As a leader, my task is to support, guide everyone else to do their role, to do their tasks well. My role is to be an enabler for them, a facilitator if that is what they need. I need to embody Master Sha's teachings and lead by example to the best of my ability. One of Master Sha's key teachings is unconditional universal service. To serve unconditionally is to expect nothing in return. Therefore, the concept of the corporate business world "reward and recognition" doesn't exist here the same way.

What we deal with on a daily basis is the effects of our service on a soul level. How does it help others to come in better alignment for their whole spiritual journey, their whole life purpose? How do our services and products enhance the quality of everyone's life on all levels: spiritual, emotional, mental, and physical? Are we guiding them appropriately to enhance their lives? Everything is to be done with love, peace, and harmony.

There is no room to rule by power, by control. Our work enables a platform for everyone to transform these aspects of our personality, our ego—in other words our karma—as part of the working process. Everyone is equal. No one is better or worse. We are all one. Master Sha teaches the concept of "Bao Yuan Shou Yi" (pronounced *bao ywen sho yee*), which literally translated means "hold both hands in a circle below the navel and concentrate on the Jin Dan, which is this area." This is the literal translation as well as a spiritual practice.

How this translates into working as a team is literally "working as one team." Truly collaborating, truly working as a team in which nobody is a winner. All are equal. All are transformed and delivered with humility, in service together for the same outcome, which is always the higher purpose of serving humanity, making others happier and healthier. If this purpose isn't achieved, then we are not providing the right outcomes, results, and services.

Every thought, every word, every action we take counts. Everyone is to self-assess every day continuously, "Are my thoughts, words, and actions contributing toward love, peace, and harmony, or are they causing negative effects on others?" These are our operating principles. These are also the way in which we conduct the business. Everyone is held with love and forgiveness, compassion, and light. This is what we focus on every day, day in, day out. It doesn't mean we are perfect at this, as we are all, each and every one of us, human beings still on our own spiritual journey. We are all transforming together, we hold each other tenderly with love and compassion and forgiveness in the process of transformation.

These are our company values, if you like, that we hold each other accountable to and support each other with love and forgiveness to call on these as an accountability when we experience or witness that we are not, that somebody is not in alignment. I am so deeply honored to be in this position, to be part of this way of working, this way of enhancing other's lives and this way of serving. I couldn't have imagined this in all those years when I was searching for the deeper meaning of life. I always held in my heart the knowing, the search that there must be more to life than what was in front of me. I just didn't know what it was.

Through Master Sha's teachings, I have found that. I have not been searching ever since I met Master Sha. This way of operating is truly different and truly unique and is extremely transforming for every single person, and to work on a level of the soul first is unique wisdom, unique knowledge that Master Sha brings to everyone at this time. Very simple, very easy, very practical, and makes a huge, huge difference to the quality of the day-to-day work. Every decision or new strategy is assessed logically, rationally from the physical world perspective as well as checked spiritually whether it is the right decision. This is the balance of yin and yang. It is a universal principle. This brings balance, harmony, and oneness. There is no balance if one only focuses on one aspect. Neither is right nor wrong. Both are equal, and you only have balance if you consider and apply both aspects.

This is accessible and available to everyone. I'm privileged to have these teachings, to have been able to apply these teachings to every aspect of my life. I am deeply, deeply grateful to have met Master Sha, to have been given the opportunity to become his Disciple, his Worldwide Representative, and to be certified as a Master Teacher on Mother Earth. I truly hold in my heart today the example Master Sha provides me every single day. Every day he teaches me more on how to offer deeper compassion for another soul and their journey of transformation. He has infinite patience. He is teaching me to grow mine daily, experience by experience, situation by situation. When I align myself with his teachings, every single situation is teaching me more and providing me the opportunity to grow further as a soul as well as a leader. Every single situation stretches my capacity and capabilities further and further. Every challenge is to be assessed on the soul level first. This brings much much deeper understanding of others. It provides the perspective of why others are suffering, which is what is manifesting in the physical-world reality when they struggle at work. I help to resolve countless challenges at work by offering blessings. This clears mind blockages for those who are working on projects. It clears relationship situations. They can release negative emotions and change instantly. Soul healing blessings only take seconds or minutes. Sometimes it feels like "magic" how instantaneously it provides relief and resolves situations. It is powerful! I feel so incredibly blessed to have these tools and this wisdom to work with in the business environment.

I now teach others how to access these teachings as well through my blog, and it is so inspiring. I see many business leaders benefiting and companies transforming with great success. The role of a leader is to bring oneness, alignment in teams and departments. This is also needed on the overall company level. The products, services, and offerings must align with humanity as well as spiritually. Otherwise, the company will not thrive. When this alignment, balance is not in place, companies can struggle greatly. This can manifest internally or externally as challenges.

Master Sha teaches that everything is made of jing, qi, and shen. Jing is matter, the physical manifestation aspect. Qi represents energy, and shen is the soul, the message. Everything in life is made of jing qi shen or can be divided into these three elements. Every organization has a soul, consciousness, and physical manifestation. When one aspect is not balanced and well, the whole organization suffers. This is why the soul is the boss. This is why we address everything on the soul level first and the rest will follow afterward. This is a powerful yet extremely simple recipe for every organization and for every person for every aspect of life.

I feel I am extremely blessed and privileged to have found Master Sha in this life and received his teachings. Whatever I can share with others by sharing my story, how I can help to serve others through what I can share with you, I am most honored and delighted to be of service in that way if that is of help. I am very grateful. I offer my greatest love and greatest gratitude to my teacher, beloved Master Sha. I cannot serve enough in return for what I have received from him. Thus, my life today is completely dedicated to serving others to the best of my ability. For this, I am very honored. I have found the meaning and purpose of life which I searched for with great desire.

With greatest love,
Master Teacher, Worldwide Representative,
and Disciple of Dr. and Master Sha,
Master Mirva Inkeri

Master David Lusch

Suffering from OCD (Obsessive-Compulsive Disorder) to Master Teacher

EVERY ASPECT OF my life has transformed through Dr. and Master Zhi Gang Sha.

Growing up in Fremont, California, USA, I was extremely loved by my parents, Roger and Diane Lusch, and my grandparents Richard and Marilyn Delfs and Joseph and Anne Lusch. I also had a loving and great sister, Erica. I had a very caring and loving extended family with my aunts, uncles, and cousins. Our family also had a dog named Belle, who I loved deeply and who taught me unconditional love in profound ways. I love all of them more than words.

My father is a dentist by profession. My mom has been a stay-at-home mother and an office manager for my dad's practice. My Grandpa Delfs was one of the original staff of doctors at Washington Hospital in Fremont. My Grandpa Lusch was in upper management at Bethlehem Steel. My sister is a dental hygienist and mother. My extended family has various professions, including dentist, nurse, lawyer, and sales representative.

At the age of eight, I became Catholic. I was raised in this faith as I grew up.

Like many young boys, I loved sports. I played baseball, basketball, soccer, tennis, golf, team handball, and I wrestled. After high school, I did some training in submission fighting. I also loved to dance. I could dance nonstop for hours.

I also actively started working out, lifting weights and engaging in cardiovascular activities, right before I turned fifteen years old. This continued as a major part of my life until I met Master Sha in June 2004. I used to read many books about lifting weights, working out, nutrition, supplements, and more. I was even a personal trainer for a while. I loved the challenge, the mental focus, and all of the aspects of lifting weights, pushing yourself further, and achieving higher goals. At my peak, I could squat and do Romanian deadlifts of about 450 pounds, three to five repetitions. I could bench press about 325 pounds, three to five repetitions.

I also had a diverse range of public and private educational experiences from kindergarten to high school. I went to Moreau Catholic High School. I graduated from California State University, Hayward (now East Bay), with a B.S. in business administration with focus on marketing and a minor in economics. I received good grades in school, mainly As and Bs. I was close to or was an honor student throughout all levels of education.

One of my passions was to do volunteer work in high school and at university. At California State University, Hayward, I was part of a coed fraternity, Alpha Phi Omega, which focused on teaching the qualities of leadership, friendship, and service. It was a fraternity focused on serving others, not primarily social. It was alcohol- and drug-free. I served as the membership vice president and co-membership vice president for two years. Some of my favorite volunteer projects were Special Olympics and Easter Egg hunts for orphaned children.

From the age of fifteen, I had various jobs working in clothing stores, restaurants, sales, gyms, and technology companies. I was a website coordinator at Twinhead Corporation and a website manager for the Institute of Soul Healing and Enlightenment.

I did my best to live a normal and active life. However, it was far from normal.

Starting at the age of ten, I developed negative, obsessive thoughts, fears, worry, and anxiety that drove me to compulsions of counting and touching things in the number of four or a multiple of four. It started with thoughts such as "If you don't touch this, then the other team will score a run or get a base hit." It quickly turned into thoughts such as "You're going to die" or "You're going to be kidnapped, molested, and killed."

These thoughts would trigger such an incredibly powerful emotional response of fear, worry, and anxiety that it would drive me to count or touch things. It literally felt so real within me emotionally, mentally, and physically.

I knew something was wrong. I knew what I was doing made no sense. However, I was unwilling to share any of this with anyone for a few years. It got so bad that it could take me an hour to get ready in the morning as a twelve-year-old. I was consumed with these obsessions and compulsions.

After it got noticeably bad, my parents took me to a psychiatrist. I had to take a multiple-choice test. Question after question I knew the correct answer. Question after question I saw a pattern. Question after question I got angrier and angrier because I knew I had a condition about to be diagnosed.

Shortly afterward, I was diagnosed with obsessive-compulsive disorder (OCD). I was angry beyond words. I had so many emotions and thoughts running through me. It was devastating and relieving at the same time.

I resisted taking medication for some time. Then I decided to give it a try. The first two medications did not work. The last one they gave me was Anafranil. It began to help some. I had not heard of cognitive behavior therapy (CBT) at that time. Therefore, I forced behavior changes to not perform the counting or thinking obsessions through willpower and self-therapy. Initially as I started to stop the counting and touching, it got much worse and more intense. After two to three months, it lightened. Within nine months, the negative, obsessive thoughts, the fear, worry, anxiety, and the counting and touching stopped. I felt like I had gone to war. It was to this day the hardest thing I have ever done.

I was supposed to be on medication every day for the rest of my life. At that young age, I was okay with it. I never wanted to go back to that other type of life where I suffered uncontrollably and constantly every waking moment of my day. I would rather die than live that way.

Over the years, I suffered from the side effects of the medication, which included being constantly tired and having dry mouth. I was always tired. It did not matter if I slept six, eight, ten, or twelve hours. I also often needed two- to three-hour naps as well. Because my mouth was dry, I always drank a lot of water. This caused me to go to the bathroom very frequently. Doing this day after day took a great toll on me.

Even with such great success, many other obsessions and compulsions continued, such as not being able to let things go, always wanting to face fear, ego, pride, and a rigid mind, that created a lot of suffering in every aspect of my life.

My relationships were challenged due to the fact I would obsess about things that occurred or I thought had occurred and be compelled to speak out about them, often in an angry, yelling, and confrontational way. Some friendships ended. Some never were the same. My family could not understand my behavior. I had a good heart and a lot of love. I also had a lot of anger, bitterness, and pain. This was all dumped into my relationships, as it is difficult not to bring your personal successes and pains into close relationships.

Financially and career-wise, it was very hard and challenging. It felt like you get up, go to work, go to the gym, go home, and go to sleep. Then do it again. This routine all happened while being incredibly tired.

Throughout this time, I had the most loving and supporting parents. They would help me in every aspect of my life. They were loving and compassionate with my behavior, activities, dreams, and more. They always encouraged me to do the best I could in everything. I cannot thank them enough for all of their support. I might not have made it if they were not so great.

As I came into my mid-twenties, I was getting angrier and unhappier with life. I felt out of control. I felt controlled by my medication and OCD. No matter what I did, where I went, or what I tried to achieve, OCD, my medication, and the side effects were always there. I could not see a future, enjoyable life this way. I no longer wanted to live this way. I wanted to be healed and off all medication.

However, there is no cure in conventional modern medicine for OCD. They teach you how to manage it.

I knew deeply within myself that I would be healed and off all medication. I did not know how or when. Where to go? What to do?

One day in 2004, I was at a pool party. I was thrown into the pool. When I landed in the water, one of my ears clogged up. I could not hear very much out of it. I could not get the water out. I tried everything I could at that moment. It did not work.

I went home and did a search on the Internet and found a spiritual and energetic healer who offered an ear candling service. I had seen it before and wanted to try it. I left a message to schedule an appointment.

The next day I was able to use a squirting suction rubber syringe to remove a chunk of wax from my ear. The relief came. However, I still wanted to have the ear candling done.

The next week I went to see this beautiful soul healer. She had an amazing Third Eye (this energy center when developed gives the ability to see spiritual images) and soul communication abilities and was a powerful soul healer.

My whole life I was someone who would ask a lot of questions. I was not easy to accept anything just because someone told me to do so. I always looked for holes or fault in things and people. I could be very skeptical. I also loved to learn new wisdom and information.

I asked her many questions. She graciously answered them. I was convinced she knew what she was doing. It helped that I had to decrease the volume on my mobile by half immediately after the first session.

She also kept telling me about her beloved teacher, Dr. and Master Zhi Gang Sha. I had resistance to get involved with anything else at that time. Ear candling and this spiritual and energetic healing I was experiencing was enough to stretch my comfort zone and mind.

However, in the third session I attended with her, she handed me a handout from Master Sha. The lightbulb turned on in my head. I was literally reading many things that I had always believed in. I also felt an incredible force urging me to find out more information and attend an event with Master Sha. I had never experienced anything like this before. I never have since.

I spent some days going back and forth in my head as to whether I wanted to do this or not. I could not shake this force. I could not outthink this force. It was always there and pushing me.

I decided to join a free teleconference of Master Sha where he offered free teachings and soul healing. During the teleconference, I was questioning and not sure I believed what I was hearing. However, I was one hundred percent sure that Master Sha believed everything he was saying and teaching. This was actually very important for me, as I knew that I could not learn or follow anyone in any capacity who had self-doubt in what they were doing.

I decided to attend Master Sha's Soul Retreat on June 8–14, 2004, at the Santa Sabina Center in San Rafael, California. I felt that I needed to explore this further in order to determine if I wanted to learn from Master Sha.

Shortly before the retreat, I knew I was going to be healed of OCD through Master Sha. I could not tell you why, how, or when it would occur. It did not make any logical sense. I just knew it would happen somehow.

When Master Sha walked into the room on the first evening of the Soul Retreat, the unconditional love, forgiveness, compassion, and light that radiated from Master Sha was unbelievable. I had never felt anything like this in this life. I could literally experience Heaven and being in the presence of a great being in ways that I had only read about in holy or sacred texts previously.

Nevertheless, I was still skeptical. The whole first twenty-four hours I tried to find something wrong. I could not do so. Everything inside me said yes, this was real and right. On the second evening, I surrendered to God. If this was where I was supposed to be, then I was going to go with it.

At this retreat, it was like I was a dirty car being taken through a divine car wash. I received Divine Karma Cleansing, Divine Soul Downloads, and Soul Enlightenment. I was empowered to do self-practice after-ward. I felt so different in so many ways. So much of the anger, emotional imbalances, and negative thinking were gone. I could literally see the world differently than before the retreat. It was so fascinating how such a deep healing and transformation could take place in one week with Master Sha.

I jumped into the teleclasses, some training programs, and made it my job to heal my OCD. I attended more events. I received more divine blessings. When Master Sha received the authority and offered Divine Soul Operations for the first time in January 2005, I knew I was healed. I worked with my Western medical doctor to get off my medication over the following months. On June 8, 2005, I stopped taking my OCD medication! This is absolutely a soul healing miracle.

In February 2009, I was approved for normal medical health insurance coverage as given to a healthy person! I was previously paying about $6,000 per year in health insurance premiums just to have coverage, not to use it, due to my medical history. This was a very special moment in my life. It was also an incredible financial blessing.

The truth is I found much more than my healing journey. I found my soul journey. I had found my beloved spiritual teacher and spiritual father, Master Sha. This is the greatest gift.

Master Sha has given me a direct connection to the Divine, the Tao, and the Source in ways that are beyond a dream. My spiritual channels have opened. My healing power has exponentially and monumentally increased. I have experienced the most amazing joys, love, forgiveness, compassion, light, gratitude, and inner freedom. I have learned that the purpose of life is to serve others to make them healthier and happier. I am now living a life of service to others.

As I have dedicated my life to this path, I have been given the honor, privilege, and authority to be a Disciple and Worldwide Representative of Master Sha, which I believe is the greatest honor anyone could ever receive. I have become a channel empowered to share in Master Sha's Divine, Tao, and Source Channel to offer Divine and Tao soul healing services. There are no words for what I have been given. It is all priceless.

In 2009, I moved to Frankfurt am Main, Germany, to help spread Master Sha's Soul Mind Body Medicine and divine soul healing system to the students and people in Germany and Europe. In June 2011, I moved to Berlin, Germany, where I currently reside, to help establish a permanent center for Master Sha. It is an honor for me to serve others in similar ways that Master Sha has served me and so many people.

I am literally and deeply touched in all levels of my being by how much unconditional love, forgiveness, compassion, and light Master Sha constantly gives to others, my family, and me. I have seen Master Sha behind closed doors working morning to night, serving emergency blessings in the middle of the night, and always creating and finding new ways to serve humanity on a larger scale nonstop, 24/7.

I will always remember a time in November 2008 when Master Sha offered me acupuncture and soul healing services at 2 a.m. after a day of fifteen hours of nonstop meetings. Even after a day like this, Master Sha stayed to assist and offer soul healing to me for some pain I had been experiencing over the last months. This service given to me has been one of the greatest teachings of unconditional universal service for my life and soul journey.

I believe Master Sha to be the greatest healer, teacher, spiritual leader, and servant of humanity, the Divine, the Tao, and the Source alive. I have tried to model my life after Master Sha. If you want to be your best and achieve your highest potential, then you need to be like the best and those living the highest potential. I have personally found Master Sha to be the best at serving others to remove their suffering, assisting them to live their dreams, and find the true meaning and purpose of their lives in serving others. Master Sha lives the highest potential of anyone I have ever known in this lifetime. It is an honor to learn and be trained directly by such a rare and special being.

There are absolutely not enough words I can express for the gratitude, appreciation, love, joy, and respect I have for Master Sha. Before I met Master Sha, I was existing, but not living. My life would probably be over if it were not for meeting and being blessed through Master Sha. Now I am living life. I am so blessed to be able to follow in the light and footsteps of Master Sha. He has given me the power and gift to serve others in similar ways that I have been served. Master Sha has empowered me to create soul healing miracles just as I have experienced.

I deeply wish for everyone to be able to have the gift and honor to be in the physical presence of Master Sha. It is a unique experience. All you need to do is open and allow the Divine, Tao, and Source to work through Master Sha to transform your life too.

I deeply wish that everyone can experience what I have received and been given out of grace. I wish for everyone to receive and experience their soul healing miracles. I wish for everyone to become the best unconditional universal servants they can be.

As Master Sha teaches, "the purpose of life is to serve others." Let us serve others together and create a world full of love, peace, and harmony.

With love and blessings,
Master David Lusch
Honored and humbled to be a Disciple
and Worldwide Representative of Master Sha
and Master Teacher

Master Allan Chuck

Total GOLD to the Divine Mission

APRIL 8, 2000, is a day I will remember, appreciate, and honor forever. On that day my late wife Mimi and I met Dr. and Master Zhi Gang Sha. On that day a new life began for Mimi and me. The rewards and blessings of this new life are like nothing I had experienced or even could have imagined. Now I devote my life to trying to bring the same healing, beauty, joy, peace, love, light, and so much more that I have received from Master Sha to others.

I did not begin this new life until I had completed fifty-two years of my old life, which today feels like a previous life. Let me share a bit about this "previous" life.

I was born in Stockton, California, in March 1948.

My parents were born, lived, met, and married in Guangdong Province in southern China. I was in my mother's womb when she first came to America accompanied by my father. I don't know the exact date of their arrival together in the United States; it was either late in 1947 or early in 1948. I don't know why they went to Stockton; they must have known someone there. To my knowledge, I had no other relatives in the United States at that time.

It was not my father' first visit to the United States. He had been here for a short while as a young boy aged eight or so with his father—my paternal grandfather. I think he also made a second visit to the United

217

States before his marriage to my mother. I don't know the reason for either visit.

As a family, my parents never shared much about their history. I don't think life had been easy for either of them, so perhaps it wasn't something they really wanted to recall or discuss.

My father told me that as a young boy coming to America for the first time, he was fiercely interrogated by immigration officials based on Angel Island in San Francisco Bay. In the prime of his life, he was a prisoner of war of the Japanese in World War II. He saw many fellow prisoners around him die of starvation and disease. My father was a survivor.

My parents had little formal education—only grade school, and their marriage was an arranged marriage, not a love marriage.

I don't think either of them had a job when I was born. When I was about one month old, we moved to San Francisco, probably so that my father could look for a job there.

My father worked as a bar boy at the famous Cliff House beside the Pacific Ocean in San Francisco, and when I was four or five years old, they had managed to save enough money to purchase a little mom-and-pop grocery store in what was then known as Skid Row and what is now the heart of downtown San Francisco. Their hard work there would sustain our family for about twenty years until "redevelopment" of the area forced them to give up the store. For years my father would open the store at 6 a.m., close the store at 2 a.m. (because these were the twenty hours during which it was legal to sell liquor), and sleep for a few hours in the back of the store before opening it again the next morning.

I grew up in the Hunters Point/Bayview district of San Francisco. It was a lower-middle-class neighborhood where most residents did manual labor. In those days it was also one of the most ethnically diverse neighborhoods in San Francisco, and probably in all of America. I grew up with African American, Armenian American, Chinese American, Italian American, Mexican American kids, and more—a true "melting pot." I learned at a young age that external appearance was just a superficial distinction. I don't recall any prejudice or disharmony among us kids based on our ethnicity, religion, or anything. I don't recall any sense of lack in myself. I was a happy and blessed child.

As with many immigrant parents, my parents' focus was to help create a better life for their children. (I have one sister, three years younger.) They emphasized education because they understood what opportunities they lacked because of their lack of education. In this and many other ways, my family story is typical of millions and millions of immigrant families to this day.

I am extremely and eternally grateful to my parents and my paternal grandparents, both of whom were able to join us and live the remainder of their lives with us. I have never really appreciated or thanked them enough. Let me do so now. Dear parents and grandparents, I thank you, honor you, and love you forever.

Thank you. Thank you. Thank you.

Love you. Love you. Love you.

I was blessed with good mind intelligence, so I did well in school and earned three degrees in mathematics. I completed graduate school, got married, and had a good career in finance, attaining an executive position in a large company to which I was loyal for more than twenty years.

My wife Mimi and I met Master Sha on April 8, 2000, in San Francisco at the Whole Life Expo, where he was an exhibitor and a featured speaker. Meeting Master Sha on April 8, 2000, would take me in a direction that I never could have imagined or dreamt. As I write this, Master Sha is again in San Francisco appearing at the New Living Expo, a successor to the Whole Life Expo. These last fourteen years have been the most eventful and blessed years I have had not only in this lifetime, but in all of my lifetimes. April 8, 2000, is a day I will remember, honor, and be grateful for forever.

At the beginning of that day, things were not so happy for Mimi and me. In early 2000 Mimi was being treated by a physical therapist for a frozen shoulder. The therapist applied some kind of release technique to her sternum. Shortly afterward she suffered from constant, severe pain that would often become excruciating. This pain functionally disabled her. She avoided riding in a car because the slightest bump in the road triggered excruciating pain. She stayed home except to visit doctors. All of her medical tests were essentially normal. X-rays, CT scans, and MRIs showed no misalignments within her body that could explain this pain. I was already depressed—without realizing it—because I had been fired from my last job in 1998 and remained unemployed. As Mimi suffered, she too became very depressed. As we went from doctor to doctor and to alternative healers without finding any explanations, much less relief, for her pain, this beautiful, ebullient, and optimistic woman also became very depressed. She wanted to end her life of misery. She had no hope. I had no hope.

Then Mimi noticed a small newspaper advertisement for a renowned qi gong master and healer, Dr. Zhi Gang Sha. We had nothing to lose. Mimi suffered through the long drive from our home in Petaluma to hear Master Sha speak at the Whole Life Expo. We also saw him demonstrate his healing on a renowned author who had suffered from chronic foot pain for years. The author received almost instant relief. We were impressed. We made an appointment for a private consultation and healing right away.

Our first meeting with Master Sha took place where he was staying, at the Hotel Renoir in San Francisco. Other than that, I don't remember any details. I only remember that he was able to do what no one else had been able to do for nearly three months: he gave Mimi some relief from her pain. Within fifteen minutes of meeting him, Master Sha gave us the biggest gift we could have received. He gave us hope.

From that moment, I knew in my heart that I could never repay this man for what he had given us. My gratitude was overflowing.

Mimi continued to need a series of consultations and healings with Master Sha. We looked forward to each one. His manner and speech were always full of care, compassion, and comfort. His healing abilities continued to help Mimi more and more. We became his students—or, rather, Mimi wanted to become his student and I accompanied her. Our first workshop with Master Sha had only fifteen or sixteen students. One by one, he asked each of us to share why we were there. I remember very clearly—and I believe Master Sha remembers as well—the essence of what I said: "Dr. Sha [we called him Dr. Sha then, and not Master Sha], I'm a very logical person. I'm not a spiritual person. I'm a very skeptical person. I don't know how much of your teaching I really believe. I'm only here because you gave my wife Mimi great healing. She wants to study with you. I'm here only to accompany and support Mimi."

As I continued to join more of Master Sha's classes with Mimi, I found that his teachings resonated with me. I found that Heaven was actually quite a logical place. I began to understand and really appreciate karma because I saw it as the ultimate fairness of the universe. "Heaven is most fair." I really liked that because I was passionate about fairness and justice.

Master Sha began working on a major book with the working title *Four Chinese Secrets*. It would be published in 2002 by HarperSanFrancisco as *Power Healing: The Four Keys to Energizing Your Body, Mind and Spirit*. One day in late May or early June 2000, for some unknown and mysterious reason, Mimi suggested to Master Sha that I could help him edit this book. Mimi and I helped do this together. I was definitely a student now, and an assistant as well.

In fact, for much of 2000 and into 2001, I was often Master Sha's only assistant. I was with him almost every day, providing customer service on the phone, booking and setting up venues, creating flyers and other promotional materials, registering participants, booking and assisting with his consultations, organizing external meetings, assisting with personal needs such as cleaning and shopping. When I wasn't with Master Sha, I was busy doing this work from home. It was my honor to offer unconditional service in whatever way I was asked. I saw firsthand how Master Sha was a tireless, unconditional servant. I saw in front of my eyes how he helped so many. Remember, I realized from the day I met

Master Sha that I could never repay him. I was only giving back a little for the huge, live-saving blessings Master Sha had given Mimi and me. I felt very honored and fulfilled to help him help others. It was my greatest honor and joy to be an unconditional servant for Master Sha, offering my services in any way needed as his assistant. Even if my conscious mind didn't fully grasp why, my soul and heart were deeply aware that I was also receiving much more than I was giving.

As I served, I gradually became aware that I was receiving direct blessings from Heaven, including energy and nourishment. I was able to serve sixteen hours a day consistently, and often eighteen, twenty, and more hours a day. I was driven. By whom? By Heaven! By my own soul! I obeyed Heaven. My soul, heart, mind, and body were aligned with Heaven. When I closed my eyes, I could see great light showering into me from Heaven. I felt so loved, so protected, and so much more. I was extremely blessed!

I was now a loyal and devoted student. When I was Master Sha's only assistant, all of his other students had left him for whatever reasons. Later in 2000 I joined seventeen others in Master Sha's first healer training course in America. Today only two of us, Master Shu Chin Hsu and I, remain.

Mimi's negative karma was very heavy. After recovering from her severe pain, she developed paranoid schizophrenia in 2001. It first manifested when she tried to jump out of our car as I was driving it. She must have heard some voices compelling her to do that. She started to yell terribly negative things about Master Sha in public. But I knew this was not the real Mimi speaking and thinking. It didn't put a single dent in my Total GOLD (gratitude, obedience, loyalty, and devotion) to Master Sha and his Divine mission. It only deepened my love and care for Mimi. I would accompany her on many visits to psychiatrists and psychologists. She would remain on medication for this condition for the rest of her life.

In 2003 Mimi was diagnosed with ovarian cancer that had already spread to other parts of her body. It would take her life the following year. Master Sha has said that losing Mimi was a big spiritual test of my Total GOLD, one of the biggest tests any of his students has had. But, Master Sha, I can honestly tell you it really was not such a big test for me. I knew that you did everything you could to save Mimi, including getting help from your most beloved spiritual father, Dr. and Master Zhi Chen Guo in China. In May 2004, three weeks before her transition, you came to our home, stood beside Mimi's bedside, and chanted Na Mo A Mi Tuo Fo for her for forty-five minutes. Her transition was very peaceful. Much of her negative karma had been cleared. Her soul had been elevated to a very high standing by your blessings. So no, Master Sha, Mimi's illnesses and death were not a major spiritual test for me at all. To the contrary, they allowed me to witness and experience once again your greatest love, greatest care, and more. This only reinforced my Total GOLD to you and your Divine mission.

I am extremely and eternally grateful to my beloved Mimi for her unconditional love and unconditional forgiveness. She was a great example of Total GOLD for me. I have never really appreciated or thanked you enough. Mimi, I thank you, honor you, and love you forever.

Thank you. Thank you. Thank you.

Love you. Love you. Love you.

Many additional teachings and blessings I have received from, and various roles and responsibilities I have been given by Master Sha, have nurtured and deepened my Total GOLD to my beloved teacher and spiritual father. Since I met Master Sha in 2000, I have been the editor for all of his books. I have held significant roles on Master Sha's business team, including co-creating his primary website, drsha.com, being his overall business manager, heading Heaven's Library Publication Corp. (Master Sha's publishing company), and heading his nonprofit research organization. I became one of his first Assistant Teachers in 2005 and his Worldwide Representative and Disciple in 2009. In addition to my business responsibilities, I traveled extensively to offer soul teaching and soul healing, including Florida, Arizona, California, Colorado, Massachusetts, Vermont, Hawaii, New York, Georgia, Alabama, Ontario, Quebec, Alberta, Germany, and India. I have shared for years that my goal in life is to be a "mini Master Sha." If my heart could hold a tiny fraction of the love and compassion in his heart, if I could offer a tiny fraction of the service he offers to humanity and all souls, I will have done very well indeed.

In December 2012 Master Sha told me that he and Heaven wanted me to serve in India. I was delighted to do this, as I felt a deep love for and connection to India during my only previous trip there, a whirlwind two-week tour for Master Sha's mission through Chennai, Mumbai, and Delhi in August 2010. Since February 2013 I have resided in Mumbai. I am both the spiritual leader and the business manager for Master Sha's mission in India.

Before I met Master Sha, I was not consciously a spiritual person. I was materially and physically oriented. I was not nourishing my soul or my heart. With Master Sha's teachings and blessings, I have undergone great transformation in the last fourteen years in every aspect of my life and every aspect of my being—all for the better! Through all of the years since 2000, challenges have come and gone. One constant is that Master Sha is always there for all of his team and students. He is there to guide us, bless us, inspire us, and empower us. He holds all of his students lovingly and tenderly. He is there to save our lives. I know that my life has been saved at least three times by Master Sha's Divine Karma Cleansing. Master Sha has saved the lives of some of his Master Teachers more than twenty times. Much more important, Master Sha has saved my soul and accelerated my soul's journey beyond words, comprehension, and imagination. I will benefit for the rest of my life. I will benefit forever. Just as important to me, I am able to benefit others as never before.

Thanks to Master Sha I have found my purpose. Through the first five decades and more of my life, I had no real purpose. As the saying goes, "If you don't know where you're going, any road will take you there." In fact, I often wondered why I was still alive. Coming of age in the sixties and seventies, two of my best friends who each lived a block from me lost their lives in the Vietnam War. One of my best friends died of a heroin overdose. Several years later, another one of my best friends contracted and died of AIDS. Several other close friends took very tragic turns in their lives at that time, never to be heard from again. Our last family home was in the Haight-Ashbury district of San Francisco in the sixties and seventies. I attended the University of California at Berkeley from 1965 to 1969 and Columbia University in New York from 1969 to 1973, so I was in the middle of the maelstrom of those years. I did all of the wild and crazy things that my friends did at that time. Why not me? Why was my sanity preserved? Why was my life spared?

In my years as a student of Master Sha, I have discovered the answers to these questions. What is my purpose? It is right there as the first sentence of all ten books in Master Sha's Soul Power Series: *The purpose of life is to serve.* I am trying to be a better and better servant. I try to help as many people and as many souls as possible to the best of my abilities. To do this is to try to be more and more like Master Sha, who is the exemplar of unconditional universal service, including universal love, forgiveness, peace, healing, harmony, blessing, and enlightenment. I can do no better than to serve the greatest servant on Mother Earth, my beloved Master Sha, with Total GOLD.

Most beloved Master Sha, I am extremely and eternally grateful to you for all you have done and are doing not only for Mimi and me, including all the blessings you have given us without my conscious knowledge. I am extremely and eternally grateful for what you have done and are doing for humanity and all souls. I have never really appreciated or thanked you enough. I thank you, honor you, and love you forever.

Thank you. Thank you. Thank you.

Love you. Love you. Love you.

Da Ai. Da Ai. Da Ai.

Da Kuan Shu. Da Kuan Shu. Da Kuan Shu.

Da Chun Du. Da Chun Du. Da Chun Du.

Da Qian Bei. Da Qian Bei. Da Qian Bei.

Da Gan En. Da Gan En. Da Gan En.

Unconditional service. Unconditional service. Unconditional service.

Total GOLD. Total GOLD. Total GOLD.

Countless bow downs. Countless bow downs. Countless bow downs.

> With the greatest honor, gratitude, and love,
> Your disciple,
> Master Allan Chuck

Master Francisco Quintero

From Middle School Teacher to Head Teacher
and Trainer for Tao Teachers and Soul Healers

I 'M DEEPLY HONORED and grateful to Dr. and Master Zhi Gang Sha
for all the love, care, and compassion that he has shown to me and all
his students around the world. He has truly touched my heart because
he has helped me to heal and transform my life. It has been more than
twelve years since I met Master Sha and I will never forget the wisdom
and teachings that I have learned from him and continue to learn.

My spiritual journey began in 2002 when I was suffering consistently
from high blood pressure. After receiving my B.S. in physics from the
University of California, Santa Cruz, I received a California Single Subject Teaching Credential in Mathematics and started to teach middle
school. During my second year teaching I had to go to the doctor for a
routine checkup and my doctor said, "You are going to have to see me
in three months to make sure your blood pressure is still not high." He
said I might have to be on medication, and I immediately thought,
"There is no way I'm going be on medication at the age of twenty-nine."
I started studying natural ways of healing and in my search found a qi
gong teacher named Patricia Smith (later also a Master Teacher of Master Sha). Patricia was teaching a qi gong class in Watsonville, California,
and she was sharing with her group a new healing technique that she
had learned from Master Sha called One Hand Near, One Hand Far.

I applied the One Hand Near, One Hand Far self-healing technique that
Master Sha teaches for one hour per day, for one year. Within one year

I was able to heal myself from high blood pressure. I also received his karma cleansing services and blessings for this condition. To this day I have normal blood pressure and did not have to take any medication. I'm deeply grateful that I found Master Sha and learned his powerful techniques for self-healing. They are beyond words.

One day Patricia invited her qi gong group to a book signing in Santa Cruz, California, in the spring of 2002 to meet Master Sha. I went to the book signing and was instantly amazed at what I had discovered, a teacher with an open heart. I was so deeply touched by the love, joy, and inspiration that Master Sha brought to the group that I decided to immediately join his upcoming workshop.

I went to my very first workshop on June 22, 2002, at the Land of Medicine Buddha in Soquel, California. The first day was on the self-healing techniques found in *Power Healing: The Four Keys to Energizing Your Body, Mind & Spirit*. I absolutely love and treasure this book. This book inspired me to continue my soul journey with Dr. and Master Zhi Gang Sha and helped me to heal from high blood pressure.

It was an amazing workshop and Master Sha made self-healing simple. I was not prepared for what was to happen the next day. The second day was on soul wisdom; this is when my heart began to open and I knew that I had found my spiritual teacher. It was the first time in my life that I had experienced unconditional love.

The second day of the workshop was filled with great joy and happiness. I felt a tremendous blessing to be in the presence of Master Sha and all of the Buddhas, holy saints, and healing angels he called upon to be present with us during the workshop. Master Sha was teaching soul wisdom and how to open our Message Center, also known as the heart chakra. I remember he had us chanting the mantra San San Jiu Liu Ba Yao Wu (3396815 in Chinese, pronounced *sahn sahn jeo leo bah yow woo*) as fast as we could and at the same time tap the middle of our chest. We would also chant "Open Message Center. Open Message Center. Open Message Center ... Fully Open Message Center. Fully Open Message

Center. Fully Open Message Center ..." It was quite an exhilarating experience.

Master Sha had a big smile on his face as he chanted with us. I experienced a profound experience that was completely new, a sensation of awe and being one with my soul. At the end of the practice Master Sha had us speak in Soul Language, and when it was my turn to speak Soul Language it sounded new but familiar at the same time. He had one of his advanced students translate my Soul Language, and the translation started with "I'm delighted to be here and to be given the privilege to open my heart." This message was simple but it touched my heart deeply and the message felt perfect for me. To this day I continue to remember that feeling, and it brings me great joy now to be able to share it with others.

During this workshop I had the opportunity to have a private meeting with Master Sha. He was offering an *I Ching* Soul Healing Blessing. I spent the whole afternoon thinking about my one request. Later in the afternoon I had the honor to meet Master Sha privately outside in a beautiful green garden next to a Buddhist stupa. He was sitting on the ground in a meditative position as I sat down next to him. He asked me what I would like the blessing for and I replied, "I would like to open my heart." He smiled upon me and let me know that was the perfect request for me. I immediately felt his love, and the light that radiated from his soul and presence was very heart-touching. I felt the presence of unconditional love that touched my soul.

Master Sha proceeded to connect to the Divine and Heaven and gave me a special paper with *I Ching* symbols. I did not know it then, but Master Sha had blessed my life so that I can have the opportunity to open my heart in this lifetime. He helped to remove soul mind body blockages to help me in my journey to give and receive unconditional love. This was my greatest wish when I first met him.

I'm so honored to have met Master Sha. I'm so happy that my first request was to open my heart to unconditional love. My life has been totally transformed since this first private meeting with him. Over the last twelve years my heart has opened more and more. I'm connecting deeper to unconditional love. I've learned to be more open to give and receive unconditional love. The process of opening my heart was not easy. There were many painful times, but also many happy and joyful times, but it was all worth it. To feel love in my heart for another soul is the most beautiful thing in life. This is something so precious that it makes it worth going through all the pain to open your heart to allow love in and out.

A few months later I experienced another special moment in my spiritual journey. It was when I received the divine transmission to become a Divine Soul Healer. During this special day my spiritual father, Master Zhi Gang Sha, had me lie down and placed his hand on my Bai Hui (acupuncture point at the top of the head, pronounced *bye hway*). He chanted a sacred mantra for about ten to thirty minutes. I remember during this time Master Sha took my soul to Heaven. He took me to the heart of the Divine. I recall seeing myself lying down in the heart of the Divine as Heaven's workers removed blockages in my soul, heart, mind, and body as they placed the Divine's love and light inside my body. I was receiving the Divine's healing power within me. I felt like I was bathed in pure love and light that wrapped my entire body. I was in the sacred heart of the Divine. I was seeing all these images with my Third Eye (energy center that allows you to see spiritual images of the Soul World).

At the end of the transmission my soul returned back to my physical body, carrying the Divine's healing power within me. The divine love and light that the transmission carries is what brings healing to others. This was such a special moment that I experienced, and I remember it so vividly. I'm so happy that I had faith and trust in my spiritual father, because he was able to bring me to the heart of the Divine. My faith in him as a representative of the Divine allowed me to grow in my spiritual journey in order to serve others. This sacred moment taught me that a spiritual father or mother can bring you to the heart of the Divine, which will allow your soul journey to be blessed and grow.

I'm very grateful to Master Sha because this transmission, Divine Soul Healer, allowed me to offer soul healing blessings to humanity and has created soul healing miracles. People around the world have healed from cancer, chronic illnesses, back pain, depression, and much more. It is very heart-touching to serve others by offering them soul healing through this divine power that was transmitted to me through Master Sha.

I'm honored and grateful for everything that my spiritual father has done for me and my family. It deeply touches my heart how Master Sha has taught me personally and helped me in my soul journey. His love and light have also helped my family. My parents were both born in Navidad, Jalisco, Mexico, and in 1964 they immigrated to the United States with my whole family and became residents of Watsonville, California. My grandparents and parents both worked as farmers when they came to the United States. My father later in life started working in computer chip manufacturing in Silicon Valley.

I saw my mother suffering from a low blood platelet condition and high blood pressure. I saw the side effects of the medication she was taking. It was difficult to see her suffer. Seeing her suffer made me want to find a natural path of healing. As I learned more from Master Sha, my sister Gloria Quintero (who is also is a student of Master Sha) and I offered her many soul healing blessings. We also had her receive many soul healing blessings from Master Sha. She does not speak English or Chinese, but my mother has used Master Sha's Divine Soul Songs to receive soul healing blessings. I have noticed a big improvement in her health since twelve years ago when I first met Master Sha. I'm deeply grateful that he has helped my family in this way. My parents, two sisters, and my brother all continue to live in Watsonville, California.

In 2008, Master Sha gave me the great honor to travel with him around the world. At that time I was working for two years as a mathematics teacher coach, going into the classrooms and working with teachers to improve their teaching skills. One day Master Sha asked me if I would like to go with him to Germany. I was very excited and quickly said yes. We made our first trip to Germany in July 2008. During this first visit to

Germany we had a series of events throughout Germany, including Darmstadt, Hannover, Stuttgart, and Hamburg. I saw many soul healing miracles happen in front of my eyes. It was always heart-touching to see the people and families feel the relief from pain and suffering.

During the German tour I saw one man who had suffered from chronic back pain for over twenty years be pain-free in front of my eyes after receiving a soul healing and karma cleansing from Master Sha. This man later went on to become a student and Divine Soul Healer. One of the most heart-touching moments was in Hamburg, when after the event we met a mother and daughter late in the night after everyone else had left. The little girl was deaf. She could not hear at all. Master Sha offered her a Divine Soul Healing Blessing and karma cleansing and afterward Master Sha asked her if she could hear. The little girl said, "Yes, I can hear Mama." She said she could hear about thirty percent better than before. This moment was so heart-touching, to see a child filled with joy and happiness and feel a moment of hope. These are the types of soul healing miracles that happen every day with Master Sha.

I've had the great honor to travel with Master Sha around the world and to learn from him personally. Two more heart-touching stories that touched my heart deeply happened in Mumbai, India. One of the miracles was of a thirteen-year-old boy who could not move his left arm. The nerve from his neck to the end of his left hand was damaged at birth. He did have mobility of his fingers, but his entire arm could not move. Before the boy received soul healing blessings from Master Sha, he was able to lift his arm about four inches. Master Sha offered him sickness karma cleansing, Divine Soul Mind Body Transplants, Divine Pearl, and also offered him his unique acupuncture to activate his arm nerve. Miraculously, the boy was able to lift up his arm to shoulder level. Master Sha offered more blessings, the crowd chanted "Ha" for several minutes, and at the end the boy lifted his arm above his head. This was truly a miracle that left the boy speechless.

The second big miracle happened privately late in the evening during our first trip to Mumbai, India. A man had multiple issues including cornea damage, diabetes, speech impairment, deafness, and heart problems. He came primarily for his right eye issue. His right eye was completely closed. He said he needed a cornea transplant because his cornea had been inflamed for several months and had been damaged. The man could not see from his right eye. Master Sha offered him a blessing and karma cleansing, and afterward the man was able to instantly open his eyes. Immediately he could start to see light and shapes. He still could not see details, but he had great improvement in his vision. The man was so happy and filled with gratitude.

These are the types of soul healing miracles that you can witness in Master Sha's presence. One of the things that makes Master Sha unique as a spiritual teacher and master healer is that he passes this Divine Soul Healing Power on to his students. I have the great honor to now be the leader of his education program and to train over four hundred Master Teachers around the world.

A Master Teacher is a divine servant who offers Divine Karma Cleansing and Divine Downloads to humanity. They are given the power by Master Sha to create soul healing miracles. I'm deeply touched to lead and help train these students around the world. Some of these students come from the United States, Canada, Peru, Taiwan, Malaysia, Japan, Australia, Germany, the Netherlands, Austria, Turkey, and South Africa. Master Sha dedicates his life to empower humanity to create soul healing miracles to transmit Divine Healing Power to those who are ready.

In August 2009, Master Sha asked me if I would be willing to move to Frankfurt, Germany, to train Divine Soul Healers and Teachers and to lead his mission in Europe. I was deeply moved by his request and that he trusted me to lead his mission in Europe. I accepted without hesitation. His service to humanity has deeply touched my heart as his love and light spread to humanity. It is my honor to dedicate my life to serve and spread his teachings.

Living in Europe has been a beautiful and wonderful experience in spreading Master Sha's teachings. In 2009 when I moved to Germany, we had two Worldwide Representatives teaching. We have grown and spread Master Sha's teachings throughout Germany, the Netherlands, the United Kingdom, Austria, Spain, and have also spread to other parts of the world, including Turkey and Kazakhstan.

One day a friend of mine was struggling in his heart to follow his soul journey. Master Sha picked up the phone and called him. I was on the phone as Master Sha spoke to my friend who was struggling deeply. My friend asked Master Sha, "Why do you spend so much time trying to help me?" Master Sha's answer deeply touched my heart. Master Sha replied, "Because I am your servant. I am the servant of humanity. I am the servant of all souls." The love that Master Sha holds for his World-wide Representatives, all his students, and all of humanity is beyond comprehension. It is unconditional love. He believes that we have the power to heal ourselves. He believes we can transform every aspect of our life. He believes that we can become unconditional universal servants. Master Sha sees our fullest potential.

The heart-touching moments of when I have seen Master Sha dedicate his time to help his students always leave me with the deepest gratitude. The love he has for his students makes me fully trust my teacher and know that he will do the best to help me in my soul journey. My spiritual journey with Master Sha has not been easy. I've had to purify deeply and open my heart completely to my teacher in order to become a better servant for humanity. Master Sha has guided me, blessed me, and helped me step by step to grow as a Master Teacher and spiritual leader. The transformation that I have experienced is beyond comprehension. I'm not the same person I was when I first met Master Sha. My heart is more open, I dedicate my life to service, and I feel happier and healthier. Master Sha is a true teacher who does not give up on his disciples and students.

In my spiritual journey I have experienced deeply the concept of "no pain, no gain." I have received the honor of being personally trained by my spiritual teacher. I have had to open my heart fully to my teacher to receive all the wisdom, knowledge, and blessings that he offers. If your heart is opened a little, you can receive little blessing. If your heart is more open, you can receive more blessings. If your heart is fully open, you can receive unlimited blessings. This was the beautiful teaching that I have learned the past years. This opening of the heart helped me to overcome challenges that I first thought were impossible or very painful to go through.

Connecting with and staying connected to your teacher is the most important commitment in your spiritual journey. To have your heart open to the teacher means you trust his or her guidance and teachings without doubt. It means you express gratitude every day, every moment for the blessings that he or she has given you for your soul journey and physical journey. I am truly blessed to have Master Sha in my life. He gives his life to teaching and training me, all his Master Teachers, all the Tao Healing Hands Soul Healers, and students worldwide. We are blessed beyond words because he gives us everything from his heart. We only have to be open to receive.

I'm filled with gratitude in my heart toward everything that Dr. and Master Zhi Gang Sha has done for me. I have gratitude in my heart for the service he has done for all his Worldwide Representatives, for all his students, for all of humanity, and for all souls. Master Sha gives hope to the hopeless. He helps people to fulfill their dreams. He helps them to heal and transform their lives. He has healed and transformed my life. I believe he can heal and transform your life and the lives of all your loved ones. I will always treasure his empowerments and spread this message to humanity.

Interview with Dr. Sha's Personal Assistant, Master Cynthia Deveraux

C YNTHIA DEVERAUX HAS worked with Dr. Sha as his personal assistant since 2009. She first encountered his books and started attending his retreats in 2006. Cynthia was born in Wilmington, Delaware. Her mother was only nineteen when Cynthia was born in the 1960s and she had her first child, Cynthia's older brother, at seventeen. Cynthia's younger sister was born a year less a day after Cynthia, so her mom had three babies to raise before she was twenty-one. The father of the children abandoned the family before Cynthia was two, and Cynthia did not even learn until she was thirteen that the man she had thought was her biological father was actually her stepdad and adopted father. Her stepdad worked for RCA and moved the family around, first to Indiana and then to Texas. After her parents divorced, her mother, brother, sister, and she moved to Ohio. Cynthia went to three different high schools in four years and never had the chance to stay in one place very long. She was expected to contribute to the family finances and started babysitting at the age of ten and waitressing at the age of thirteen. Most of the money she made she turned over to her parents.

Despite the tumultuous circumstances of Cynthia's childhood, she was a good student in school and was deeply connected with God and the Divine. This connection started at the early age of three or four. She explained that the Divine would speak to her in the silence of her bedroom. He told her that Mother Earth would have to change; humanity would have to wake up and open their hearts and souls if Mother Earth and humanity were to survive. This made a huge impact on Cynthia's consciousness as these conversations with the Divine would continue.

Her parents used Sunday church services as a babysitting service and would pack the kids off on whatever church bus would take them for the morning. Cynthia experienced a wide variety of church services and did not significantly connect with any single church or denomination. As a young child Cynthia contemplated becoming a nun and felt that her mission in life was to help the world evolve to a better place through opening people's hearts. When she sought inner guidance on her plan to be a nun she was told by the inner voice, "not in this lifetime." Even as a young child Cynthia felt that somehow her life's challenges and suffering at the hands of her parents and others was not about anything she was doing wrong in this lifetime but perhaps in other lifetimes. She had a sense that she had a soul and a sense of compassion whenever she saw suffering. She was aware of everything that she did and everything that she spoke and felt she had to give more love, forgiveness, and compassion to her family and others. Cynthia lived her life based on her conversations with the Divine as well as how he would allow her to see the "soul" of those around her causing her great pain.

She had waitressing to do and high school courses and soon a part-time job as a sales assistant while still in high school. When she graduated from high school, she found work in a title agency and then in a law firm, where she mastered the skills to be a legal secretary. She moved to New York when she was just twenty-one to pursue a modeling career, but that was not meant to be, so she moved back to Wilmington, Delaware, where her great-aunt and uncle lived, and was soon working for a legal firm again. At the age of twenty-four she met a client of the law firm and dated him for eight years before they married. He had been married before and had three children and was sixteen years older than Cynthia, but she felt comfortable with him and had decided as a child that she never wanted to have children of her own, so marrying an older man with children allowed her to participate as a parent without raising young children. The marriage had high points and low points and lasted seventeen years. Cynthia continued to work throughout the marriage and helped her husband go into his own franchising business, which became highly successful. Cynthia was able to pursue her spiritual path and volunteered to work with different spiritual organizations. In 2006, just as her marriage was beginning to lose its purpose, she started working as a volunteer for Dr. Sha's Institute of Soul Healing and Enlightenment. Two years later she was offered a full-time position as an employee and not long after was selected to serve as Dr. Sha's personal assistant.

The following are the questions I asked Master Cynthia, and her intriguing answers.

Bill: In working with Master Sha as his personal assistant, what do you feel is the greatest blessing for you?

Master Cynthia: First, I want to start by sharing my story of the first retreat I attended with Master Sha in November 2006. My soul was beyond excited to attend the Soul Enlightenment Retreat being held in Mt. Shasta, California, after meeting him at a book signing in August 2006. Each day of the retreat was such a life-changing experience for me. I had been with a spiritual teacher for about twelve years before meeting Master Sha. The teachings were based on karma and reincarnation as well as service. Master Sha's teachings were also based on karma and reincarnation, and he stressed the "soul" just as powerfully. He especially emphasized unconditional service to humanity and all souls.

What touched my heart during that retreat was Master Sha's availability to connect with all of the participants. I had been lucky in all of the twelve years of my previous studies to actually "meet up close" my previous teacher two times. Yet here was a master who was so open, so caring, so real, and so giving that it took my breath away. My soul and heart have always known truth and when something or someone is real. My soul and heart knew that Master Sha was the "real deal" and what I was receiving every day was a most blessed gift. I cried endlessly every day of the retreat. I did not cry for just moments at a time, but for hours. I could not really explain to anyone what I was experiencing or feeling, for many would have thought I was losing my mind or going crazy. I remember thinking and knowing deep within that I was communing with a divine presence unlike any I had ever come into contact with in this or any other lifetime, as well as many other lifetimes. My soul knew I had been searching for truth, for wisdom, and for the expansion of my soul to go higher, and the most precious door to all of this had opened to me through this master.

I had been searching since I was three when the words of the Divine so deeply impacted my being, and now the words rang so true to me as I was face-to-face with this most magnificent presence whose mission was to open the hearts and souls of all humanity and bring love, peace, and harmony to all. I knew in every cell of my being that Master Sha was so divinely touched and appointed that my own soul had been divinely touched and transformed beyond all of the twelve previous years in just the very short time of that retreat. The keys to unlocking so many of my questions, so many of my soul's desires were about to be given to me and I knew it was a once-in-a-lifetime opportunity. The journey had just begun.

So for me, each day I know it is an honor and blessing for me to be alongside Master Sha as I watch him considering everyone else; offering healings, blessings, teachings, wisdom, and more in such a powerful and unique way to empower every soul he comes into contact with. He does this without any thought of his own gains or by having a "what is in it for me" attitude. Master Sha is an unexpected example of a true unconditional servant in the world in which most normal people are focused on their own self-interests. Master Sha's humility and the great joy he expresses when helping others touch my heart and soul deeply. What is most humbling and the greatest blessing to me is to wake up daily and know I work beside and am in the presence of Heaven, and this presence of Heaven is embodied in Master Sha, who is a devoted, compassionate, magnanimous, and loving unconditional servant.

Bill: What have you learned that is of greatest value to you?

Master Cynthia: I have been given the opportunity to learn every day. I have been given the opportunity to transform every day. Master Sha has been my greatest gift in this lifetime and my greatest teacher. He has taught me to always look at myself. If I have a problem, if I have issues with anything or anyone, I must look deep within myself.

Master Sha taught me the deepest wisdom and practice in his workshops. He has said, "What challenges you have in your life, including health, relationships, finances, and every aspect of life, are what you have given to others in all lifetimes, including past lifetimes and this lifetime. When the challenges come, appreciate the challenges. These challenges are the reminders for you that you could have harmed others before. These challenges are the blessings for you to clear your negative karma. Therefore, deep forgiveness practice is the key to transform all challenges." This profound wisdom and practice have been kept in my soul, heart, mind, and body all of the time. I follow this teaching and practice. Whatever challenge I am facing, I do the forgiveness practice. The result is so heart-touching. I cannot express my greatest gratitude for this invaluable teaching.

Bill: I know that Dr. Sha sometimes works around the clock. Describe the longest single day of work that you have experienced as his assistant and tell us what you and Dr. Sha did in one day.

Master Cynthia: Honestly, there are no hours in the day that are counted. In all of the years I have been with Master Sha, time is never counted. It is only the service that matters. Master Sha's soul, heart, and consciousness are always serving. When he is serving, there is no thought of food for nourishment, time for sleep, or any of the other mundane aspects of daily life. He truly only thinks of what it is that he can give more of to serve all souls that he is giving to.

For example, in February 2014 he held an advanced retreat in Canada. He had started the last day of the retreat around 10 a.m. He continued to offer powerful teachings, blessings, and even signed books until 5 p.m. the following day. He signed books for everyone, which lasted hours. He signed every single book someone brought to him and gave a blessing to every object people brought to him. He was extremely patient. This moved every participant so deeply. This is his unconditional love, blessing, and service to every participant. He offered this unconditional service with no sleep and had to be forced to take a few short breaks to eat. Most heart-touching is Master Sha's unconditional love to his students and to everyone who needs his help.

In 2013 he was in Germany with about 180 students. He asked the participants, "Why do you want to

study with me?" Almost everyone responded together, "Because of your love!" That was such a
heart-touching moment.

Bill: Are there many days almost as busy as that day?

Master Cynthia: Yes, whenever Master Sha is serving, the days are
filled endlessly. He never tires of this unconditional
service to his students, his clients, and their loved
ones. I would like to say, "Master Sha loves everyone. He loves humanity. He loves all souls." In his
Soul Healing Miracles book he said he is "an unconditional servant of humanity and all souls." I am
working beside him. He always does what he says.

Master Sha has saved so many people's lives. There
are hundreds or more people who have had emergency conditions and searched for Master Sha's
emergency blessing to save their lives or remove
their suffering. Many people have had serious conditions including heart attacks, inability to breathe,
a stroke, are paralyzed or in a coma. I would like to
say almost every day Master Sha has requests for
emergency blessings in the last few years. Master
Sha serves everyone unconditionally. Some emergency requests come at midnight or between 2 and
5 a.m. He has told me, "Call me anytime if there is
an emergency blessing. People could lose their life
in such a short time when they are in the emergency
room. If I can save one person's life, that is my greatest honor." It touches my heart and soul so much
that Master Sha serves selflessly that it leaves me
speechless.

I would like to share one emergency case. A lady in
Australia was in a coma. The daughter asked for an
emergency blessing from Master Sha. He instantly
offered the Divine Karma Cleansing and Divine
Soul Mind Body Transplants. Within two days the

lady woke up. The doctors also discovered that she had blood clots and a brain aneurysm. Master Sha offered the divine blessings. The woman then went for surgery. Surprisingly, the doctors could not find the blood clots anymore. The brain aneurysm was also avoided and no operation was required.

In the last six years Master Sha has traveled ten to eleven months each year. At the beginning of every year, he always consults with Divine, Tao, and Source to ask how many months he must travel and he receives the answer. Then he receives the guidance on where to go. He never tires of what he does daily and what is asked of him. He has been committed to fulfill whatever tasks have been given to him from the Divine, Tao, or Source.

Bill: I have noticed that Dr. Sha does many healings, consultations, teachings while writing his books and organizing his events. How are you able to shift focus so quickly as his assistant and keep up with him?

Master Cynthia: I was blessed before meeting Master Sha to have worked in many different areas as an executive assistant and legal secretary. All of the people I had worked for had given me many different tasks to accomplish at the same time. This allowed me to learn flexibility as well as being able to multitask. This has been a great gift, but in all honesty, it has been through Master Sha's blessings that I have been able to keep up and shift with the ever-changing frequencies, vibrations, and the daily requirements needed. Master Sha has blessed me beyond my own imagination, allowing me to excel daily in my duties.

Bill: Dr. Sha has told me that when he has written major books, there is spiritual opposition. Could you share with us some specific instances and how you have assisted?

Master Cynthia: Whenever there is a new book that Master Sha has been divinely guided to write, spiritual opposition can arise. I have had the honor of typing a number of Master Sha's books that he has flowed. The experiences with each one are very different.

For example, when he wrote *Soul Healing Miracles: Ancient and New Sacred Wisdom, Knowledge, and Practical Techniques for Healing the Spiritual, Mental, Emotional, and Physical Bodies,* the amount of spiritual opposition was enormous. We could see the darkness did not want this book to be written.

During this intensive writing period, there were often times that Master Sha had requests to offer emergency blessings to help someone who was experiencing great challenges, and most of the time these challenges were life-threatening.

During the flowing of the book there were approximately twelve to fifteen different episodes where Master Sha was called upon to offer these emergency blessings. Each of these requests was life-threatening and afterward the energy would be so enormously intense that he would be knocked out. It did not matter what time of the day the emergency was needed, Master Sha would stop flowing the book and offer whatever was needed. He tried his best to save each of the people's lives.

When people have an emergency condition, they need to go to the emergency room for a life-saving service. Master Sha has thousands of students worldwide. When they are suffering with an emergency condition, they want Master Sha's divine blessings to serve their condition. Master Sha would then offer divine negative karma cleansing, protection, and divine systems, divine organs, and other divine soul treasures to serve their needs. He would then require a few hours' sleep and would awaken and continue flowing the book.

I would like to share with the readers that Master Sha's flowing of the books is unique. He connects with the saints, Divine, and Tao and there are usually thirty or forty of them above our heads. We can see them very clearly. They give Master Sha the contents for the book and he then flows from them. It is so fascinating to experience and witness this again and again. Generally speaking, he flows a two-hundred to three-hundred-page book within seven days. The speed to accomplish the book is beyond people's comprehension. He is a true flower of Divine and Tao.

When Master Sha flows his books, I can see clearly in my Third Eye there are countless saints and Heaven's generals and soldiers who are surrounding us. The field of Divine and Tao are exchanging and accelerating all of the time. The frequency and vibration can become so strong that it can knock us both out. Some of his Disciples and advanced students around the world can also feel this frequency and vibration.

Bill: I have personally found that being in Dr. Sha's energy can be deeply purifying. Is this the case for you?

Master Cynthia: Congratulations! I am happy to hear you say this. It is truly a blessing to be purified and allow the transformation to take place in the presence of Dr. and Master Sha.

Yes, as I explained earlier, when I first met Master Sha and went to my first retreat, it was the beginning of my deep purification process that has continued over the course of all of these years since 2006. I have been deeply purified in my soul, heart, mind, and body, as well as in every aspect of my life.

I did not come to seek another spiritual master at that time in my life to heal me. I wanted another spiritual master in my life who would help me on my soul journey. Many have come to Master Sha to seek help and healing with their physical, mental, and emotional challenges. In turn, they have also opened up to their soul and its higher purpose and journey.

Master Sha touched my heart and soul deeply at that first retreat. I knew I was in the presence of a divine being, someone who would be able to guide and accelerate my soul's journey. I had an experience during that retreat that to this day I knew and continue to feel with every ounce of my being that I was touched by the Divine's love and the Divine's heart in a way that forever changed me. This was the beginning of my deep purification process that continues to this day. I can recount the feelings and details of that moment when through an Order given by Master Sha, my soul and all those in attendance were uplifted to a more enlightened state.

I physically felt my soul uplift in my body from my heart up to my throat and felt burning in these areas like I had never felt before. It was as if thousands of suns and the light from them had blasted these areas and were opening them further. Of course, I had felt burning and the opening of my heart many times before, when the Divine would allow me to see through a human being and look at their soul, but it was only for a moment when the Divine needed me to be more aware, more awakened to things around me and within other people.

At that specific time in 2006 I had not actually felt, up to that point, the intensity of love given to me when the Divine actually told me he had given me his heart and his love. It was profound. And with that profoundness my soul knew of the great purification that I was about to enter. My soul knew through this beloved Master I had been granted the gift of being truly touched in a way I had desired all of my life. I had always wanted the love and the heart of the Divine to touch me in a more profound and deeper way. But I was not ready even if I wanted it.

My soul, after receiving this great gift, at that moment was shown in my spiritual eye and in my own deep knowing the purification of what I was about to undertake. It would be a great test for me, as everything from that day was forever changed in every aspect of my life. I had been dedicated to my spiritual path my whole life, but actually what took place would test my dedication to my soul, to the Divine, and to a path I knew was right.

Each day I have purified through the knowledge of Master Sha's teachings and great wisdom. He has given me the tools and awareness of what I must do to make a difference. It is not up to anyone else to change me and the course of direction that I take moment by moment, but it is I who must always be aware. There are principles and laws that must be lived by that make a difference if one truly desires the deepest love, the deepest compassion, and the deepest forgiveness to be within their lives. Master

Sha is the greatest example of this. I have had to purify every aspect of myself and with great truth. I can't hide my head in the sand and not hear or understand what I am being given and guided to change.

When a true master comes in, the presence of this soul ignites purification. A true master can "see" and "know" what needs to be purified to bring you up higher. This is what has taken place with me through Master Sha. I can't hold on to the pain, the wounds, and I can't blame others. I must take accountability and responsibility for what decisions I have made not only now and in this lifetime, but in other lifetimes that have caused others pain. This is what purification is all about. That is why I cried for days during that first week in the presence of Master Sha for the first time many years ago. My soul knew without any doubt I had been given an opportunity to purify.

Is the purification easy at times for me? No, it is not. I have always been extremely sensitive and emotional when it comes to what I have done because I feel it so deeply. At times this is a gift because I know immediately when I have gotten out of integrity of bringing good, doing good, or speaking good. At times it can be difficult, as the need for deeper forgiveness must be given not only for the souls I have done a wrong to, but also for my own self.

So, purification is a daily process. It is not something you go through in a day. It is a moment-by-moment analysis of things that need to be transformed. And in the presence of Master Sha we are gifted with the acceleration of that purification because of his frequency and vibration.

Bill: How many words a minute do you type?

Master Cynthia: What is so funny about this is that I never understood why I had to take typing when I was a senior. I had to take one of two electives to graduate from high school, one of them being typing. So I chose typing thinking, "Oh my goodness, what will I ever need this for?" It was amazing because back in the '70s we had the real typewriters where you had to pound the keys and hit the return bar, working with carbon paper! My fingers flew over the keys like they were my long-lost friends. It was only after high school that I started my lifelong journey with these "keys," graduating from the old typewriter to my current MacBook Pro, typing away through the years, never paying attention to how many words I type a minute. I have been asked many times if I have been a court stenographer, but the answer is always "no."

Actually, when I type it is as if I am in flow with the channel of Master Sha. I don't think about anything and actually just connect and let my fingers do the walking.

Bill: Do you think your typing and organizational skills have improved since being Master Sha's assistant?

Master Cynthia: Oh yes, most definitely. Master Sha has blessed me beyond my dreams with special blessings. He does that for his entire business team. We are beyond blessed to be able to receive these blessings to help us fulfill our daily tasks in a more efficient and effective way.

Bill: What is the happiest moment you have had working with Master Sha?

Master Cynthia: Actually, every day I am extremely happy working with Master Sha. It is an honor and I am most humbled to have been given this task at this time no matter for how long. I have been blessed beyond my wildest dreams. To me I have been given one of the most blessed opportunities and I don't take it for granted ever. My life has been changed. My life has been saved. My soul has been forever granted an opportunity that I may never have again. This is what brings happiness to me every moment.

Bill: You work with Master Sha closely. Could you tell me what is Master Sha's true mission and what is his heart service?

Master Cynthia: Master Sha's truest mission and heart service is to serve you and every soul, all of humanity as an unconditional universal servant in order to create the Love Peace Harmony World Family. He truly wants to empower souls in every aspect of their lives. He is tireless in that service and devotion. His devotion to remove the suffering of humanity and Mother Earth, and his love, forgiveness, compassion, and light to transform humanity and Mother Earth are beyond comprehension as he gives immediately back in service with whatever he has received in wisdom, knowledge, power, frequency, and more from Divine, Tao, and Source. His generosity to share the sacred ancient wisdom and new wisdom from the Divine and Tao, as well as his willingness to uplift his disciples' and students' healing power, has touched his thousands of students' hearts and souls. There is not one selfish part of Master Sha that holds on to anything. He is a unique channel who does not think about receiving from others, but only what it is that he can do to empower and serve you!

Bill: Why do you think you were chosen both as a personality and as a soul to work as Dr. Sha's assistant?

Master Cynthia: That is a hard question to answer. I think Master Sha should answer this question, not me. But you asked me and I will answer.

I believe we all have specific roles in our lives and a specific task to offer to humanity. I feel that I have a lot of service to offer to many, many, many souls on Mother Earth. As I have explained, I knew as a child I had karma and that this was not my only lifetime. I believe I have been granted the opportunity to work as Master Sha's assistant so that I can know firsthand what it means to serve unconditionally, love unconditionally, and forgive unconditionally. I feel as I travel around the world with him, I too am in service to any soul and all souls asking for their forgiveness and offering my love as a return for anything that I have done that has hurt or harmed them in any way. This is one of the golden opportunities that Heaven has given me. I am extremely honored to be Master Sha's assistant.

Master Sha's mission is my mission. Master Sha has thousands of totally devoted students who think the same thing. I have devoted my life to serve Master Sha's mission. I serve from my heart and soul. Master Sha has given me so many blessings. I am growing every day. I have been empowered more and more to be a better servant. I have gained deeper wisdom for my spiritual journey and for my physical work. I am extremely grateful.

Bill: What questions are you most asked by people about Dr. Sha?

Master Cynthia: I am often asked by new people, "Is he really like this all of the time?"

I smile and say, "Yes, what you see with Master Sha is what he is 24/7. He is an endless stream of boundless love, offering all that he has to every soul."

I am also asked, "Can I see Master Sha, or will he offer me any personal time to bless me?"

I again smile and explain to them that I will try my best to help.

Bill: What changes have you seen in Dr. Sha since becoming his personal assistant?

Master Cynthia: Master Sha has grown deeper in his dedication and his devotion to his disciples and students, as well as to everyone with whom he comes into contact. His heart has expanded beyond what I can put into words. Master Sha has no boundaries. He can't say "no." He just continues to give.

I have recognized more and more over these last few years when new people come into his presence, they are astounded and are quickly moved to tears. Many have expressed that they have looked for many, many years and sometimes their entire lifetime to find a master or teacher. They often remark that when they see and hear Master Sha their soul immediately knows "he is the one" and their great joy and their emotions are heart-touching.

His desire over the years to teach and empower each of his disciples and students to be the best and most powerful teacher and healer is priceless. He guides, teaches, and offers unparalleled wisdom to open each of our hearts more and more, removing our own blockages that we have within our soul, heart, mind, and body.

He takes no credit for anything that he does or for what he receives. He gives every credit for everything he has accomplished and for what he receives to the Divine, Tao, and Source. In turn, he teaches that same principle to each of his disciples and students. We truly are not the ones offering anything, be it wisdom, a teaching, or a blessing. We are able to offer the wisdom, the teaching, the knowledge, or the healing and blessing because we have received the opening of our spiritual channels and been given a spiritual ability through a Divine and Tao Order and blessing from Master Sha's Divine and Tao Channel.

Bill: Master Sha is a tireless worker. I heard that he often works fifteen hours or more a day. It is hard to understand how a normal person can work such long hours. He has worked like this for many years. Can you explain how Dr. Sha can work these long hours?

Master Cynthia: Master Sha is truly divinely guided. I have been witness to it and seen as he has worked twenty hours a day and more, he is totally recharged from a higher power. For example, during retreats that last two weeks and sometimes longer, he is continually uplifted and recharged through a higher power that feeds him a source of energy that we are not able to see with the normal human being's sight. Every part of his body is recharged and nourished, down to the tiniest space, constantly from Heaven.

Master Sha shared with the public and said, "People charge their cell phone every day. I am receiving the charge from the Divine and Tao all of the time. If I do not receive this kind of special nourishment, the way I work, I would not be here on Mother Earth anymore."

Bill: Master Sha tells everyone that giving unconditional service is the highest virtue. I have observed that you also have given unconditional service to Master Sha's mission. Could you explain how you feel about your role?

Master Cynthia: Again, I can honestly say I can only give unconditionally because I stand beside Master Sha, who gives and serves unconditionally more than anyone

I have ever known. If I am tired, if I don't want to serve, I could ask myself, "What would Master Sha do?" But I don't do that. I only know deep within what I have been given. I don't take it for granted because I could be in a different position tomorrow. I must take every opportunity I can to serve to the best of my ability and serve unconditionally. I have no expectations. I have no desires. I have no attachments. That is also part of the purification process you asked me about earlier. It is only to serve and be the channel of what service I am to give at any moment.

Master Sha is the embodiment of Divine and Tao service on Mother Earth. I want to emphasize again that:

- I have never known anyone who works tirelessly and for so long as he does. He never complains. He is truly an unconditional universal servant.

- I have never known anyone who is totally committed to serve and empower his students to gain their healing abilities and life-transformation abilities to serve.

- I have never seen anyone who is so extremely generous and shares the sacred wisdom so easily with everyone. In ancient times, true masters kept their sacred wisdom their whole lives until they transitioned only to give the secrets to one or two disciples.

- I have never seen anyone who is as fearless as when he offers Divine and Tao Karma Cleansing. I have seen numerous times Master Sha being attacked from the darkness when he offers Divine and Tao Karma Cleansing, including having chest pains, difficulty in breathing, and difficulty in thinking.

Master Sha's unconditional service has deeply touched my heart and soul. He is the great example in my heart. I always feel that I cannot serve enough. I will continue to learn and serve together with Master Sha. I am so honored.

Bill: Dr. Sha has taught that divine love melts all blockages and transforms all life. Describe how you have seen Dr. Sha provide divine love to humanity.

Master Cynthia: This question actually brings tears to my eyes. Divine love is something I feel every soul since the time of inception has wanted. As we grow up, throughout all of our years we only want to receive a pure love that will nurture and feed us, wrapping us in a blanket of this unconditional love.

I believe Master Sha was chosen as a divine servant because of his ability to embody pure love and divine love, which is unconditional love. I believe that all of his testing and his deep tenacity to learn all of the ancient arts such as tai chi, qi gong, kung fu, *I Ching*, and feng shui were stepping stones for the higher power to come in and accelerate. I believe his training as a doctor of modern medicine and traditional Chinese medicine were the preparation for him to create Soul Mind Body Medicine and co-create Soul Mind Body Science with Dr. Rulin Xiu.

It is because of his deep purity and desire to serve unconditionally that he has been able to embody this divine love. Therefore, he receives higher and higher frequencies and vibrations of divine love that souls who come into contact with him can actually feel. This divine love that Master Sha embodies is real and cannot be forged. He has shown his deep love, divine love to humanity and all souls as he has offered approximately ten divine treasures to all humanity and all souls without asking anything in return. This includes pets and all inanimate objects. They too are being served unbeknownst to their own soul, heart, mind, and body. Unconditionally he serves all souls at any time through his blessings.

Bill: In my personal experience, Dr. Sha is almost always smiling and laughing, even when providing great healings. Why is he laughing most of the time?

Master Cynthia: Master Sha feels great joy in service to you and everyone. His soul is so very happy. Therefore, he is always smiling. You rarely ever see Master Sha not smiling. He is like the young child offering his innocence and love to the world, not caring what he receives in return. The purity of his heart shows in his smile and the joy that comes from his laugh.

I have heard so many people say in the events, "Master Sha's smile has healed me." Some people also say, "I came to this event just to see Master Sha's smile."

Bill: When Dr. Sha is faced with a major blockage with a healing, what does he do?

Master Cynthia: When faced with a major blockage with healing, Master Sha will continue to offer services. He never gives up. No matter what, he will do what he can to help a soul with unhealthy conditions. I have witnessed this many times. Sometimes he has spent a few hours offering healing blessings to one person for their condition, not stopping at all. This kind of devotion is amazing because he offers this kind of service daily.

Bill: A year ago, when Dr. Sha first started to learn calligraphy, did you have any idea that the calligraphy would become one of the most powerful healing methods?

Master Cynthia: Yes, I actually did. I saw the power through my Third Eye images and experienced the healing power myself as he created the Tao Source Calligraphies.

When Master Sha was writing the book *Soul Healing Miracles: Ancient and New Sacred Wisdom, Knowledge, and Practical Techniques for Healing the Spiritual, Mental, Emotional, and Physical Bodies,* my body started to go through deep purification. As Master Sha started to flow the book, all of a sudden things started to happen to me physically, mentally, emotionally, and spiritually. The purification process started immediately when the guidance was received that Master Sha had to start flowing. There were times I could hardly get up out of the chair. Master Sha would stop and write a calligraphy for me and ask me to chant. I saw the enormous power in the calligraphy and would chant, receiving immediate results. This continued throughout the writing of the book. I am most grateful for the healing, for I was able to experience firsthand the extreme power of all of the calligraphies as they were created. I was shown beautiful images of the future and how these calligraphies would assist humanity in their own healing process. It was very, very beautiful.

Master Sha's Source Ling Guang Calligraphies are extremely powerful. Calligraphy is artwork. The uniqueness of Master Sha's calligraphy is that Master Sha is the channel of Divine and Tao. He has been given Divine and Tao authority to offer Divine and Tao transmissions to the calligraphies. He sent Divine and Tao Orders to gather countless saints, countless saint animals, countless soul treasures, and for some extremely special calligraphies his Divine and Tao Order has gathered countless planets, stars, galaxies, and universes to the calligraphy. Imagine the power within each of Master Sha's Source Ling Guang Calligraphies.

Bill: I have observed that Dr. Sha is always evolving and growing. Do you have any idea what he will do next?

Master Cynthia: Master Sha is always in flow. He is the only person I know who follows exactly what the guidance is from the Divine, Tao, and Source. He does not question anything. He trusts totally in every aspect of what is given him and because of that he is able to receive more. I believe what is coming next is the awareness within more people and their own acknowledgment of what Master Sha has to offer to them to transform their own lives. I also believe that as other great masters walked this earth many years ago, having every obstacle thrown at them from non-believers, that more non-believers and those who have questioned will realize that within our midst is a true Master who gives tirelessly from his heart and soul to awaken and empower each of us in this most desolate time on Mother Earth.

As the words of one well-known Indian government official stated after attending a seven-day retreat of Master Sha's in 2013:

I have traveled all over India, been to many ashrams, and visited many Masters. I have had the opportunity and been asked to live in my own private housing, which would have been built for me at these ashrams and have politely declined. But being here at this retreat with Master Sha for these last seven days, I want each of you to know he is the first Master I have encountered who is without ego.

That statement was huge and made each of us stand up with great honor in our hearts for having been in the presence of this great Master for one hour, one day, or for years. We were in the presence of a master who serves without ego and loves without ego. This was finally recognized and acknowledged by someone else who had great integrity and wisdom. This soul was able to see and feel and know within seven days the essence of this master I so wonderfully and humbly serve.

Master Sha, being without ego, will not plan what is next, but will receive his guidance. He will continue to follow that guidance. He will continue to love and offer all that is given selflessly and unconditionally.

Bill: My last question. What does your heart and soul want to share with the readers of this book?

Master Cynthia: My heart speaks volumes when I share my experiences about Master Sha. I often, if not all of the time when I speak of him, cry. It is because my heart has truly been opened and touched by this divine soul who loves each of us so purely and gives unconditionally. My soul has been nourished. My soul has been fed. My soul continues to be fed and stripped of what is no longer of use. I am becoming what I have always desired deep within the recesses of my heart and soul, a human being free of the blockages that have bound me, kept me from accelerating in my previous lifetimes and in this one.

Divine and Tao have heard my cries and calling. I have been granted the greatest gift of working beside a very, very, very special soul, a master who selflessly embodies what is the essence of Divine and Tao. To sit at the feet of the master is to be cleansed and to feel and become the truest essence of his or her soul.

Master Sha has embodied the essence of his soul for many years now and it is only becoming more and more powerful. His soul exudes more and more love and forgiveness, more and more the burning desire to serve even endlessly. It touches my heart deeply to see how he offers this and more to souls he has just met as he connects deeply with his eyes, his soul, and his heart. His great soul is everywhere, deeply moving about, searching and giving what is needed at any moment that will best serve appropriately.

Time and space are nothing. What matters most is the saving of all souls; the saving of Mother Earth and beyond. That is the goal of this most beloved and highly evolved master that humanity has walking in their midst. I am not delusional or making flowery statements, but am speaking my truth in what I have witnessed and experienced. We are blessed. Humanity is truly blessed to have a soul who offers hope to those who have nowhere to turn, who offers wisdom to those who desire more answers, who offers a journey that will bring their soul higher and higher to a path that will bring transformation at the deepest and most profound levels.

Yet in the end the ultimate is to live on this most beloved planet and with one another in the greatest love, the greatest peace, and the greatest harmony. When we can have that, then we will know and experience even more from this most beloved spiritual teacher and master, Master Sha.

For that I am forever grateful and will serve all I can endlessly and unconditionally to awaken each soul to this awareness. Master Sha is leaving huge footprints upon this Mother Earth. We only need to step onto this path and realize as we do the door and

keys will be given for the greatest and most profound transformation, healings, blessings, and wisdom to be received.

We are all truly blessed.

Thank you for the opportunity to share a small part
of my experiences with my most beloved spiritual
father and teacher, Master Sha. It is my desire that
all souls can experience his greatest love, his greatest forgiveness, his greatest compassion, his greatest
light, his greatest humility, his greatest commitment, and his unparalleled greatest and most magnanimous heart to create the Love Peace Harmony
World Family and the Love Peace Harmony Universal Family.

> *I love my heart and soul*
> *I love all humanity*
> *Join hearts and souls together*
> *Love, peace, and harmony*
> *Love, peace, and harmony*

Love you. Love you. Love you.

Thank you. Thank you. Thank you to my most beloved Master, Divine, Tao, Source, my colleagues,
humanity, and all souls.

Because Master Cynthia is the person who in my presence has given the
Akashic Record readings, I also wanted to ask her about those readings.
Interestingly, just as this book was about to go to press, I received a
phone call from Naada Guerra, the young woman we met at the start of
my journey whose left eye had been injured while riding in an open-air
double-decker bus. This chapter will end after a brief analysis of Cynthia's relationship with the Akashic Records with the account from
Naada of her reading from Master Cynthia and her acceptance both then

and now of the seeming correctness of her reading. I am happy to report that Naada continues to make progress and expects to regain full use of her eye.

In 2009 as part of Cynthia's training she was taught how to access the Akashic Records. This is an essential component of the teachings Dr. Sha provides to the four hundred Master Teachers he is training to help heal and teach self-healing. I asked Cynthia if she is ever wrong when she accesses the Akashic Records, and how she would know if she is right or wrong.

"I am not in a trance when I access the Akashic Records but I have no memory of what I report to others. I have no direct way to know if I am right or wrong in any specific reading and I assume that I cannot be one hundred percent accurate all the time, but the results of my readings have never been challenged to me personally, so I think at some level I am mostly accurate. What I see in my Third Eye is what I share. I trust my readings but I cannot claim I have one hundred percent accuracy. I only access the records with a pure heart and intent to help those who seek healings with Master Sha.

"I personally believe in the law of karma and think my readings help people. Dr. Sha encourages all of his Master Teachers to do readings, and when there is a retreat, there are often as many as six Master Teachers who will do readings for a single healing. We are all trained as healers to read the Akashic Records and we work together to provide the best possible advice we can. I do not think we are infallible, but we provide our services with a pure heart and pure intent," she explained.

Update on Healing of Naada Guerra's Left Eye

I had not contacted Naada at the time I started writing this book and did not have her contact information until just a few days before this book had to go to press. When I reached Naada, she reported that her eye was healing nicely and that she was scheduled for another surgery in just a few weeks. She explained the experience of the healing in the Beverly Hills Hotel as follows:

"As you know, it was a very last-minute decision to see Dr. Sha. My friend Amish called me at the last minute and said he was meeting with an oriental healer and that I should try to join him for lunch. I did not recognize the name Dr. Sha but I have always trusted Amish, so thought why not. It was only while I was walking into the hotel that I realized that I had actually read one of Dr. Sha's books about three years ago and even done some of the exercises in the book. I had felt good about the exercises but had stopped doing them and had not thought about Dr. Sha for at least two years before the accident. On October 27 I had been riding on the upper deck of a bus when a tree branch crushed the bone in my left eye socket. The doctors had done emergency surgery on October 31, inserting titanium mesh to prevent my eyeball from sinking into my sinuses. I met with Dr. Sha in early December, and at that time I could not look down at all and there was tremendous swelling above and around my eye. In addition to the discomfort, I felt anything but beautiful when I or anyone else looked at my face.

"The actual healing was almost comical. We were in the Beverly Hills Hotel, right in the lobby just a few hundred feet away from the registration desk. People were coming and going, but Dr. Sha just ignored the traffic and with his assistant Master Cynthia took me aside and explained that the problem was my karma. Master Cynthia did a karma reading and told me that in a past life I had been an abusive overseer in a factory and been unkind to many of the employees. She also told me that I had been a soldier in another lifetime and whipped my horses so mercilessly that several of them died. My karma was indicating that I was destined to go blind not only in this lifetime but in an additional seventy-two future lifetimes. Having read Dr. Sha's book, I was not unfamiliar with his concept of karma cleansing and the law of karma, so I thought that this might be correct. I was initially heartbroken but then Master Cynthia explained that Dr. Sha had the ability to heal not only this lifetime but future lifetimes as well. He did a karma cleansing for me and then had me hold the calligraphy in his new book Soul Healing Miracles to my face while he held his hands above my head and yelled 'spiritual transmission' right there in the lobby of the hotel. He was so intense

in his efforts and so innocent in his approach to healing me. I was touched and also thought the whole episode somewhat humorous.

"Much to my surprise and delight, immediately after Dr. Sha applied an acupuncture needle, I was able to move my left eye for the first time since the accident, and the swelling noticeably shrank. I am scheduled for surgery now several months ahead of schedule and anticipate a positive outcome. I am so grateful to Dr. Sha. There is no doubt that my prognosis is far better today because of his intervention. To have so much karma cleared is truly a miracle."

Master Peter Hudoba's Enlightenment Experience

THE GOAL OF many world religions, especially Asian religions, including Buddhism, is to attain enlightenment. I have spoken with Dr. Sha about the purpose of his own journey, and when he is ready Dr. Sha will reveal to his students and others who he is and what he represents from the perspective of an enlightened being. I do not want to define enlightenment in this book, as the subject of enlightenment deserves at least a book or several books to just touch the surface of this elusive topic.

I also do not want readers to lose the focus of Dr. Sha's message. Dr. Sha can do soul healing miracles. You can do soul healing miracles. Together we can do soul healing miracles and create a healthier and happier world.

But I recognize that for those readers on a spiritual path, Dr. Sha is not just a miracle healer but also a spiritual teacher. Dr. Sha can and has assisted others to reach enlightenment. Peter Hudoba is the first of Dr. Sha's disciples to publicly share his enlightenment experience. Dr. Sha asked me to include this experience in this section of the book to help his students and others better understand the ultimate reward of being of unlimited service to others. Without ever focusing on your own reward or achieving enlightenment, you may actually achieve this rare state. I thank Peter for sharing this account, which was previously published in his own book. Before presenting his story, I present some background information about Peter so skeptical readers can better evaluate that this story is grounded in fact and not fantasy.

One of the most interesting of Dr. Sha's students is Peter Hudoba. Peter was trained as a neurosurgeon and had a thriving practice in Canada when he decided to seek a spiritual master to allow him to pursue his spiritual goals. Peter is married with a child and lives a harmonious and peaceful domestic life. Although Peter had an academic appointment at a major Canadian university hospital to continue his profession as a neurosurgeon, he chose instead to resign his position and study exclusively with Dr. and Master Sha. This career change occurred in 2000. Since that time Peter has learned how to perform soul healing miracles himself and become an expert on the techniques Dr. Sha teaches and practices. Knowing more about how and why Peter made such a massive career shift will help us better understand Dr. Sha and his unique teaching.

Peter Hudoba was born in Czechoslovakia in the 1950s. His parents were teachers and there was nothing extraordinary about Peter at birth. He was born a few weeks premature, and as a toddler was little and weak. At the age of five he caught the flu, was given penicillin, and had an allergic reaction that nearly killed him. Other than that incident Peter had an uneventful early life. His parents were extremely loving and kind to both Peter and his younger brother. He was secretly baptized soon after birth.

At the age of ten Peter and his family moved to a new subdivision where there was a street gang, just young kids into bullying others, not the kind of street gangs that were killing people and dealing drugs, but still a challenge for the new kid on the block. Peter's father saw how frightened Peter was when he ran home one day just barely escaping the wrath of the gang. "What's wrong?" his father asked.

"Those kids are after me. If they catch me, I know they are going to beat me up. Other kids at school have warned me of what they have done to them. Why did we have to move here?" Peter sobbed.

"Peter, you do not need to be frightened by these bullies. I noticed there is a gym down the street that teaches judo. Judo is an ancient Japanese art. Once you learn judo you will be able to defend yourself and never have to worry about these bullies again," his father reassured him.

Within two months Peter had learned rudimentary judo. His judo teacher was amazed at Peter's rapid progress. Peter was the youngest student in the class and was often competing against boys five or even six years older. One day at school one of the bullies from the street gang attacked Peter. Peter, who has a devilish sense of humor, laughed and smiled at the memory as he told me, "There was blood and teeth on the floor. That bully never approached me again. None of the bullies did. I did not know it at the time, but I was using the energy that Dr. Sha has taught me as Tao. I have never felt physical fear since my early mastery of judo."

An indirect consequence of learning judo was that Peter also learned to meditate at the same time. Only ten years old, Peter was full of energy during his judo classes, and his teacher realized that Peter had to learn to channel his excessive energy. Meditation was the teacher's solution for Peter, and Peter incorporated meditation into his daily practice. He would only meditate a few minutes at a time, but the meditation practice connected Peter with his inner stillness. One day a year later while reading a book about Christmas, Peter experienced an awareness that years later he would recognize as "unity consciousness."

Peter recounts his experience vividly. "As I was reading the book, I started to notice that the snow was falling gently outside my bedroom window. There was complete silence and stillness all around me. I had a sensation that the scene I was reading in the book and the moment I was living in my bedroom was the same moment. There was no difference and there was a feeling of complete peace and awareness of the interconnectedness of all life and all matter. I felt a kind of emptiness that was also a sense of complete knowingness. In that moment I felt a complete bliss and calm that I have been seeking ever since."

"Did that experience immediately change your life?" I asked.

"Not immediately and to some degree not at all," Peter responded. "I was still only eleven years old. I did what eleven-year-olds do. I had lots of hobbies and interests. A few years later I learned how to play the bass guitar and joined a rock band. I studied classical guitar, had girlfriends, played soccer, and led a normal life."

"What kind of a student were you?" I inquired.

"I was always an excellent student. My favorite subject was biology. When I was thirteen, I read an article that explained how to make amplifiers and speakers for my rock band. I was fascinated and even more intrigued when I read an article about a neurosurgeon in New York State in America named Dr. Cooper. Dr. Cooper was putting wires in his patients' brains as a way to stop tremors in their hands. His success amazed me, and after reading that article, while still a teenager I resolved to become a neurosurgeon and to move to America, where I would teach and perform surgeries just like Dr. Cooper. Much to my surprise, within twenty years I had accomplished these goals," Peter recounted.

"You must have been driven as a student," I commented.

"Not really," Peter replied. "I just loved learning about the human brain and doing research on advanced topics on the frontiers of science. In 1978 I wrote a research paper in which I analyzed how electrodes could be used in neurosurgery. The paper was submitted for a science contest that covered the entire university. My paper won first prize. Later the paper was submitted to a science contest for all universities throughout all of Czechoslovakia. Again my paper won first prize. With so much recognition I felt a greater sense of responsibility toward my studies. I gave up my rock band, playing soccer, and even judo and karate. It did not seem to be a sacrifice. I loved what I was doing and was soon enrolled in a Ph.D. program to become an expert on strokes and how to treat them. The political situation was less and less tenable in Czechoslovakia, and together with my family we migrated first to England for a year and then to Canada. The least expensive plane tickets were to the town of Hamilton, Ontario. There was a university there, and I applied at the Department of Neurology for a research position. The professor interviewing me asked me questions about my reasons for wanting the position and how I had become interested in neurosurgery. I explained my fascination with the research of Dr. Cooper. My interviewer laughed and told me, "Almost all of the patients on whom Dr. Cooper has done his electrode surgeries have been my referrals. Dr. Cooper and I are not just colleagues but close friends. I am sure you will be successful working here."

And sure enough, that was the case. Peter thrived, and by the time he was thirty he was considered one of the top neuroscientists at McMaster University in Hamilton, Ontario. He was working with his boyhood idol, Dr. Cooper, who was still active, and he was offered additional training first at the University of Toronto and then a major staff position at the University of Saskatchewan, also in Canada. He had married, and with his wife had a beautiful home, a son, a dog, and all the family and material success that a refugee from Czechoslovakia could have dreamed for. Peter had even been able to arrange for his mother to come and live with his family after his father had passed. Life was complete in almost every way and Peter was able to nourish his second passion— to study Tao and learn the ancient Buddhist and Taoist teachings. He would race home after work and translate ancient texts and practice meditations. But one thing was missing. He did not have a spiritual teacher to guide him on his path.

Peter decided he needed to find a teacher. He approached several teachers ranging from qi gong experts to Buddhist masters. After each encounter he would consult the ancient Chinese Oracle of the book of *I Ching* and ask if he had found his teacher. Each time the *I Ching* said "no." Peter had been using the *I Ching* since he was a teenager and trusted in the answers he received. In each case he turned down these teachers and continued his search. But he could not find the right teacher. Finally, he consulted the *I Ching* and asked the *I Ching* where his teacher was. The *I Ching* told him he would find his teacher in Vancouver, Canada. Peter believed so strongly in the *I Ching* that he immediately put his home on the market and told his wife that she should make arrangements to move to Vancouver. Peter was going to dedicate himself to his spiritual path and being a stay-at-home dad. The *I Ching* had told him his teacher was in Vancouver, and he had faith he would find his teacher there.

Shortly after making this commitment Peter was told to call a man named Dr. Sha. Peter flew to San Francisco to meet Dr. Sha, but Dr. Sha had an emergency meeting and had to fly to Canada where Peter had been. Peter waited in San Francisco and met Dr. Sha in the San Francisco airport. Despite the public venue, Peter immediately felt a tremendous peace in Dr. Sha's presence and had an inner knowing that Dr. Sha was in fact the teacher he had been seeking. The year was 2000, and Dr. Sha was using acupuncture to heal and had not yet received Divine power to offer divine healing to the masses. But even in 2000 Dr. Sha had discovered the principle of karma cleansing. He explained to Peter that the unhappiness that Peter was experiencing in his life despite his material and career success was due to past karma. Peter explains his first real teaching with Dr. Sha in the following words:

"I went to his apartment and we had a few words and tea. He asked me why I came to see him. I said there was an evil force that was destroying my life. I had peaks of joy and then big disasters. I explained that I felt fragmented by this evil force and wanted his help. 'There is no evil force. It is just you,' Dr. Sha explained. 'You have done wrong in past lives and this negative energy is coming back to you now. All you have to do is to ask the Divine to forgive you.' It seemed too simple, but I respected Dr. Sha and accepted his advice. I began to ask for forgiveness every day. I began to see positive results.

"Two years later I realized that just asking for forgiveness was not sufficient to truly save my soul. I asked Dr. Sha what I must do to save my soul and his answer was again very simple. 'You must chant every day and dedicate your life to a life of service. Every day you must find a way to heal and help others. These acts will bring light to your soul and nourish your soul,' Dr. Sha told me.

"Ever since that day I have dedicated my life to healing others and to performing the chants and teachings that Dr. Sha has given me. I now have the ability to heal others, and what is most fascinating to me as a scientist is that Dr. Sha is always evolving his techniques and his knowledge. The basic premise of karma cleansing is simple, but there are many ways to achieve this goal. Every time I see Dr. Sha, he has elevated his own vibration and I am challenged to raise mine. The way I raise my vibration in my knowledge of healing is to learn what Dr. Sha is teaching. Just recently he has begun using ancient calligraphy as part of his soul healings. I would never have imagined calligraphy as part of the therapeutic process, and yet I see the results and realize that Dr. Sha is ever evolving as a healer. In my dedication to Dr. Sha and to healing I have found true joy. I enjoy my wife and family. My home is full of love and laughter. Every home can be full of love and laughter when those in a family are aligned with their soul's purpose. Not everyone is inclined as I am to be a healer. That is my soul's purpose. That is Dr. and Master Sha's soul purpose. Each of us must find our soul purpose and in finding that purpose align ourselves with the purpose of the Divine. This may seem too simple for your readers but it is the truth of my experience."

Peter's Enlightenment Story

My enlightenment process actually happened in three stages. As I have shared, I met Master Sha for the first time on October 15, 2000. Within two days, all my energy centers, all my chakras opened. It was a totally amazing, shocking, and extraordinary experience. Little did I realize that this was just preparation for what was to come.

We did not talk only about energy issues at our first meeting. Master Sha asked me, "Why did you come to see me?" I said, "You know, Master, there is some evil force that is destroying my life. It has been sabotaging me throughout my life. I understand that this is karma, but I do not know how to get rid of it." Master Sha looked at me and said, "There is not an evil force; it is you. It is the result of your wrongdoings of your past lives and in this life, and that is what is coming at you to make you suffer."

This answer shook me to my core, but it rang true because it did reflect some wisdom from Buddhism, and I accepted what he said. I asked, "What can I do to dissolve my karma?" Master Sha gave me an answer that didn't make sense to me at the time. He said one sentence:

"Ask God to forgive you."

I couldn't understand this; it seemed too simple. I had read in the holy books that one had to sit and meditate, do special practices, and suffer to clear bad karma. I was thinking, "My goodness! A saint like Shakyamuni Buddha sat in a forest, tortured himself with ascetic practices for five years and almost died, then sat under the Bodhi tree for forty-nine days until he became enlightened. Milarepa sat in a cave for twenty-five years. He had to spend so much time to become enlightened." It did not make sense to me that dissolving karma could be as simple as sincerely saying one sentence: "God, please forgive me!"

At our first meeting, Master Sha gave another key instruction to reaching enlightenment. He said that when we chant a mantra such as A Mi Tuo Fo (pronounced *ah mee twaw faw*), we need to give our total self to A Mi Tuo Fo and become totally filled with the mantra; then we are A Mi Tuo Fo. We become the mantra. As with the first instruction, my awareness was simply not opened enough to understand this teaching fully.

I left this meeting for my home in Canada to finish my work. I was just winding up my academic position at the university.

Three months later, I returned to meet Master Sha for a second time. I spent a weekend with him as he offered public lectures. As one lecture was taking place, I suddenly started to feel extremely sorry for all the wrongs I had done. It is very hard to explain this clearly, as this is a very special condition to be in. It is not a state you merely want to get into, but is something you may suddenly find yourself in.

As we were chanting, I suddenly felt very sorry that I had so many weak points, that I had so many negative feelings or thoughts. All sorts of mistakes I had made in my past came to mind, and I felt such regret about my behavior. I felt deep pain that I still had bad attitudes in my mind despite years of effort to purify myself.

I responded to this pain by saying I was so sorry to all of Heaven. In my heart, I felt that I had done so much wrong in this life and in my past lives. I bowed to God. I felt deep regret and apologized to God from my heart. I told God, "You give me so much, yet I still have this negativity in me, and I feel very sorry for that."

For a fleeting moment, I went into a unique state that I could not understand.

When I finished the meditation, Master Sha looked at me, smiled, and said, "Well, it looks as though you have reached something new."

I was so moved! When I tried to explain what and how I felt about myself, one of his students, Shu Chin Hsu, said to me, "How could you say that? You are such a nice person. Why would you think you are mean? Why do you feel that you are bad to people? You should not feel that way. It is not like you."

At that moment, I did not know what to think. The only thing that was true and I was vividly aware of was that I had reached some state in my mind, and when I was in that state, I was very sorry for everything that I had ever done wrong.

Master Sha just smiled and said nothing. We parted, I returning to Canada and he to his work in San Francisco.

When I got home, I desperately wanted to become enlightened. I was so into that pursuit that I cleaned up a shed in our garden, covered its walls in white, put in a new floor, and brought in a meditation mat.

From that January in 2001, I spent most of my time in that shed. Every morning, I sat there for two or three hours, emptying my mind and trying to reach enlightenment. I took a break at noon and resumed this practice after lunch for the afternoon.

As time went by, I slowly became calmer but could not reach that big emptiness of mind or any enlightenment either. I had several moments while chanting A Mi Tuo Fo when a big lotus suddenly opened in my chest, but I did not know what it meant. I continued to purify myself and continued to meditate. Eventually, I started to practice Zen meditations. I tried to empty my mind. I thought this was the only way to become enlightened, but it just didn't work. The more I tried, the worse it got. My mind was filled with racing thoughts.

In August, Master Sha called me to meet him again in San Francisco. I arrived on a Friday morning and we had lunch, followed by a little rest. Then Master Sha said, "Let's go outside and meditate."

We walked together toward the Golden Gate Bridge, sat down on the beach, and meditated for two hours. While I was sitting next to Master Sha, I noticed that I could enter into the state of emptiness almost instantly. My mind just went blank instantly!

It was much later that I understood that just being in the presence of an enlightened being purifies the mind. It is because an enlightened being shines light from himself, and that creates a very special energy field. In this special field, I was able to reach emptiness right away.

We meditated for about two hours. Then Master Sha said, "Let's go home and finish the meditation there." We were walking in the marina, alongside the boats, when Master Sha suddenly said, "Peter, you are so stuck! Why are you trying to follow only one way? You are trying to empty your mind, using only one technique. I can learn from anything." And then, he just opened his arms and turned around in a circle. He said, "I can learn from the whole universe. There are so many different ways. You are just stuck on one way—to empty your mind." I looked at him and completely stiffened up. Then Master Sha touched my chest and said, "Why don't you just open?"

As soon as he touched me, there was a blast! It was as if I was encased in a glass bell that suddenly broke apart. Instantly, I felt completely free and open—united with everything around me. My heart felt connected to the whole universe. There was complete openness, without any boundaries.

This is a difficult experience to explain unless you have personally gone through it.

Until then, I was not at all aware that I was closed, that I was isolated from the outside. But as soon as this isolation fell apart, like a glass wall shattering, I suddenly felt totally open.

Master Sha and I just looked at each other and laughed and laughed spontaneously like two little children. We went home, had dinner, worked on something, and then went to sleep.

In the morning, we went to the home of one of Master Sha's students who later became my very good friend. This was a workshop with a doctor who wanted to have a private teaching. It soon became obvious that those private teachings happened in a very special way. Master Sha gave a talk like never before—a very deep teaching.

Then we began to chant God's Light. After ten minutes of chanting, I started to cry. I felt embarrassed and felt much pain in my heart for the many mistakes I had made in my life and for the hurt I had caused so many others. I started to see things that I had done that I would never before have considered bad. I thought of arguments where someone had made me mad and I felt fully justified to zing them back with sharp words, saying something to put them in their place, and I felt right and justified in doing so at the time.

Memories of many things like that which had happened in the past came to my heart like attacking beasts. I felt so sorry for everything I had done: the many blunders in my life, the many mistakes.

Then I thought about my previous lives. What had I done in those lifetimes? I started to cry again and felt so sorry for my wrongdoings in all my lifetimes. That special feeling I had experienced in January returned again, but this time it was much stronger. I had no idea what to do, but suddenly I recalled a sentence that Master Sha had told me in October 2000:

"Ask God to forgive you."

I bowed down to the floor and asked God for forgiveness. I said, "God, I love you so much. Please forgive me. I don't know what else I can do. I fully realize that I was so bad in my life and in my past lives, and I am truly and sincerely sorry for that. Please forgive me."

And boy, what happened! The light in the room was like an explosion. There was golden light and purple light everywhere; the whole room resonated with light. My whole body vibrated like crazy, and I just kept crying and crying. Then, while we were meditating further, I suddenly noticed a golden buddha sitting in my chest, and from my chest a huge lotus opened up and enveloped the whole room.

Master Sha had opened my heart the day before, and the next day, his chanting produced such a powerful light field that my soul became purified to the degree that it became enlightened and slowly moved up from my abdomen to my Message Center.

The enlightenment process continued the following day. We started to meditate, and within a short time, I noticed that I was becoming a golden buddha. I was aware that my hands were turning golden, then my face and whole body were becoming golden as well. I was like a golden buddha sitting on a lotus. That was something!

I approached Master Sha and asked, "Master Sha, could it be possible that I have become enlightened? I mean, I am golden all over. I sit on a lotus, and I am like a golden buddha." Master Sha smiled at me, checked with God, and said, "Yes, congratulations! Finally, it came to your awareness." This is the process. If you were to just kneel down and ask God to forgive you, it probably would not work. You first have to get into a very special state of mind.

It is not a matter of logically understanding it or wanting to be in that state. You need to completely open your heart and soul and be in the appropriate pure field; only then can you get into that very special state. When you are in that special state, if you ask God to forgive you, it will be valid.

However, I remember vividly that on both occasions when I was in that state, I had absolutely no understanding or awareness that I wanted to become enlightened or that I wanted to get something. Absolutely, definitely not! This was a state where all I felt was sincere sorrow for all that I had done. Then somehow, the idea had trickled into my mind that I should ask God to forgive me for all my wrongdoings.

If you are not feeling that intense sincerity and you are not in that unique condition, your request will probably not work. You need to be in that state first.

The process of enlightenment is in fact very simple. However, to actually reach enlightenment is extremely difficult, and to do it alone is almost impossible. That eventful Friday morning on the beach, when Master Sha touched my Message Center saying, "Why don't you just open?" caused my Message Center to open up. When Master Sha opened my Message Center, my mind opened completely, and I reached unity consciousness with the universe.

Once my mind had opened, it was a matter of opening my heart. My heart opened when I was in that intense condition where I felt regret and sadness over all the wrongs I had done. I opened my heart, felt sincere sorrow, and wanted to apologize to just about everyone I had ever offended. That opened my heart even further.

While we chanted God's Light, Master Sha invited the Divine and many holy beings, saints, and buddhas to come. The Divine and the saints were flooding me with an incredible amount of light and virtue, which further purified my soul. Once the Divine and holy beings see a sincere heart moving toward enlightenment, they will grant enlightenment.

In the Lotus Sutra, there is a perfect description of Shakyamuni Buddha's enlightenment. When he was being enlightened, gods were showering flowers on him. When they wilted, they showered even more flowers on him. This went on and on. Those flowers are symbols of virtue and light.

Once God and the holy beings blessed my soul so that it became pure enough, my soul slowly ascended higher and became seated in my chest. I had reached soul enlightenment. Once my soul reached soul enlightenment, I was ready to go on to the next stage.

The first was an opening of the heart; the second was purifying the soul so that it rose to the empty and purified heart. Finally, there was the third stage, of which I had to reach a realization myself. Master Sha didn't tell me; he led me to open my awareness so that I would understand who I was. That was the final stage.

It was very difficult for me to accept that I could become enlightened. How could I deserve that? As soon as I became enlightened, compassion further opened in me. My heart opened and I felt guilty that I could have what others wanted so much.

During the precise time I became enlightened, my whole family back in Canada went suddenly berserk. Once I knew that I had reached enlightenment, I phoned my wife and said, "You will not believe what happened. This visit, I became enlightened." My wife replied, "Yes, you know, we all went totally berserk around that time. Your mother and I just couldn't stop laughing and the dog and our son were wildly running around the table. Mathias was chasing the dog, who kept barking like crazy. It was just one big rampage, like someone had filled the room with laughing gas!" My family had perceived very clearly what had happened to me, even though they were three thousand miles away. So that was the process of my soul enlightenment.

Immediately after enlightenment, I became incredibly happy. I had a feeling of happiness that is hard to describe. It was like being a ten-year-old again and awakening to a warm May morning. You open your bedroom and look into a garden full of blossoms. The sun has just come up, the birds are chirping, the bumblebees are buzzing; you see butterflies fluttering all around. You feel young and so alive.

You have absolutely no plans for the future, and no worries; you just look at the beautiful garden and bathe in the light. You are full of beautiful strength, peace, and joy, and resonating with vibrant youth, bliss, and a happy mind. That is how I felt.

As well, the concept of time ceased. Time stood still. I had no feeling of yesterday, today, tomorrow, morning, noon, or evening. It was all just one big nothing.

Again, this is very difficult to explain. You have to be in that state where you feel no relationship to what is going on now, to happenings in the past, and have no thoughts of future consequences for your current actions. You just exist. This incredible feeling lasted for days and days.

When I went home, my wife wanted to celebrate this very special occasion, so she borrowed a lovely movie from the library called *Little Buddha*. As I watched it, I again felt a pain in my heart. I saw Tibetan monks living in a monastery from childhood to old age and death. Every day, they sat and meditated, chanted mantras, and memorized holy books in their search for the enlightenment that I now had. I literally felt a pain in my heart. How was it possible that I could reach that state and they hadn't?

The desire to teach and help everybody reach the level of happiness that I now have is one of the strongest motivations in my life.

PART FOUR

Master Sha's Growing Influence as a World-renowned Healer

Master Sha's Growing Influence
as a World-renowned Healer

I N THE TEN years since writing the first edition of *Miracle Soul Healer*, I have had additional opportunities to interact with and learn from Dr. and Master Sha. He has become a true friend and colleague and we share a mutual desire to raise the consciousness of human beings as quickly as possible. This desire is based on our observations that the human species has been acting in ways which jeopardize both human and planetary survival. If a majority of human beings truly understood the fundamental principles which govern the laws of the universe, there would be less suffering, less destructive behavior, greater cooperation, and greater love, peace, and harmony throughout the world.

My commitment to the goal of raising human consciousness is through my publishing and film company, Waterside Productions Inc. Waterside has long maintained a corporate mission to assist authors and publishers to create and distribute books and products which will create a better world. Master Sha's focus is on healing, training others to heal, and teaching the sacred ancient wisdom embodied in the work of Lao Zi as presented in Lao Zi's sacred *Dao De Jing* more than 2,500 years ago.

Waterside has thrived over the last ten years and in addition to agenting, Waterside is rapidly becoming one of the fastest-growing independent publishers in the world, while also developing a robust film division, online education division, non-fungible token division, and event division. Master Sha has been even more innovative in these last ten years, further refining his abilities as a Tao Grandmaster serving thousands of students through Tao Calligraphy, Tao Song, Tao Water, Tao Calligraphy NFTs, and countless classes for the general public on the nature of the Tao itself.

In the last two years, Master Sha and I have collaborated on providing a free Facebook class on "The Power and Wisdom of *Dao De Jing* through Tao Calligraphy and Tao Song." Collaboration is too strong a word, as this is really one hundred percent the teachings of Master Sha while I serve as host and, whenever possible, capture and share the essence of each lesson in a short overview. I feel honored to participate in this unique class and I have gained deep and powerful insights into the nature of reality from my participation. Each class provides an analysis of a single chapter or, in some cases, a partial chapter of the eighty-one chapters of Lao Zi's *Dao De Jing*. The chapters are short but profound. Master Sha provides examples as do I at times of modern equivalencies for the metaphors used by Lao Zi more than 2,500 years ago. Although Lao Zi was writing for the rulers of China more than two millennia ago, the wisdom and advice are timeless and relevant to our present personal and world circumstances.

As a student of philosophy as an undergraduate at Yale College, I studied the great Western philosophers from Socrates and Plato to Kant, Spinoza, and many others. In learning the wisdom of Lao Zi, I am able to recognize the similarities at the core of both western philosophies and ancient Chinese traditions and am of the opinion that Lao Zi's teachings not only incorporate the wisdom teachings of other great philosophers but exceed them. Lao Zi in many ways anticipated the findings of quantum physics and new post-materialist science.

As host for the Power and Wisdom of Dao De Jing course, I have learned that Master Sha is the 373rd-generation lineage holder of the teachings on immortality of Peng Zu. Peng Zu was an ancient renowned Tao saint who created "Zhi Qi Zhi Dao," which means *The Tao of Governing, Managing, and Controlling Vital Energy and Life Force*. He has been honored throughout Chinese history as the "longevity star." This extraordinary connection that Master Sha shares with Peng Zu and Lao Zi is likely the reason why Master Sha's interpretation of *Dao De Jing* is so provocative and powerful. Many have interpreted Lao Zi throughout the centuries but few have grasped the true essence of his teachings as profoundly as Master Sha. But even more powerful than Master Sha's ability to teach and interpret Lao Zi is Master Sha's commitment to use his Tao Calligraphy and Tao Song to allow those taking the course to experience an actual connection to the Tao. Lao Zi explains in *Dao De Jing* that the Tao that can be discussed is not the authentic Tao, as the true Tao cannot be seen, heard, or touched. The best any normal teacher can do is provide approximations and metaphors. But Master Sha is not an ordinary teacher. Master Sha has dedicated his life to connecting with the Tao. It is through this connection that he is able to provide healing experiences. Master Sha creates a Tao field and enables others to experience the energy of this field. Combining this experience of the Tao through calligraphy and song is what makes the course on "The Power and Wisdom of *Dao De Jing* through Tao Calligraphy and Tao Song" so fulfilling and effective.

In addition to hosting the Dao De Jing course, I have been collaborating with Master Sha on creating TAPPING THE SOURCE SUMMITS. The first summit was held in July 2022 and included participation from Dr. Ervin Laszlo, Dr. Deepak Chopra, Dr. Rulin Xiu, myself, and Master Sha. The focus of the summit was on the true nature of reality. Dr. Rulin Xiu presented the basic principles of Tao Science which, as a UC Berkeley-trained physicist, she developed in partnership with Master Sha. This unique science attempts to explain grand unified field theory from the perspective of the concept of the Tao. Dr. Laszlo presented the newest findings from quantum science which suggest that the ancient concepts of the akashic records and other traditions are reflected in new scientific concepts such as the zero point, quantum entanglement, and non-local transferal of energy. Deepak Chopra discussed the intriguing concept that all is consciousness and that the universe or multiverses we study and experience are actually illusions. Master Sha provided the context for the discussion and, through his Tao Calligraphy and Tao Song, provided an experience of the unlimited power of the vacuum which can be accessed through the Tao field which Master Sha is able to create.

Master Sha and I intend to provide future Tapping the Source Summits to explore how modern science and ancient wisdom are merging. Although I did not know Master Sha when I co-produced with my wife Gayle the award-winning film "Tapping the Source," I now realize that what I was exploring in this film as the Source is analogous if not identical to what Master Sha has been describing when he explains and utilizes the Tao in his healings. The Tao is the source that provides the infinite energy which generates both the world of things and the world of emptiness. We may speculate that the Tao is the consciousness from which all arises but of course, as Lao Zi has warned us, in the moment of attempting to define the Tao we are limiting our understanding and likely making if not an incorrect at least an incomplete formulation.

I mention these activities as they further illustrate the unique gifts which Master Sha is providing not just through his position as the most powerful healer on our planet at this time but also as one of the most insightful teachers and visionaries. In the following short chapters, we will further explore why although Master Sha remains a mystery, he is quickly becoming a legend. There is no other healer or spiritual teacher who has been able to innovate and expand his healing and teaching modalities as quickly and effectively as Master Sha has over the last decade.

Is Master Sha a Living Legend?

W E DESIGNATE THOSE who achieve great results as legends. Tiger Woods in his prime was a legendary golfer. Tom Brady is considered the GOAT (Greatest of All Time) in American football. Michael Jordan in basketball, Pele in soccer—legends can be found in almost any field of endeavor, athletic and beyond. They all achieved legendary results, performances that had never been imagined possible until they accomplished their extraordinary athletic feats.

It is in this context that we must consider Doctor and Master Zhi Gang Sha a legendary healer. There have been legendary healers throughout history, such as Edgar Cayce. who achieved miraculous results for decades. There is no question that Master Sha's credentials elevate him to legendary status as a healer equal to or greater than Edgar Cayce. Master Sha has directly healed thousands. Moreover, he has trained thousands of healers who collectively have now healed tens of thousands of people. Many of these healings are documented with videos available on YouTube and other sites. In many instances, these healings were for serious and even life-threatening conditions, including advanced cancers.

I have researched other prominent healers and cannot find any with results comparable to those achieved by Master Sha. In my opinion, Master Sha is a legendary healer based purely on his own direct healings. However, his ability to train other healers puts him in a unique category which has never been rivaled. Perhaps even more legendary has been Master Sha's ability to bring healing energy to calligraphies, song, and even water.

In the last several years, Master Sha has refined his calligraphy so that the energy in the calligraphy is now powerful healing energy. I observed this first hand when Master Sha created a special calligraphy for my daughter the week before her wedding. That week, Tara had an accident that left her unable to walk without crutches. She was told she would not be able to walk down the aisle. Once she received and, over the next three days, traced the calligraphy from Master Sha, she was able to walk without pain. Not only did she walk down the aisle, but she danced until four in the morning. She did require additional time for full recovery but there was no disputing the "medical miracle" from the perspective of traditional medical doctors who were certain she would require months to recover from her injury.

Tara is just one of hundreds of individuals who have experienced calligraphy-based healings. There are also those for whom calligraphies have benefitted their personal relationships or financial status. One of the most striking examples is that of David Meltzer. David was cofounder of Sports 1 Marketing. During the great recession that started in 2008, David suffered several financial reversals which he had not recovered from when I introduced David to Master Sha in 2014. The purpose of the introduction was so that David could provide Master Sha with access to several of the injured NFL (National Football League in the United States) Hall of Fame players David had represented. Master Sha wanted to demonstrate his healing abilities to this group of elite athletes. After successfully treating several of these world-class athletes, Master Sha asked David, "How can I serve you?" to show appreciation for the connections David had made. David was frank and told Master Sha that his primary concern at that time was recovering from his recent financial challenges: "I want more money." Master Sha right away opened his case of calligraphy materials and wrote a unique and very powerful Tao Calligraphy, *Tao Ye Chang Sheng*, which means "Tao career is flourishing." Then, David asked, "What am I going to do with this calligraphy?" Master Sha said, "Tao Calligraphy creates a Source field. Calligraphy is art. Tao is the invisible Source. Tao Calligraphy means Source invisible love, light, frequency, vibration, and information, energy, and matter of financial flourishing have been put into this calligraphy. Connect with the financial blessing Source field of this Tao Calligraphy. Put five fingertips of one hand together to trace this calligraphy for ten minutes a day."

David did not believe that tracing the calligraphy would have any impact at all on his financial situation but loved the calligraphy as art and hung it in his office. His wife also loved the calligraphy and encouraged David to follow Master Sha's guidance and trace for ten minutes a day. David later told me, "I didn't really believe it was going to work but I didn't see how it could hurt so I started to trace every day. My wife Julie would ask me after work when I came home if I had traced so I never missed a day. Nothing happened the first several weeks but then almost as if by magic, our business started booming. I have continued to trace this calligraphy every day for the last eight years. I cannot believe the effortless financial abundance that has come forth in these eight years and continues to flow. Millions and millions of dollars have come to me. But even more than such great financial abundance, ever since starting to trace this calligraphy, every aspect of my life has flowed effortlessly and joyfully. My relationships with Julie, with my children, and with my clients and business associates have been joyful and fulfilling beyond any previous level. I am so grateful to Master Sha and encourage everyone to experiment with his calligraphy and his healing blessings. For me, Master Sha is the most important contributor to my health and happiness of anyone on this planet except my wonderful wife Julie."

Another context in which I view Master Sha as a legendary personality is as a spiritual teacher and philosopher. I studied philosophy at Yale University and was exposed to a wide range of thinkers ranging from Plato to Immanuel Kant to Spinoza. I learned much from each but it was not until I discovered the teachings of Lao Zi as presented by Master Sha that I began to understand the true nature of reality. It is remarkable that Lao Zi was able to intuit so many truths about the nature of man and the universe. It is equally remarkable that Master Sha has been able to bring Lao Zi's eternal teachings to the present day and even enhance them. Wisdom is eternal. We can use metaphors to explain specific teachings but the teachings themselves are eternal. This is especially true when presenting the wisdom of Lao Zi's eighty-one chapters in *Dao De Jing*.

True understanding of Tao is impossible. The most we can hope for as human beings is to appreciate an approximation of what the Tao is and represents for human existence. Master Sha has had direct experience of Tao states and considers being a true messenger of the Tao his greatest service to humanity. As explained in the previous chapter, Master Sha is the 373rd-generation lineage holder of Peng Zu, an ancient Tao saint known throughout Chinese history as "The Longevity Star." This in and of itself is a remarkable gift. Even more remarkable and legendary is Master Sha's ability to translate these ancient teachings into modern times and share these insights with the world. Even more than Master's Sha's accomplishments as a healer, a teacher, and a creator of healers, I believe his legacy as the foremost teacher of the Tao is what over time will ensure Master Sha's own legacy as a true treasure for humanity while in human form.

The details of how Master Sha has been able to achieve such success in so many different modalities, as a healer, trainer of healers, Tao grandmaster, master calligrapher, creator and singer of Tao Song, creator of Tao Science, and teacher of Tao may never be fully understood. This is why Master Sha will always remain a mystery. But I predict his ultimate legacy will be less as a mystery than as a legend whose service to humanity was truly unprecedented.

Tao Science:
The Tao Healing Field

T HIS BOOK WOULD not be complete without a brief explanation of Tao Science and the unique qualities of the Tao Healing Fields which Master Sha has been able to create. There are complete books on Tao Science which Master Sha has co-authored or is presently writing with Dr. Rulin Xiu which explain in detail the scientific breakthrough in postulating a scientific theory for the otherwise elusive qualities of Tao healings. In this chapter we will only present the overriding principles which those interested in scientific explanations and theories can explore more fully in those other books.

Tao Science postulates that all universes are united through the existence of the Tao. Master Sha and Dr. Rulin Xiu have formulated the equation $S + E + M = 1$ to explain the unique relationship that when the mind, heart, and soul of a human being (S) are infused with energy (E) and matter (M) and all are aligned, the result is equal to one, where "one" represents the steady state of the Tao, the Source and container of all existence and non-existence. For many, the concept of a source which contains and has created both the universes of things as well as the universes of emptiness may be difficult to comprehend. But the proof of the correctness of this formula lies in the ability to actually access the Tao or oneness in our own universe of human reality.

Using ancient Chinese concepts, Master Sha explains that all human beings and all matter have components of soul, heart, and mind. The soul is the most important of the triumvirate. The soul informs the heart and together the soul and heart inform the mind. Our minds are often ego-driven and do not always recognize the importance or even existence of a heart and soul connection. However, evidence from other scientists is demonstrating the connection between heart and mind corroborating the postulates from Master Sha and Dr. Xiu. Energy and matter are the "stuff" of our universe. When we combine and align our inherent soul nature with our energy and matter, we are able to reunite with the profound true nature of reality itself—the Tao.

Traditional science is only now beginning to understand that even quantum physics and string theory are limited and incomplete. There is a new scientific movement of post-materialist science which is beginning to explore phenomena which until now have been incompatible with or unexplainable by traditional science. Just as we have discovered that Newtonian principles of basic material interactions—although effective at a certain level of reality—are inadequate and in fact incorrect when viewed from a more complete perspective that includes information only now being discovered about the nature of quarks, quantum entanglement, and other concepts from quantum physics. We are now learning that even these new scientific breakthroughs are also incorrect from an even more universal perspective. I forecast that that the explanations being suggested by Tao Science will ultimately be considered cutting edge and more useful than other theories.

Once you understand the principles of Tao Science, you have the elements for the paradigm that explains the nature of forming a Tao energy field and why, once formed, that energy field is able to serve as a healing modality. The Tao energy field can be created through Tao Song, Tao Calligraphy, or, remarkably, by inputting the Tao energy field into basic substances such as water. Master Sha is able to access the Tao. Whether this is by creating a vortex of energy which he has cultivated over the past five decades of his individual training or through other factors, we may never know. However, as they say, the proof is in the pudding or, as Master Sha likes to say, "If you want to know if a pear is sweet, taste it."

From personal experiences as well as from dozens of illnesses which I have confirmed to have been "miraculously" healed, I can confirm that the pear of healing offered by Master Sha through the creation of the Tao healing fields tastes very sweet indeed. My hypothesis is that Master Sha creates a vortex of energy—whether through song, calligraphy, or other means—which allows each individual to interact directly with the energy of the Tao. Master Sha actually has never claimed to heal anyone. He admits freely that all healing is generated by the healing energy of the Tao field. He takes no credit and seeks none. As a humble servant, Master Sha serves as a catalyst to open the field to others. Since the Tao has no time or space, the energetic exchange once it occurs is internal. Other factors enter into any healing, including the presence or absence of negative energy.

For Master Sha, the source of any negative energy is negative karma from the current or past lives of the individual seeking treatment. I am still uncertain I agree completely with this belief as from the perspective of the Tao there is no past or future. However, in that human beings live in a world of illusion that is a reflection of the deeper reality of the Tao—but not the Tao itself, it is possible that karma does exist at the level of reality in which human beings live, die, and perhaps reincarnate. I am not sure we will ever have the means to test the hypothesis of karma itself but I must admit that even if not completely accurate from a scientific perspective, the concept of karma is useful in approaching the creation and utility of interacting with Tao energy fields for measurable results.

Master Sha has always maintained that any healings or energetic shifts require not just the initial connection with the Tao but also an active continuing commitment, whether through tracing Tao Calligraphy, listening to Tao Song, or drinking Tao Water by the petitioner for blessings. This is logical from my perspective, as the expression of gratitude and appreciation is aligned with the Tao itself and cements the lasting connection to the Tao energy field as well as to the Tao itself.

Tao Water

O F ALL THE healing modalities Master Sha has developed, Tao Water has the greatest potential to serve hundreds of millions and perhaps even billions of people. Every human being requires water to survive. Every animal, every plant also requires water. Water is the most ubiquitous element on Earth. It is also perhaps the most endangered. Because of industrialization, even "pure" water is almost never truly pure. Whatever modest pure water reservoirs we might still retain, whether from deep in caverns or trapped in glacial formations, are rapidly dwindling. Many strategic advisors to governments predict that the next great wars will be over water reserves not oil reserves.

All efforts to remove pollution from water must be accelerated. Efforts to remove plastics from oceans, lakes, and rivers should be given the highest priority. In addition to these activities, attempts to provide spiritual uplifting to water should be given high priority as well. Every ancient culture studied by anthropologists has had rituals to generate and purify water. Pure water has been considered sacred across the world for thousands of years.

In writing *Dao De Jing*, Lao Zi comments extensively on the Tao nature of water. According to Lao Zi, there is no element on earth more attuned with the Tao than water. Water seeks the level of its environment. Water will flow to the lowest and most polluted areas on the planet. Water will purify itself through its own movement. Water serves all life selflessly. Alan Watts, the great popularizer of the Tao for western audiences, also wrote extensively about following the course of water as a metaphor for human behavior.

Master Sha has recently developed a technique to bless water so that the water becomes a healing tool. We know from the work of Masaru Emoto that water receives and carries messages. When water receives words and images of love and is frozen, exquisite, orderly crystals form, but when anger or hate are directed towards water, there is no sign of any organization or harmony in the frozen structures. Master Sha has done research with Dr. Emoto on the effects of his remote blessings from Canada to water in Dr. Emoto's laboratory in Japan. The effects of Master Sha's remote blessings were very clear. Afterward, Dr. Emoto said, "Dr. Sha is an important teacher and a wonderful healer with a valuable message about the power of the soul to influence and transform all life."

We may not be able to scientifically understand how Master Sha is able to input positive information into water across thousands of miles, but we already have hundreds or perhaps thousands of testimonials to the effectiveness of Tao Water.

Every day at 6 p.m. Eastern Standard Time, Master Sha give a five-minute blessing to those who subscribe to his Tao Water blessing. The blessing is given to as much as four liters of water and remains in the water for exactly one week. In the near future, Master Sha will offer these blessings free to a well being built in Africa for the people living in a village represented by Queen Diambi, the esteemed author of the foreword. These villagers have had to walk for hours to access clean drinking water for thousands of years, so this new well will save significant effort on obtaining water for thousands of people. In this instance, the water will be blessed by Master Sha for improved health and well-being. This pilot program could lead to more such charitable acts to bring clean and blessed water to millions around the world.

Master Sha has dedicated his life to serve humanity. He continues to develop his abilities to reach more and more people throughout the world. His Love Peace Harmony Foundation is dedicated to providing free services to communities in need. To learn more about the Love Peace Harmony Foundation, visit lovepeaceharmony.org.

As Master Sha evolves his Tao field healing activities, he has become a major musical performer. His first international Tao healing concert was held July 22, 2022 in Toronto to a capacity audience at the Aga Khan Museum, with an additional audience of about six thousand viewing online. Future concerts are planned for New York, San Francisco, London, and Berlin. Wherever you are in the world, make an effort to attend in person or online. These are unique concerts in which Master Sha performs Tao Songs especially created to inspire, enlighten, and heal. The first concert focused on transforming anxiety and depression. Future concerts may focus on healing fear, anger, and other emotions, on rejuvenation, or on longevity. Visit taohealingconcert.com to learn more about these upcoming concerts. In fall 2022, Master Sha's first Tao Song album will be released by E. Broad Records. This unique album will provide access to the Tao healing field.

I cannot predict what additional activities and modalities Master Sha will develop in the future. I can predict that the impact from present and future Tao services will touch millions and leave a lasting imprint on the world. Master Sha will always be a mystery but his legend will grow over time and those who will have had an opportunity to interact with him directly or through his concerts, calligraphies, and teachings will cherish those opportunities.

We are all here on this Earth to experience joy and happiness and to serve others. The greatest joy comes from serving others, so please spread these unique teachings and blessings from Master Sha with everyone you can. I bless each of you and thank you for the joy that each reader brings me in allowing me to play a small part in a much greater unfolding that is intended to relieve suffering on this Earth. The Tao is unconditional love. The Tao is accessible to us all. Master Sha can initiate you on your first steps towards understanding and experiencing the magic and wisdom of Tao consciousness. It is this state of consciousness that we all seek and it is this Tao consciousness that will provide the highest and most integrated evolution for each of us as individuals and as part of the miraculous world in which we live.

Tao Song

ONE OF MASTER Sha's most remarkable modalities for providing healing is Tao Song. Every major culture studied by anthropologists has developed songs and chants for rituals, as well as many for healing. In today's modern world, song connects us. Whether religious songs in churches or secular songs heard on the radio, music inspires and soothes us. For those of my generation, the music of the Beatles and other groups represented a new culture and new values emerging in the 1960s. The contemporaneous music of Bob Dylan and Joan Baez was used to protest against established customs and practices ranging from racism to war.

From almost any perspective, the power of music is one of the most powerful energetic exchanges human beings experience. Of course, birds and other animals are famous for their songs, which are often connected with mating rituals or survival warnings. In the case of Master Sha and Tao Song, we have a truly extraordinary blend of high-vibration music and extraordinary musical skills. The great songwriter and Grammy award-winning singer Roberta Flack was introduced to Master Sha in 2010. Master Sha sang a Tao Song for Roberta and she was astonished. She told Master Sha that she was aware of only a handful of singers with voice quality equal to his, among them the renowned operatic tenor Luciano Pavarotti. At that time Master Sha was more focused on developing his other healing modalities but he did initiate his Tao Song and Tao Dance initiatives. Roberta wrote the following foreword to Master Sha's book *Tao Song and Tao Dance*:

Master Sha is divinely blessed and guided to heal the world and every-thing that is in it. From the smallest situation to the largest, he has the faithful gift of power to make things right.

Nothing in Master Sha's voice interferes. When the voice is completely free of interference, the voice simply is. His voice is incredible and carries incredible power. His vowel sounds are so clear and strong. Every sound from Master Sha's voice is so pure. This can only be because his voice is from and of the soul. Only the soul can produce sounds like that. His voice is amazing.

The Tao Song that Master Sha sings is a musical gift beyond the sound of any voice singing that you can hear every day. It holds a purity and a resonance that only he can lay claim to. His voice is beyond anything and that is what makes him the great teacher and healer.

His voice is like the voice of God singing. God's voice in his body is so unique that it is definitely a healing sound.

Roberta Flack
Grammy Award–winning American songstress and humanitarian

This is remarkable praise from such an accomplished singer and per-former as Roberta Flack. What is perhaps even more remarkable is that it is only in the last year that Master Sha has once again focused on sing-ing as one of his most important gifts to humanity. In July 2022, Master Sha performed the first-ever Tao Song Healing Concert with Queen Di-ambi hosting and her sister Princess Isabelle performing. Princess Isa-belle is one of Europe's foremost opera soloists and she, like Roberta Flack, was impressed with Master Sha's ability to fill his music with such power and energy.

In October 2022 Master Sha is releasing his first Tao Song album, *The Way of All Life, Volume 1*, through E. Broad Records. According to Whit Whitley, founder of E. Broad Records and Executive Producer of the al-bum, the first meeting with Dr. and Master Sha felt like a predestined moment.

I will never forget the first time I heard Dr. and Master Sha sing. I'd never heard anything like it before.

Immediately I knew that millions and millions of people from all over the world are going to be healed by Dr. and Master Sha's voice and Tao Song.

Whit Whitley

The Way of All Life, Volume 1 features healing mantras interwoven with otherworldly yet musically familiar soundscapes on themes of unconditional love, joy, faith, compassion, calling in your higher self, wholeness, healing depression, healing grief, healing trauma, and hope. Dr. and Master Sha's powerful and soothing voice will immediately benefit listeners. Tao Song is a gift to humanity.

If you would like to listen to one of Master Sha's Tao Songs, you can visit www.ebroadrecords.com/mastersha. If you are fortunate to live in one of the major cities (New York, San Francisco, London, Berlin) where Master Sha is planning major concerts in 2023 and 2024, I strongly encourage you to attend one of these Tao Song Healing Concerts. You will be entertained in a way that will inspire and perhaps even heal you. For more information, you can visit taosonghealingconcert.com.

The True Miracle: Selfless Service

IN ANALYZING THE phenomenon of Master Sha, the concept of self-less service stands out as the most important lesson we can learn from Master Sha. Master Sha states in many of his books and teachings, "The purpose of life is to serve. To serve is to make others healthier and happier. To serve is to empower and enlighten others." This seems so simple but putting selfless service into action remains a challenge for most human beings. Master Sha's life and daily routine are a dynamic demonstration of selfless service in action. From the morning into the evening, Master Sha is constantly serving. His service includes private healings, teachings, online workshops, creating calligraphies, blessing water, directing the activities of his Love Peace Harmony Foundation, writing books, recording Tao Songs, and being available to his students whenever they are in crisis. I have never met a human being with as much energy and commitment to service as Master Sha.

In a paradoxical way, Master Sha's unlimited service to others may be the source of his own unlimited energy. Master Sha is constantly in a state of joy. He loves teaching others the essence of the Tao. He loves teaching the ancient secrets he has learned from his own teachers, including many of the top masters in China. He loves writing calligraphies. He loves singing. He loves creating new modalities to heal others. He loves the creative potential of the universe and he loves enabling others to not only heal but thrive so that they too can heal others. And behind all this is the clear understanding that serving others is ultimately about creating greater happiness for the entire world.

If you observe Master Sha creating a calligraphy, you will see a true master in action. It is as though we were watching Picasso paint. Master Sha's brush strokes are elegant and effortless. When creating calligraphy, Master Sha is connected to the Tao. That is why the calligraphies have so much power. The Tao cannot be seen, heard, or touched. The Tao does not communicate through normal means, not even in a mountain, a lake, or a sunset. The Tao does however communicate through Tao Calligraphies. The reason is that Master Sha through decades of service and dedication has become a true Tao Grandmaster. This is one of Master Sha's highest aspirations. Because Master Sha understands the Tao, he remains humble. He knows that he will never completely master his access to the Tao. But because Master Sha is extremely ambitious and dedicated, he will never pause his mission to learn more, master more, and serve more.

I have had the pleasure of co-hosting Master Sha's free Facebook online course, "Power and Wisdom of *Dao De Jing*," every Monday at 2 p.m. ET for the last year. This course has taught me more about the true nature of the Tao than I could have learned in decades of self-training. Master Sha has an extraordinary ability to present complex concepts in simple terms. This was the unique gift of Lao Zi, who wrote *Dao De Jing* more than twenty-five hundred years ago. Master Sha, as the 373rd-generation lineage holder of Peng Zu, the legendary "longevity star" of ancient China, is continuing this legacy of making the complex simple and the unknowable knowable. For me, this course is perhaps the greatest gift that Master Sha is providing to humanity. Wisdom is eternal. An individual healing may be a miracle and should certainly not be taken for granted. However, learning the essence of existence, where we come from, why we are here, and how we can live in accordance with nature's way—these are eternal truths which have even greater value as they empower each and every one of us to align with our higher purpose to create a better world not just for other human beings, but for all of existence in all realms even beyond the boundaries of our earth planet.

This course on *Dao De Jing*, like so many other of Master Sha's activities, is provided free through the internet. Master Sha has embraced the power of the internet like no other healer. Every Saturday morning at

11:30 a.m. ET, Master Sha appears live on Instagram with Queen Diambi on "Tao Source Healing with Master Sha and Queen Diambi" and every weekday at noon ET, Master Sha provides a major blessing in his brief "Experience the Power of Daily Blessings," also live on Instagram.

In addition to these and many other examples of selfless service, Master Sha founded the Love Peace Harmony Foundation. The Love Peace Harmony Foundation is dedicated to providing compassionate support through the practice and application of Master Sha's teachings to communities all around the world. For example, the foundation has supported the planting of hundreds of thousands of trees around the globe. It is committed to building some wells to provide clean drinking water to communities in Africa and intends to create Tao Calligraphy Healing Centers to help those with limited or no access to medical resources or who are seeking alternative and complementary approaches to healing. The foundation is passionately committed to providing blessings to help humanity and our planet in new and innovative ways.

Below are links that will enable you to connect with these and other Master Sha activities. I encourage you to take advantage of these opportunities to connect with one of the true legendary healers and humanitarians of the twenty-first century, Dr. and Master Zhi Gang Sha.

- Facebook: drandmastersha
- Instagram: masterzhigangsha
- YouTube: DrandMasterSha
- Twitter: drandmastersha8
- TikTok: masterzhigangsha
- Love Peace Harmony Foundation: lovepeaceharmony.org

The Value of Tao Calligraphy

WHEN WE GO to world-renowned museums such as the Louvre in Paris, the Prado in Madrid, or the Museum of Modern Art in New York City, we are often told that the art works on display, whether from Michelangelo, El Greco, Goya, or other master artists are "priceless." Technically, nothing is priceless, since even if the art work is not for sale, if someone offers a billion or more dollars for it, likely there will be a transaction. However, in the deepest sense, these masterworks of art are in fact priceless. No one will ever be able to replicate the original Mona Lise should it be destroyed or stolen. The world would lose access to a work of art which is truly priceless because no amount of money would make it possible to recreate such a world treasure.

Though it may be bold, let me opine that the Tao Calligraphies created by Master Sha will within decades be considered priceless artistic treasures. Early collectors have already paid as much as a million dollars for a single Tao Calligraphy. With Master Sha's renown growing daily and major art collectors beginning to collect his calligraphies, it is just a matter of time that the calligraphies as works of art will become priceless treasures. In the case of these Tao Calligraphies, the value is even beyond their value as works of art. More and more experts and many others have realized and experienced that Master Sha's calligraphies are "art beyond art." The concept of art beyond art conveys the reality that the calligraphies are not just masterworks of art but also masterworks of healing. Because Master Sha accesses the Tao when creating his calligraphies, each calligraphy can embody the power of the Tao and serve specific healing, relationship, or financial needs.

In chapter thirty-six, you have read about David Meltzer's experience after dedicatedly tracing the financial abundance calligraphy he was gifted eight years ago. In just eighteen months, his annual business revenues increased from $1.5 million to $60 million. After a few years, David's financial situation improved even much more dramatically. After Master Sha released his first-ever non-fungible token Tao Calligraphy for financial abundance, hundreds of early purchasers reported immediate financial windfalls, unexpected tax refunds, new job opportunities, new clients, and many other forms of financial flourishing. In most cases, it was not sufficient to just own the calligraphic images (NFTs are electronic images only, not physical calligraphies) to generate these wonderful results. Master Sha explains that his blessings and his calligraphies are only the gateways to creating the desired results. At least fifty percent of the outcome is determined by using the calligraphies to connect with the energy they contain. The best way to connect is not just by viewing the calligraphies, but by tracing the calligraphies. There is a video available at this link which illustrates how to trace the calligraphy for maximum results. The technique is the same whether you are tracing a physical calligraphy or tracing the electronic image of the calligraphy in an NFT.

Because very few individuals can afford one million dollars or more to purchase a great work of Tao Calligraphy, Master Sha intends to release a series of future NFTs. His first financial calligraphy NFT was priced at two thousand dollars in 2021 and the entire print run of five thousand NFTs sold out in a matter of weeks.

In this book, Master Sha has generously agreed to share an example of one of his calligraphies. I encourage you to trace this calligraphy for ten minutes a day and observe the impact your connection to the calligraphy has on your life. Kindly share your experience at drsha.com/share-your-stories. Most likely you will be skeptical as I was that a calligraphy can have dramatic influence on your health, your relationships, your career, or your finances. Most likely you will learn, like me, that the calligraphy will in fact have dramatic impact on your life and will be grateful you allowed your curiosity to overcome your skepticism.

The Importance of Wisdom

IN HOSTING THE course "Power and Wisdom of *Dao De Jing*" with Master Sha, I have come to more deeply appreciate the wisdom of Lao Zi as well as the wisdom of Master Sha himself. Wisdom is ultimately more important than any material possession or specific knowledge or information you may pursue. Knowledge is fleeting. Technology that was important one hundred years ago is now in many instances obsolete. Possessions come and go. Eventually every material possession you own will cease to exist either during your lifetime or afterward. Money itself is just a human construct. The value of money fluctuates with inflation and economic cycles.

But wisdom is eternal. Wisdom like the Tao is timeless. But unlike the Tao, wisdom can in fact be seen, heard, and in some ways touched. Wisdom is the closest human beings can come to truly understanding the nature of the human condition and their own existence here on earth. Why are we here? What is our purpose? How do we act, think, and live to enhance not only our own well-being but the well-being of everyone and every living creature on planet Earth? These are deep questions and fortunately many of the answers are available to us in this masterful class exploring the teachings of Lao Zi from more than 2,500 years ago.

Human nature has not changed significantly in 2,500 years. Human beings require love and a sense of belonging to thrive. Lao Zi explains that these fundamental needs can best be met by following nature's way. But what is nature's way? Western scientists have adopted the paradigm of the "survival of the fittest" but is that truly nature's way? How does nature define the fittest and do the "fittest" truly survive? Even more importantly do we ever ask what survival means? To exist in my mind is not necessarily survival, especially if in order to exist one must act in ways that create suffering for others or contribute to the pollution and destruction of our planet. Many ancient and modern indigenous cultures were more connected to nature and realized the eternal nature of existence.

Lao Zi and Master Sha present a much more loving and humble model of nature. Nature like the Tao itself does not judge. Nature like the Tao supports all life. Water is a primary metaphor in Lao Zi's teaching. Water will flow to the lowest and most polluted areas of the planet and not complain. Water is here to serve. Over time, water can change boulders into sand. Water over time can turn deserts into thriving forests. Be more like water: patient, gentle, and selfless.

My favorite book of all time is *One Hundred Years of Solitude* by Gabriel Garcia Marquez. *One Hundred Years of Solitude* was first published in 1967 as *Cien Años de Soledad*. I was a freshman at Yale College in the fall of 1968 and because I had lived in Spain as an exchange student in Barcelona, I was fluent in Spanish and was granted access to a special graduate level course taught by the famed literary critic Emir Rodriguez Monegal. Reading *Cien Años* was a revelation. The ability to capture the essence of the lives of the fictional settlers of Macondo was remarkable. Even though *Cien Años* was a novel, the characters were more real and more revealing than any descriptions from histories of the actual people and events which the novel was depicting with what at the time was considered a new form of literature which was named "magical realism." Magical realism was an apt description because some of the events in the novel were clearly magical, such as the ascent of one of the characters in physical form to the sky because of her unimaginable beauty or the constant appearance of hordes of butterflies whenever she appeared, but the essence of each character was based on real people and each event in the novel no matter how outrageous and "miraculous" was based on actual historical events.

Gabriel Garcia went on to win the Nobel Prize for Literature for *Cien Años* and his other novels. The award was much deserved and was based on his extraordinary writing talent. For me however, the true genius of his writing was his ability to fully capture the human condition and explain to readers the essence of what being truly human entails. As human beings, we get angry, joyful, and come up with brilliant solutions to everyday challenges, as well as commit follies, suffer, and in the end are totally alone with our inner emotions, thoughts, and beliefs.

The teachings of Master Sha have qualities that resonate with magical realism. Many of his results seems magical and yet they are based on actual disciplined proven practices. Many of these practices were initiated by Lao Zi and other ancient teachers in China. It is no accident that Master Sha focuses on power and wisdom in his course of teaching. Wisdom will bring power but not necessarily power in the sense that the majority of people consider power. For Lao Zi and for Master Sha, power is power to be authentic and to serve the Tao. In serving the Tao, all that is meant to be experienced in your lifetime will be experienced. Wisdom is the key. True power follows naturally.

Tapping the Source

IN ADDITION TO the many free classes, healings, and blessings that Master Sha provides, he is now participating in several Tapping the Source Summits with other major thought leaders. My wife Gayle produced the film "Tapping the Source" several years before I met and began working with Master Sha. In that film more than one hundred visionaries and thought leaders were interviewed, representing fields ranging from business to film to art, health, and literature. The premise of the film was to ask each participant what their source of happiness was and how they stayed connected to that source on a daily basis. At the time I had little knowledge of the Tao and did not refer to the Tao in any of the interviews that I conducted with each participant. The framework for the film and the interviews was provided by The Master Key System created by Charles Haanel more than one hundred years ago. Charles Haanel was the first author in America to present concepts from India and other eastern cultures in the context of European and North American values. The Master Key System has been used throughout the last one hundred years and was publicly acknowledged by Napoleon Hill as being the basis for his own landmark work, *Think and Grow Rich*.

As the film evolved, Gayle and I learned that for most participants their key to happiness was finding a way to express gratitude every day and to be of service to others. Several years later, when I discovered the teachings of Master Sha, I was delighted that his two primary directives—seek forgiveness and be of service to others—were so closely aligned with the information we had generated in filming "Tapping the Source." Master Sha is also a major proponent of expressing gratitude and has created special Tao songs and calligraphies focused on gratitude as well. It is almost as if Gayle, who was focused on creating a film that would be directed by the Source itself, and Master Sha were working on the same project—bringing the essence of the Tao or Source to the general public—without any actual connection in time or space.

Given this wonderful complementarity of what Master Sha teaches and the purpose of the "Tapping the Source" film and interviews, Waterside and Master Sha and his team have combined our resources to promote a series of Tapping the Source Summits. The first summit was held in July 2022 with Dr. Ervin Laszlo, Dr. Deepak Chopra, and Dr. Rulin Xiu participating with Master Sha. The primary topic was to explore the nature of reality and the importance of consciousness in human evolution. The online summit was attended by several thousand and was of great value to those attending. Based on the feedback and success, we will be holding a second Tapping the Source Summit in October 2022 and several more throughout 2023. The purpose of these summits is to introduce additional thought leaders to Master Sha and Master Sha to additional thought leaders so that we can create a community of dedicated teachers and visionaries to bring a higher level of awareness to as many people as possible as quickly as possible.

To learn more about these summits, go to tappingthesource.org. Master Sha and I welcome your suggestions for additional speakers and panelists and specific topics for future summits. I want to publicly thank Master Sha for participating in these summits and donating his share of the proceeds to his charitable organization, the Love Peace Harmony Foundation. The other participants, including Waterside, are also donating their proceeds to like-minded charities which help to raise the consciousness of humanity at this critical moment in time.

Death Be Not Proud

O NE OF THE most famous poems in the English language is "Death Be Not Proud" by the English poet John Donne. Donne captures the reality that all humans must die without capitulating to the fear that is often associated with death. Master Sha in his teachings focuses on the soul journey, which transcends the temporality of human life. Master Sha wants us to focus on the higher dimension of the Tao, the timeless dimension which is truly eternal. All great saints and teachers have reflected on the ephemeral nature of human existence. Even if we live one hundred years that is but a blink of an eye in the timeless eternity of the Tao. That is why Lao Zi and Master Sha constantly focus on letting go of human attachments, letting go of the desires for wealth, fame, and material comforts. There is nothing wrong with acquiring wealth and respect from others but ultimately none of your possessions or praise will follow you to your next stage on your soul's journey.

The concept that this life is but a dream has been presented by many great thinkers, philosophers, poets, dramatists, and spiritual teachers over the last several thousand years. Buddha was clear in presenting human life as an illusion from which few awoke. The great Spanish dramatist Calderon de la Barca in his play *La Vida Es Sueño* (Life Is a Dream) provided the sage wisdom which I translate loosely as, "What is important is to do good works, for if life is a dream then you may wake and find that this was a test and if life is not a dream then clearly you will want to have done good works." Plato in his parable of the cave and shadows expressed similar thoughts. Master Sha has declared in all of his books, "The purpose of life is to serve. To serve is to make others happier and healthier. To serve is to empower and enlighten others." For Master Sha, this is divine guidance that was given to him more than twenty years ago. Master Sha has been truly selfless in serving others nonstop.

Interestingly, Master Sha as a Tao Grandmaster does not limit his service just to those of us living on this human plane. Master Sha has given blessings to those who have reached the end of their lives so that they will ascend to the Buddhaland on their soul's journey. The Buddhaland is the realm of no attachment and joy. Saints immediately ascend to this realm but not all humans. When discussing esoteric matters relating to the soul, it is not possible to prove the validity of such concepts in the language of material science, which is limited to earthly proof. Neither Master Sha nor I ask you to believe. However, I want to relate a recent incident that for me provides evidence that indeed it is our soul's journey that ultimately should be the center of our attention.

Last March my wife's ninety-eight-year-old mother, Doris Wilkinson, had a fall and nearly died. Given Gayle's and my close relationship with Master Sha, we asked if Master Sha could provide a blessing since it seemed Doris was ready to pass. Master Sha immediately gave a special blessing so that her journey to Buddhaland would be effortless. He warned us however that it might not yet be the time for Doris to transition. Only Doris and the Tao controlled the timing of her passage. Doris remarkably recovered and, after one month of intensive physical therapy, was able to move back into her home in Laguna in which she had lived for more than fifty years. Doris had often shared that she wanted to die at home and that it was important to her to return to her home no matter what the circumstances. Doris lived by the motto "someone to love, something to do, and something to look forward to." This had for her been the key to the twenty-plus years she lived alone after the death of her beloved husband Richard. When Doris returned in late April to her Laguna home, she was restricted to minimal movement and required full 24/7 assistance. For the first time in her life, she felt she no longer had "something to do and something to look forward to." Until her fall, Doris had been an active reader of manuscripts for our publishing company, Waterside Productions Inc. Doris would write her critiques in long hand and provided two full critiques a week for the last ten years prior to her fall. Unfortunately, the fall exacerbated her failing eyesight and in those final months she was no longer able to read and provide critiques. For the first time in her life, Doris no longer had something to do and something to look forward to.

Doris still had people to love but she decided that it was time to move to the next adventure on her journey. She called Gayle on a Friday and told her she was ready to pass and that Gayle should come to her home to be with her for her last days on Earth. Gayle arrived and assisted to ensure that Doris was not in any pain. Within forty-eight hours, Doris passed with a smile on her face and contentment in her heart. She had lived a life of service and purpose. She had been born just before the great economic depression of 1929 and had lived in foster homes because her parents were unable to provide a home and basic nutrition for her as a young child. Doris had worked her entire life, bore four children, was a homemaker, secretary to the dean of a local college, and helped her husband rise in his career. Doris was also looking for ways to be of service. During World War II, she volunteered to work in a veteran's hospital where she wrote letters for injured and dying soldiers. When economic circumstances allowed later in life, Doris volunteered as a patrol and clerical assistant for the Laguna police department and later at both the local library and hospital. When Doris passed, she had more than forty grandchildren and more than twenty greatgrandchildren and great greatgrandchildren. From any reckoning Doris experienced a life well lived.

After Doris passed, unusual events began to occur. When talking about Doris or a decision to be made related to the memorial Gayle and I were planning to honor her, lights that had never flickered in our home flickered. One time a pocketbook jumped off the couch, signaling us that Doris was present in spirit. Everything related to her estate was effortlessly resolved, including the sale of her home to a neighbor who greatly valued his connection with Doris. Additionally, the fire alarm in our home—which had never gone off—would beep when we discussed Doris or her last wishes. When Gayle was on the phone with one of Doris's closest neighbors, her phone would have static and then a voice would take over the phone for a few seconds before the phone went dead. For several weeks, a small hummingbird would fly to our patio and remain motionless while Gayle did her morning meditations. Once when Gayle was on the patio, the colors of the sky changed dramatically and Gayle felt she was experiencing the magical presence of her mom who was now in a place of beauty and joy. When neighbors came to Doris's Laguna home to pay condolences after her death, they each commented on the light they felt emanating from the home. Although each was saddened by her passing, they commented on the joy they felt in the home. They had each in their way loved Doris and it was clear that Doris's passing was a moment of joy not sadness.

We cannot know precisely how much Master Sha's special blessing has aided Doris in her soul's journey but it seems likely the blessing has had major significance. As Master Sha explains, whenever he gives a blessing, half is the blessing and another half is the active participation of the recipient of the blessing. In the case of Doris, she was no longer actively participating but her ninety-eight-year-long life of service was her participation. Had she had a less giving life, it is unlikely the blessing would have been as effective.

Just last month, her Royal Highness Queen Elizabeth II of England passed at the age of ninety-six. Like Doris, Queen Elizabeth had led a life of service and gratitude. We can only hope that Queen Elizabeth's soul journey is as joyful as that being experienced by Doris. It does not matter if you are a queen or a commoner. Your actions while on Earth determine your soul's journey. None of us as human beings is expected or able to be meticulous in every moment of existence Neither Doris nor Queen Elizabeth were perfect individuals. They had moments of disappointment and likely errors in judgment. But both were loving individuals who dedicated their lives to serving others and finding in their hearts ways to love and accept other and their own shortcomings.

Personally, I have had many close friends and colleagues pass in the last three years. My younger brother Tom, my very close friend Barbara Marx Hubbard, my good friends Bob Proctor and Bernie Dohrman, my first-ever client David Loye, and one of my closest friends and colleagues Michael Gosney have all passed just recently. It is difficult to accept the passing of so many good friends.

But there is a lesson in death and that lesson is that death is not eternal. Death is but the passing of the body. I still communicate with those who have passed. I still reflect on the wisdom they shared with me while they were present. At times I find myself conversing with them and feeling their presence as strongly or even more strongly than when they were alive.

Master Sha has reaffirmed for me the reality of the soul's journey as the most significant aspect of our human experience. When I had my near-death experience at the age of fifteen, I was gifted with the knowledge that life is truly eternal and joyful. We may never know with exactitude our true destinies, but I encourage all readers to seriously consider the wisdom and teachings of Master Sha in perfecting your own lives and the journey that awaits you beyond the earthly realm.

Acknowledgments

F IRST AND FOREMOST I must acknowledge and thank Dr. and Master Sha. Without him I simply could not have written this book. His generosity of spirit and of time, his sharing of personal memories, and his constant focus on the true nature of his service and his purpose as a miracle soul healer were gifts beyond measure. His sense of humor and his loving nature made this project a joy. I know that beyond all other connections, we will forever be true friends. I have learned more from Dr. and Master Sha about the nature of reality and my own true nature than from any teachers, masters, or experiences I have had previously in my life. I believe that working closely with Dr. and Master Sha on this book has healed aspects of my life and my own soul journey that would never have otherwise been healed. My life is even more joyous now because of this experience. Thank you is really not enough.

I want to also acknowledge Master Cynthia. She is a tireless worker and supported this project from its inception. Without her I would have never captured the information in the interviews not just with Dr. Sha but also with Dr. Peter Hudoba, Dr. Rulin Xiu, and Professor Gary Schwartz. She is a most amazing typist, going at two hundred words or more a minute with flawless accuracy. She is an even bigger star as a human being. Her good humor, support, and kindnesses throughout the creation of this book were invaluable. Without Master Cynthia this book could not have been written. Thank you, Master Cynthia.

My biggest supporter for the last twenty years of my life has been my wife Gayle Gladstone. Without her in my life I would never have been in a position to write this book or truly appreciate the unique gifts of Dr. and Master Sha. Gayle was the first reader for most of the chapters in this book, and my first critic. Her insights, contributions, and encouragement were invaluable. She has been by my side every step of this amazing journey and made sacrifices without which this book could not have been written. Again, thanks alone is insufficient.

I do not believe in overly long acknowledgments but want to thank every single person who appears in this book, from the Master Teachers to those who have shared their healing experiences with me. Especially for this updated, revised edition, I am very grateful to Master Allan Chuck, Master Lynda Chaplin, and Master Elaine Ward whose editorial assistance has been invaluable.

About the Author

WILLIAM GLADSTONE IS a prolific author, literary agent, publisher, and filmmaker. He has degrees from Yale College and Harvard University, where he studied medical anthropology. His background as the original researcher for the NBC television special hosted by Rod Serling, *In Search of Ancient Mysteries*, prepared him for the research and analysis of Dr. and Master Sha and his miracle soul healing accomplishments. Mr. Gladstone is known for his philanthropic activities and commitment to helping authors publish books that contribute to the well-being of others and to our planet. His personal clients in addition to Dr. and Master Sha include Eckhart Tolle, Neale Donald Walsch, Thom Hartmann, Barbara De Angelis, Jean Houston, Linus Torvalds, Tom Anderson, Peter Norton, Hunter Lovins, Dr. Michael Tobias, Dr. Paul Ehrlich, Dr. Ervin Laszlo, and many authors whose books have contributed to increasing knowledge and well-being for hundreds of millions of readers.

Mr. Gladstone lives with his wife Gayle in Cardiff-by-the-Sea, where he enjoys golf, tennis, and the beach. His daughter Tara Rose Gladstone is a writer and editor, and his son Cyrus Jay Gladstone is a post-production film expert. His greatest joy is playing with his grandson Titus Gladstone and his granddaughter Arella Gladstone.

Other Books
by William Gladstone

Tapping the Source. New York: Sterling Ethos, 2010. Reprint, New York: Jeremy P. Tarcher/Penguin, 2014.

The Power of Twelve. Dallas: BenBella Books, Inc., 2013. Reprint, Waterside Productions, 2022.

The Twelve. New York: Vanguard Press, 2009. Reprint, Waterside Productions, 2018.

The Golden Motorcycle Gang (with Jack Canfield). Hay House, 2011.

Test Your Own Mental Health. New York: Arco Publishing Company, 1978. Reprint, New York: New American Library, 1979. Reprint as *Test Yourself with Nell Daly*. Waterside Productions, 2021.

Selected Other Books by
Dr. and Master Sha

Soul Mind Body Medicine: A Complete Soul Healing System for Optimum Health and Vitality

Soul Mind Body Science System: Grand Unification Theory and Practice for Healing, Rejuvenation, Longevity and Immortality

Soul Healing Miracles: Ancient and New Sacred Wisdom, Knowledge, and Practical Techniques for Healing the Spiritual, Mental, Emotional, and Physical Bodies

Tao Science: The Science, Wisdom, and Practice of Creation and Grand Unification

Tao Calligraphy Healing Field: An Information System with Six Sacred Tao Techniques to Empower You to Heal and Transform Your Life

Tao Calligraphy to Heal and Rejuvenate Your Back

Tao Calligraphy to Heal and Transform Depression and Anxiety

More information about Dr. and Master Sha

- Facebook: drandmastersha
- Instagram: masterzhigangsha
- Twitter: drandmastersha8
- YouTube: DrandMasterSha
- Website: drsha.com

Master Sha's Impact on Distinguished Thought Leaders

"The Universe is not made of matter. It is made of information. Information that is aligned with the structure of the universe heals. The Tao Calligraphy of Master Sha is aligned with the structure of the universe. It heals. Dr. and Master Sha is an authentic Dao grandmaster."

— Dr. Ervin Laszlo
Founder of the Club of Budapest and
the Laszlo Institute of New Paradigm Research

"Dr. and Master Sha's unconditional love for humanity will open your heart and touch your soul. He is one of the most extraordinary and powerful human beings I have ever met."

— Barbara De Angelis, PhD
New York Times bestselling author

"We, the human race, need more Zhi Gang Sha."

— Maya Angelou
Award-winning author of *I Know Why the Caged Bird Sings*

"Dr. Sha is an important teacher and a wonderful healer with a valuable message about the power of the soul to influence and transform all life."

— Masuru Emoto
Author of *The Hidden Messages in Water*

"Dr. Sha offers a clear, practical path to learning the secrets of self-healing."

— Marianne Williamson
Author of *A Return to Love*,
former candidate for United States President

Love Peace Harmony Foundation

Founded by world-renowned healer, humanitarian, doctor, and author, Dr. and Master Zhi Gang Sha, the Love Peace Harmony Foundation is a nonprofit devoted to service by creating a more loving, peaceful, and harmonious world using a special song and the Tao Calligraphy Healing Field.

Our mission is to empower people, organizations, and communities to cultivate an environment of love, peace, and harmony through our transformative song, calligraphy art, and movement.

The Source song, "Love, Peace and Harmony" and the *Love Peace Harmony* calligraphy hold a high frequency and vibration which have the ability to transform negative information, energy, and matter into positive information, energy, and matter. Using the song and calligraphy, we can transform the information in the field of our health, relationships, finances, and more to uplift our lives. This is supported by quantum physics and through the life experiences of thousands of people worldwide who use these healing tools for life transformation every day.

We are committed to take the concept of world peace from a theory to a practice. When we are dedicated each day to our inner peace, this creates a ripple impact among families, friends, communities, organizations, countries, and ultimately the world.

With this understanding, we are empowered through our own speech, thoughts, and actions to impact great change and transformation, especially when we align our hearts and souls in this mission of collectively embodying and creating a more loving, peaceful, harmonious world for all.

The Love Peace Harmony Foundation has hundreds of volunteers around the world who continually give back in their respective communities. They are sharing the positive message of the "Love, Peace and Harmony" song in schools, institutions, community centers, and beyond. We are helping children in areas around the world, including Africa, India, Ecuador, and Bhutan by supporting educational opportunities, improving their environment, and engaging them in positive activities. They in turn are reaching out to seniors to let them know they're not alone and provide a resource to bring them greater peace in their formative years. Love Peace Harmony Foundation volunteers take action right where they are to make a significant impact and be the representations of love, peace, and harmony.

With our song translated into more than fifty languages *and* with representation in hundreds of communities on every continent except Antarctica, we are truly empowering humanity to empower themselves to live a move loving, peaceful, and harmonious life.

Love Peace Harmony Foundation collaborations and partnerships with like-hearted organizations continue to grow, extending our network worldwide to make a significant positive impact on humanity and Mother Earth's evolution to oneness.

With the escalating rate of challenges and disasters, we have made a conscious decision to wake up every day and use these powerful tools to enact change, taking a stand for a world free of suffering. Although it sometimes may seem impossible, we believe that together, anything is possible! Do you believe? Visit us at www.lovepeaceharmony.org to find out more and experience it for yourself!

With love, peace, and harmony,
Penelope Mathieson
Managing Director
Love Peace Harmony Foundation